Ten Theories of
Human Nature

Ten Theories of Human Nature

Fifth Edition

LESLIE STEVENSON

DAVID L. HABERMAN

New York   Oxford
OXFORD UNIVERSITY PRESS
2009

OXFORD
UNIVERSITY PRESS

Oxford University Press, Inc., publishes works that further Oxford University's
objective of excellence in research, scholarship, and education.

Oxford   New York
Auckland   Cape Town   Dar es Salaam   Hong Kong   Karachi
Kuala Lumpur   Madrid   Melbourne   Mexico City   Nairobi
New Delhi   Shanghai   Taipei   Toronto

With offices in
Argentina   Austria   Brazil   Chile   Czech Republic   France   Greece
Guatemala   Hungary   Italy   Japan   Poland   Portugal   Singapore
South Korea   Switzerland   Thailand   Turkey   Ukraine   Vietnam

Published by Oxford University Press, Inc.
198 Madison Avenue, New York, New York 10016
http://www.oup.com

Oxford is a registered trademark of Oxford University Press

Library of Congress Cataloging-in-Publication Data

Stevenson, Leslie Forster.
    Ten theories of human nature / Leslie Stevenson, David L. Haberman. — 5th ed.
    p. cm.
    Includes bibliographical references and index.
    ISBN 978-0-19-536825-3 (pbk. : alk. paper)   1.   Philosophical
anthropology.   I. Haberman, David L., 1952- II. Title.
    BD450.S766 2009
    128—dc22   2008028648

9 8 7 6 5 4 3 2

Printed in the United States of America
on acid-free paper

*To my daughters, Sonia and Lydia, who have,
of course, taught me much about
human nature*
L. S.

*To my parents, Reuben and Ruth,
in many ways the sources of my own
human nature*
D. H.

Contents

Preface to the Fifth Edition

Why a fifth edition so soon after the fourth? It is mainly in response to reactions from users who found the Darwinian chapter too disjointed and the Historical Interlude too superficial, and from many who suggested a chapter on Buddhism.

I am delighted that David Haberman has been able to supply the latter. Perhaps I should explain that, for better or for worse, we have not collaborated in any of the writing, so apart from the first three chapters, which are David's, the rest of the book is entirely my responsibility (Leslie Stevenson).

I have completely reorganized and rewritten the chapter on Darwinian theories, in terms of three main waves of evolutionary theorizing about human nature: roughly, (a) 1800–1900, the first theories of evolution; (b) 1900–1950, the reaction in favor of culture and society; and (c) 1950–present, the return of biology into theories of human nature. I have benefited from comments on this chapter from Kevin Laland in St. Andrews, as well as Richard Joyce, Edouard Machery, and Patricia Turrisi, who have helped me do better justice to this complicated and crucial set of issues.

I have retained the Historical Interlude, still feeling the need for some filling of the gap between early Christianity and the eighteenth century (without extending the book), but I have omitted some sections that were ridiculously brief and tidied up the others.

To make room for David's chapter on Buddhism, I have reluctantly decided to omit that on Freud. The other candidate for demotion was Marx, but I decided that biological theorizing about human nature was already well represented in Chapter 10, and that Marx, for all his faults, provides a social and historical dimension that would otherwise be somewhat lacking in this book. Besides, I feel that his diagnosis of the human effects of capitalist economies may still have something to teach us, even if his own prescription was way off target. (I found a similar thought or two in Adam Smith, of all people!)

I have also done some tidying up, clarification, and rewriting of the chapters on the Bible, on Kant, and the Conclusion. The others have only a few cosmetic changes.

St. Andrews   L. F. S.
November 2007

Preface to the Fourth Edition

It is a long time since the summer of 1967, when I first had some of the thoughts that inspired this book. America was riven by the Vietnam War and by race riots in cities, and I was an aspiring but uncertain graduate student of philosophy at Oxford, spending my summer vacation on a cross-continental tour of the United States. Between experiences of the cities of the East and the amazing scenery of the West, and brief encounters with cowboys and Indians, anti-war campaigners and hippies, I remember jotting down some structural comparisons between Christianity, Marxism, psychoanalysis, and existentialism.

In the early 1970s, as a raw young lecturer at St. Andrews University, I found myself faced with large numbers of first-year students who were compelled, under the traditional Scottish system, to take a philosophy course. I wondered what was appropriate for such an audience of conscripts, most of whom would study no further philosophy. My response was to broaden a conventional philosophy of mind course into a critical examination of rival theories of human nature. The first edition of this book emerged from that pedagogical experience. Thirty years have passed since publication, and the book is still, apparently, found useful for many courses in various countries.

It is a rare privilege to be read by so many thousands of students, and I have a corresponding responsibility to update and improve the book as best I can. The differences between successive editions are getting larger, in fact. The second edition made only cosmetic changes, leaving the seven main chapters untouched. In the third edition, I updated my treatment of those seven theories, I added a new chapter on Kant, and David Haberman of the Department of Religion at Indiana University at Bloomington was enrolled to contribute chapters on Confuciansim and Hinduism (thus seven theories became ten).

This fourth edition is still more radically changed. I have at last decided to drop Skinner and Lorenz from the pantheon, and have replaced those chapters by a single long chapter on evolutionary ("Darwinian") theories of human nature. This new chapter contains sections on Skinner and Lorenz, along with various other influential figures, with special critical attention being given to E. O. Wilson. I have written a completely new chapter on Aristotle. And I have added a "historical interlude" to fill the otherwise huge gap in the history of ideas between the ancient world and the Enlightenment: in this section I offer thumbnail sketches of some of the most influential movements and thinkers.

I have also rewritten the other chapters very thoroughly, deepening the treatment (I hope), while still keeping the level introductory. In particular, I have extended my (far from impartial!) account of the Bible, suggesting a distinction between spiritual and supernatural interpretations of Christianity; I have tried to clarify my account of Kant, concentrating on the theme of reasons and causes and adding a comment on his philosophy of history; and I have added sections on Freud as moralist and on Sartre's first and second ethics. David Haberman has also made some clarifications and additions to his chapters on Confucianism and Hinduism.

There are, of course, many plausible candidates for extending the list of theories beyond our chosen ten. In view of the resurgence of the influence of religion in the contemporary world, Islam and Buddhism would be obvious choices, but our editors wanted to keep the theory count to ten (perhaps the fifth edition will be more inclusive). Meanwhile, we can recommend the "Very Short Introductions" on the Koran, Islam, the Buddha, and Buddhism, published by Oxford University Press. (By the standards of that series, the chapters in this book are *very, very* short introductions!)

With the addition of Aristotle and the historical interlude, the center of gravity of the book has perhaps moved backward in time—but that may not be a bad thing! There is a prevailing obsession with being up-to-date with the very latest scientific research or fashionable speculation. But in our rush toward the future, there is the danger of a parochialism of the present that forgets—or is simply ignorant of—the wisdom of the past. I would like to hope that this book will help readers to see presently influential ideas in a more historically informed context, and to evaluate both science-based and religion-based conceptions of human nature in a deeper, more philosophical way.

Comments from various people have suggested more adequate treatment in some places. I hereby thank my St. Andrews colleagues for their reading of the relevant chapter drafts: Sarah Broadie (Plato and Aristotle); David Archard (Marx); Jens Timmerman (Kant and Sartre); Malcolm Jeeves (Darwinian theories); and Gordon Graham, now at Aberdeen (the

Bible). I would like affectionately to remember here my father, Patric Stevenson (1909–1983) for his fastidious attention to matters of style and readability in the first edition, which I hope has rubbed off through me into subsequent editions. I also thank Emily Voigt and Robert Miller of Oxford University Press in New York for their encouragement and support in the writing of this fourth edition.

St. Andrews   L. S. F.
July 2003

Introduction: Rival Theories and Critical Assessments

This book is meant for anyone who is looking for a "philosophy of life," that is, an understanding of human nature that gives some guidance for how we should live. Such a *prescription* is often based on a *diagnosis* of what tends to go wrong, which in turn presupposes some sort of *ideal* of how life ought to go or how human beings ought to be.

We are using the title phrase "theory of human nature" in a wide sense to cover ancient religious traditions, some classic philosophical systems, and more recent theories that try to use scientific method to understand human nature and find guidance for human life and society. This is to stretch the meaning of the word "theory" beyond purely scientific theories. We could substitute the word "philosophy" in its classical sense of *philo-sophia* (love of wisdom), or perhaps the concept of a "worldview" (derived from the German term *Weltanschauung*) or "ideology" (the beliefs and values by which a certain society or community lives). In our wide sense, a "theory of human nature" encompasses:

1. a background metaphysical understanding of the universe and humanity's place in it;

2. a theory of human nature in the narrower sense of some distinctive general claims about human beings, human society, and the human condition;

3. a diagnosis of some typical defect in human beings, of what tends to go wrong in human life and society;

4. a prescription or ideal for how human life should best be lived, typically offering guidance to individuals and human societies.

Only theories in this wide sense that combine such elements offer us hope of solutions to the problems of humankind. For instance, the single assertion that everyone tends to be selfish (i.e., to act only for our own self-interest) is a very brief diagnosis, but it offers no understanding of what makes us selfish and no suggestion as to whether or how we might overcome it. The statement that we should all love one another is a prescription, but it gives no explanation of why we find it so difficult (and no gloss on what sort of "love" of others we should aspire to) and it offers no help in achieving it. The theory of evolution says important things about the place of human beings in the universe, but does not in itself offer any prescription; as a purely scientific, causal explanation of how the human species came into being, it does not attempt to tell us the purpose or meaning of our life—what we should try to do or be.

This book is not a conventional introduction to philosophy in the narrower sense of the academic subject as it is often defined these days, with its divisions of logic, philosophy of language, metaphysics, theory of knowledge, philosophy of mind, ethics, political philosophy, aesthetics, philosophy of religion, and so on. We will touch on topics in many of those areas, but our primary concern is to focus on ten selected systems of thought that offer answers to the sorts of existential, life-relevant questions that motivate many people to study philosophy in the first place. What is our place in the universe? Why are we here? We ask in both the causal sense "What brought us into being?" and the purposive sense "What—if anything—are we here for?" (What should we do, or aim at? What should we avoid?)

It is obvious that much depends on what theory of human nature we accept: for individuals, the meaning and purpose of our lives, what we ought to do or strive for, what we may hope to achieve, or to become; for human societies, what vision of human community we hope to work toward, what sort of social changes we favor. Our answers to these huge questions will depend on whether we think there is some "true" or "innate" nature of human beings and some objective standards of value for human life. If so, what is it, and what are they? Are we essentially products of evolution, programmed to pursue our self-interest, to reproduce our genes, or fulfill our biological drives? Or, is there no such "essential" human nature, only a capacity to be molded by society and its economic, political, and cultural forces? Or, is there some transcendent, objective (perhaps divine?) purpose for human lives and human history?

RIVAL THEORIES

On these fundamental questions there have been, of course, a variety of views. "What is man that Thou art mindful of him . . . Thou hast made him a little lower than the angels, and hast crowned him with glory and honor," wrote the author of Psalm 8. The Bible sees human beings as created by a transcendent God in His own image, with a God-given purpose for human life. There are also the great philosophical systems of Plato, Aristotle, and Kant, which set out supposedly objective standards of value for human lives and societies to aspire to.

"The real nature of man is the totality of social relations," wrote Karl Marx in the mid-nineteenth century. Marx denied the existence of God and held that each person is a product of the particular economic stage of human society in which he or she lives. "Man is condemned to be free," said Jean-Paul Sartre, writing in France in the Second World War. Sartre agreed with Marx's atheism, but differed from him in holding that we are not determined by our society or by anything else, rather every individual person is free to decide what he or she wants to be and do. In contrast, would-be scientific theorists of human nature such as E. O. Wilson have recently treated humans as a product of evolution, with biologically determined, species-specific patterns of behavior.

It will not escape the notice of contemporary readers that these quotations from the Bible, Marx, and Sartre all use the word "man," where the intention was surely to refer to *all* human beings, including women (and children). Such traditional usage has come under criticism for contributing to questionable assumptions about the social and familial dominance of men and the consequent neglect or oppression of women. These are, of course, important issues that involve much more than linguistic usage. We will not address feminist themes head-on in this book: there is no chapter on specifically feminist theories of human nature (which now differ among themselves). But we will note what our selected "theories" have to say about commonalities and differences between men and women. We will try to avoid sexist language ourselves (but it cannot always be avoided in quotations).

Different conceptions of human nature lead to different views about what we ought to do and how we can do it. If an all-powerful and supremely good God made us, then it is His purpose that defines what we can be and ought to be, and we must look to Him for help. If, on the other hand, we are products of society, and if we find that many human lives are presently unsatisfactory, then there can be no real solution until human society is transformed. If we are radically free and can never escape the necessity for individual choice, then we have to accept this and make our choices with full awareness of what we are doing. If our biological nature predisposes us to think, feel, and act in certain ways, then we had better take realistic account of that in individual choices and in social policy.

Rival beliefs about human nature are typically embodied in different individual ways of life and in political and economic systems. Marxist theory (in some version) so dominated public life in communist-ruled countries in the twentieth century that any questioning of it could have serious consequences for the questioner. We can easily forget that a few centuries ago Christianity occupied a similarly dominant position in Western society: heretics and unbelievers were persecuted and even burned at the stake. Even now, there is in some places a Christian consensus that individuals can oppose only at some social cost. In many Muslim countries, Islam occupies a similarly dominating position. In traditionally Catholic countries (like Italy, the Republic of Ireland, and Poland) the Roman Catholic Church has exerted considerable social influence and limits state policy on abortion, contraception, and divorce. In the United States, a Protestant Christian ethos underlies much public debate and has influenced policy, despite the constitutional separation of Church and State.

An "existentialist" philosophy like Sartre's may seem unlikely to have social implications; but one way of justifying modern "liberal" democracy is by the philosophical view that there *are no* objective values for human living, only subjective individual choices. This assumption is highly influential in modern Western society, far beyond its particular manifestation in European existentialist philosophy of the mid-twentieth century. Liberal democracy is enshrined in the American Declaration of Independence, with its acknowledgement of the right of each "man" (i.e., *person*) to "life, liberty and the pursuit of happiness"—usually interpreted as the right of each individual to pursue his or her own *conception* of happiness. It should be noted, however, that those who believe there *are* objective moral standards (whether religious or secular) may still defend a liberal political system if they think it unjust or unwise to try to *enforce* those standards. So although value-subjectivism supports political liberalism, the reverse is not the case.

Outside the Western tradition, there have been other theories of human nature, some of which are still very much alive. Islam, which shares origins with Judaism and Christianity, is undergoing a resurgence of popular strength as the peoples of the Muslim world express their rejection of some aspects of Western culture (and we are thinking here not primarily of terrorists, but of the more moderate defenders of Islamic cultural identity). Islam has spread into the West with immigration and has gained some new adherents there. In India, Hinduism is resurgent, sometimes in fundamentalist or nationalist form. Buddhism, originally an Indian religion, spread into the far East, China, and Japan, and has gained publicity and converts in the West. As the influence of Marx and communism wanes, some in Russia have looked for guidance to their Orthodox Christian past and others to a variety of modern forms of spirituality. And, as China modernizes and looks beyond Marxism for guidance, the ancient Chinese philosophy of Confucius has been looked at again.

We have selected ten theories (philosophies, worldviews, or ideologies) for detailed examination. In each case we provide some critical discussion that will, we hope, encourage readers to think for themselves (and there will be ample recommendations for further reading). We will not endorse any one theory as the "best buy," but will leave our readers to make up their own minds—though there are some suggestions for synthesis in the Conclusion. Before we begin our main business, let us review the prospects for impartial, rational assessment of these controversial matters.

THE CRITICAL EXAMINATION
OF RIVAL THEORIES

Many of these theories are (or have been) embodied in human societies and institutions. If so, they are not just intellectual constructions, but ways of life, subject to historical change, to growth and decay. A system of beliefs about the world and human nature that is held by some group of people not in a purely intellectual, academic, or scientific way, but as giving rise to their way of life, has often been called an "ideology."

When a belief is an ideology, used to justify the way of life of a social group, it will be difficult for the members of that community to consider it objectively. There will be strong social pressures to conform to it and acknowledge it. People will feel that their set of beliefs, even if perhaps open to some theoretical difficulties, contains vitally important insights, a vision of essential truths that have practical importance. For many people, to question their theory of human nature is to threaten what gives meaning, purpose, and hope to their life, and thus to cause them psychological discomfort or distress. Inertia, and unwillingness to admit that one is wrong, often play a part here. If one has been brought up in a certain belief and its associated way of life, or if one has converted to it and followed its precepts, it takes courage to question or abandon one's life commitment.

The prospects for impartial, rational, "purely philosophical" examination and evaluation may not seem bright, then. In so many discussions and debates (in public or in private), one feels that people's fundamental positions have already been decided (often by social conditioning of one sort or another) long before, and that all one gets by way of "debate" is a restatement of prejudices on all sides. Thus, one finds people maintaining and defending their favored ideology or theory of human nature (e.g., Christianity or atheistic humanism) in the face of intellectual and moral objections.

First, believers typically look for some way of explaining the objections away. The Christian may say that God does not always prevent evil or answer our prayers, and that what seems bad to us may ultimately be for the best. Human suffering under a political regime has often been excused by its propagandists as the necessary birth-pangs of a new world-order. Preachers and politicians become well practiced at such justification of the ways of God and His Church, or of the ruling party and its leader.

Second, the believer can take the offensive by attacking the motivation of the critic. Christians may say that those who persist in raising objections are blinded by sin, that it is their own pride that prevents them from seeing the light. The Marxist may claim that those who do not recognize the truth of Marx's analysis are deluded by the "false consciousness" typical of those who benefit from capitalist society. In the case of Freudian theory, critics of psychoanalysis have often been "diagnosed" as motivated by unconscious resistance to it. Thus a critic's motives are analyzed in terms of the very theory being criticized.

If a theory is defended by these two devices:

1. not allowing any evidence to count against the theory and always assuming that there must be some way of explaining away putative counterevidence,

2. answering criticism by analyzing the motivations of the critic in terms of the theory itself,

we can say that it is being held as a "closed system." This does not mean, however, that all believers in a theory (e.g., Christians, Marxists, or Freudians) have to hold it in that closed-minded way.

Is it possible, then, to discuss various theories of human nature rationally and objectively, as we are setting out to do in this book? When such theories are embodied in ways of life, belief in them seems to go beyond mere reasoning. The ultimate appeal may be to faith or authority, to community membership, loyalty, or commitment. There may be no answer to the questions "Why should I believe this?" or "Why should I accept this authority?" that will satisfy someone who is not already a member of the relevant group or tradition or finds herself attracted to it.

In the contemporary world, rival traditions and ideologies are as influential as ever. Religious, cultic, political, national, ethnic, psychotherapeutic, and gender-based dogmas are asserted with various degrees of aggression or politeness, crudity or sophistication. The media of the so-called "global village" usually seem to bring different cultures together only by way of confrontation, rather than genuine dialogue, mutual listening, and understanding. Many people feel the attractions of certainty, commitment, identity, and membership of a strongly defined community— notably in various forms of "fundamentalism," making appeal to what are seen, rightly or wrongly, as the fundamental, essential, defining themes of one tradition or another (Protestant or Catholic Christianity, Judaism, Islam, Hinduism, Marxism, "free-market-ism," American nationalism, or whatever).

In reaction to this, skepticism and cynicism are very tempting. Nowadays they tend to take the form of cultural relativism or postmodernism, according to which no particular cultural tradition (or ideology or theory of human nature) can have any more rational justification than any other. One of the most influential prophets of this trend was the nineteenth-century German philosopher Friedrich Nietzsche, who has been described as a "master of suspicion" because he was always ready (like Marx before him and Freud after him) to diagnose an unacknowledged ideological commitment or psychological need behind claims to supposedly "objective" truth or morality. If we jump to the relativist conclusion that there can be no such thing as a true account of human nature, or rational discussion of rival theories about it, the project of this book may seem doomed from the start.

We want to suggest, however, that such despair would be premature. For one thing, not all the theories we discuss are the ideologies of any identifiable social group, and in those cases there is less likelihood of their being defended in the closed-minded way. But more importantly, even if a theory is held by many people as a closed system, some degree of rational evaluation is still possible for those who are prepared to try it. We can always distinguish what someone says from their motivation for saying it. Motivation will be relevant if we wish to understand the personality and social background of the speaker. But if we are concerned with the truth or falsity of what a speaker says, and hence with whether there are any good reasons for believing it, then his or her motivation can be ignored. Someone may have admirable motivation for saying something that is nevertheless false, and someone else may be saying something true, even if his or her motivation for saying it is questionable. Criticism is not refuted by dislike of the critic. The most annoying critics are those who are (at least partly) *right!*

So, if the discussion is about whether the theory is true, or whether there are good reasons for believing it, then the objections that anyone produces against it must be replied to on their merits, regardless of motivations. And if motivation *is* considered, to analyze it in terms of the theory under discussion is to assume the truth of that theory, and thus to beg the question (i.e., to argue in a circle). An objection to a theory cannot be rationally defeated just by reasserting part of the theory. The second feature of closed systems—the technique of meeting all criticism by attacking the motives of the critic—is thus rationally unsatisfactory. It is open to us to make the effort to discuss and evaluate on their own merits the propositions that anyone asserts (with all due politeness to the assertor).

As to the first feature of closed systems—the attitude of always trying to find some way of explaining away objections—we can always ask whether the proposed "explaining away" is successful. It is not enough just to find some rhetorical flourish, a "one-liner" or "sound bite" that may temporarily surprise critics and allow one to escape with the impression that one has successfully maintained one's position. Rational, philosophical discussion—unlike "debates" in the media—is open-ended, there is always the possibility of making further points and of reexamining what has already been said to see if it can stand up to detailed scrutiny. So, any attempt at "explaining away" can be held up to careful examination, to try to decide whether or not it is really convincing. Many people do not have the time, patience, or willingness to engage in that kind of open-minded debate—but that does not prevent others from trying their best to do so. The ancient Greek philosopher Socrates gave us this method of "Socratic dialogue" (see Chapter 4). Jesus also set an example of being willing to talk and argue seriously with anyone, however socially outcast, with concern for their spiritual well-being.

So we say to the committed (including fundamentalists of various persuasions): we are not asking you to give up your commitment, but to think about it. You can compare it with other theories, considering how far you would agree or disagree with them. You can think about how best you can reply to objections to your own theory. You can think about which parts of your tradition you want to say are really essential or lay hold of some fundamental truth, and which parts are in some sense optional— perhaps historically important, but not needing to be imposed on everybody. It is up to you, at every stage, to make up (and perhaps change) your own mind about exactly what you want to affirm.

To the uncommitted (including relativists or postmodernists) we say: everybody has to have some sort of theory of human nature or ideology or philosophy to live by; you must have some conceptions of what affects human well-being, and some views about what is most worth doing—even if only about what your own long-term well-being or happiness consists in. We invite you to consider these various systems of thought we put before you, to compare your present view (however minimal or relativist it is) with them, and to try to rationally evaluate the differences. No human being who lives at a more than animal level can completely opt out of offering reasons for his or her beliefs and actions.

1

Confucianism: The Way
of the Sages

No other single figure has had more influence on Chinese thought and civilization than Confucius (551–479 B.C.E.). Little is known for certain about this important figure who came to be regarded as "the teacher" in many periods of Chinese history. He was born into the aristocratic yet poor K'ung family in the state of Lu, now part of the province of Shantung. We are told that as a youth he was orphaned early and was very fond of learning. Later in his life he left his home state of Lu and traveled through-out several regions of China offering his service as an adviser to feudal lords; however, he was never successful at obtaining a position that would allow him to put his ideas into practice and so returned to Lu to devote the remainder of his life to teaching. It is useful to keep this failure in mind while considering certain aspects of his teachings. Confucius be-came honored in Chinese chronicles as the Great Master K'ung, or K'ung Fu-tzu, better known in the West in the Latinized form "Confucius."

By all accounts the text known as *Lun Yu*—usually rendered into English as *The Analects*—is the most reliable source of Confucius's ideas. The *Analects* consists of scattered sayings of the Master that were com-piled by his disciples after his death. It is a matter of scholarly debate whether any or all of the *Analects* can be regarded as the actual words of Confucius, and many will argue that some of the chapters are later additions. Although Confucianism is a complex tradition with a long history of development, the *Analects* gives voice to early and central Confucian ideas that continued to define the tradition for many centuries. Therefore, for the purposes of this introduction, I focus exclusively on the *Analects*, treating the text as a whole, and use the name "Confucius" to refer to the source of the sayings recorded in the *Analects*. Two later developments within Confucianism that pertain to theories of human nature are explored toward the end of this chapter.

THEORY OF THE UNIVERSE

The main emphasis in the *Analects* is on humanism, not metaphysics. That is to say, Confucius was concerned primarily with basic human welfare and spoke little about the ultimate nature of the world in which we live. When once asked about worship of gods and spirits, Confucius replied: "You are not able even to serve man. How can you serve the spirits?" (XI.12). And when asked about death he said: "You do not understand even life. How can you understand death?" (XI.12). Avoiding metaphysical speculation, Confucius instead advocated good government that would promote the well-being of the common people and would bring about harmonious relations among citizens. Confucius did, however, recognize that there are forces in the universe that determine our lives. He characterized these by employing two related meanings of the term *ming*: the Decree of Heaven (*t'ien ming*) and Destiny (*ming*).

Confucius insisted that we live in a moral world. Morality is part of the very fabric of the universe; for Confucius, there is something ultimate and transcendent about ethical conduct. He once remarked: "Heaven is author of the virtue that is in me" (VII.23). The concept of the Decree of Heaven was widely accepted in China during Confucius's day. The Decree of Heaven was generally understood to mean a moral imperative for governance, based on the belief that Heaven cares profoundly about the welfare of the common people. Heaven would support an emperor only so long as he ruled for this higher purpose and not for his own benefit. Confucius added to this doctrine by extending the realm of the heavenly mandate to include every person; now everyone—not just the emperor— was subject to the universal law that obliged one to act morally in order to be in harmony with the Decree of Heaven. Ultimate perfection, then, for Confucius, has to do with cultivating a transcendent morality authored by Heaven. It is possible, however, to resist or disobey the Decree of Heaven.

Nevertheless, there are certain dimensions of life that are beyond human control, areas in which human effort has no effect whatsoever. This indeterminate dimension of human life falls under the heading of Destiny, that aspect of Heaven's design that is beyond human comprehension. One's place in life, social success, wealth, and longevity are all due to Destiny. No amount of struggle will make any difference in their outcome; these things are simply determined by one's fate. Whereas the Decree of Heaven can be understood—although with great difficulty—Destiny is beyond comprehension. The distinction between the Decree of Heaven (to which humans can conform or not) and Destiny (which is beyond human agency) is fundamental for Confucius, for if one understands that the material comforts of life are due to Destiny, one will recognize the futility of pursuing them and will devote all one's effort to the pursuit of Heaven's morality. Morality, then—which has nothing to do with social success—is the only worthy pursuit in life. Confucius argued that it is necessary to understand the nature of both the Decree of Heaven (II.4) and Destiny (XX.3), but for different reasons. The Decree of Heaven is the true object of ultimate concern, whereas Destiny is simply to be accepted courageously.

Before we move on to look at Confucius's views of human nature, it is useful to examine another of his concepts: the Way (*tao*). Although the term *Tao* did come to be used in China as an abstract metaphysical principle (especially by the Taoists), for Confucius it primarily meant the "Way of the sages," those ancient rulers of earlier ideal times. The Confucian concept of the Way is linked intimately to the concept of Heaven in that it involves the path of proper conduct. Although it is difficult to discern, the Way of Heaven can be known through the previous actions of the sages. Regarding the sage Yao, Confucius is recorded as saying: "Great indeed was Yao as a ruler! How lofty! It is Heaven that is great and it was Yao who modeled himself upon it. He was so boundless that the common people were not able to put a name to his virtues" (VIII.19). Accordingly, the ancient sages—who modeled themselves on Heaven—become models of the Way to human perfection in the present, the Way to be followed by all people (VI.17). In the end, three related things warrant reverence according to Confucius. He is recorded as saying: "The gentleman stands in awe of three things. He is in awe of the Decree of Heaven. He is in awe of great men. He is in awe of the words of the sages" (XVI.8).

THEORY OF HUMAN NATURE

Confucius seems to have been very optimistic about potential human accomplishments. In fact, the goal of much of Chinese philosophy is to help people become sages. Confucius's remark that "Heaven is author of the virtue that is in me" demonstrates his conviction that human beings have access to the ultimate reality of Heaven's morality. For Confucius, every person is potentially a sage, defined as one who acts with extreme benevolence (VI.30). That is, all human beings have the capacity to cultivate virtue and bring themselves into harmony with the Decree of Heaven. Confucius indicates that the result of following the Way of Heaven is the subjective experience of joy. Optimism regarding human potential, however, is not the same as optimism about the *actual* state of human affairs. The truth is, Confucius went on to attest, that a sage is a very rare being. He declared: "I have no hopes of meeting a sage" (VII.26). Although all human beings are potential sages, in reality this is an uncommon occurrence. Most human beings exist in a dreadful state.

What is it that enables potential sages to be so misled? Confucius said very little directly about human nature, causing his disciple Tzu-kung to remark: "One can get to hear about the Master's accomplishments, but one cannot get to hear his views on human nature and the Way of Heaven" (V.13). His dearth of statements on human nature allowed widely divergent theories to develop in later Confucianism. Despite his lack of explicit statements about human nature, however, it is clear from Confucius's sayings that in certain areas of life human beings exercise a freedom of will. Although we have no control over our Destiny—we cannot, for example, determine our social status or longevity—we are free to reject or pursue morality and proper conduct. That is, we have the ability to resist or conform to the Decree of Heaven, the very source of virtue. While acknowledging that human beings have no significant choice as to the circumstances of the life they live, Confucius stressed that we do have a choice as to *how* we live in any given situation.

While he did not define human nature in any detail, Confucius insisted that all human beings are fundamentally the same. We simply become differentiated due to our different ways of being. "Men are close to one another by nature. They diverge as a result of repeated practice" (XVII.2). What this means, among other things, is that human beings are extremely malleable. We can become almost anything. We are unfinished and impressible, and in need of constant molding to achieve our ultimate end of moral perfection. In accord with modern sociologists and psychologists, Confucius seems to be suggesting that our environment and ways of being significantly determine our character. Thus his great concern with paradigmatic figures—the sages—and the role they play in shaping the ideal human life. Human life without carefully crafted culture produces disastrous results. The subsequent state of problematic social conditions is taken up in the next section.

Two additional matters are worth mentioning in regard to Confucius's views of human nature. First, the ideal moral figure for Confucius is the "gentleman" (*chun-tzu*). This term is decidedly masculine. While the term might be applied in a manner that includes both genders, it is clear that Confucius used the term in an exclusive way. He has little to say about women, and when he does speak of them he frequently does so in unflattering terms. On one occasion, for example, he lumps them together with "small men" and warns that in one's household both are "difficult to deal with" (XVII.25).

Second, although Confucius informs us that human nature is fundamentally uniform, he does not clarify whether this is a good nature that needs to be guarded carefully or a bad nature that stands in need of serious reform. His lack of specificity on this issue spawned much heated debate in later Confucianism. We see what two major thinkers in the Confucian tradition have had to say about this important issue in the last section of this chapter.

DIAGNOSIS

Although the sayings of Confucius are predominantly prescriptive, they give a clear indication of what is wrong with human life. Generally speaking, the human condition is one of social discord caused by selfishness and ignorance of the past. Stated perhaps more succinctly, human beings are out of accord with the Decree of Heaven. Consequently, human interaction is marred by strife, rulers govern with attention only to personal gain, common people suffer under unjust burdens, and social behavior in general is determined by egoism and greed. Such is the dismal state of human beings.

What are the reasons for these distressing circumstances? At least five causes can be discerned in the *Analects*: (1) people are attached to profit; (2) society lacks the respect of filial piety; (3) the connection between word and action cannot be trusted; (4) ignorance regarding the Way of the sages prevails; and (5) benevolence is absent from human affairs. Let us examine these causes one by one.

Confucius said: "If one is guided by profit in one's actions, one will incur much ill will" (IV.12). One of the central tenets in Confucian thought is the opposition between rightness and profit. "The gentleman understands what is moral. The small man understands what is profitable" (IV.16). Ordinary human behavior is driven by a strong concern for the outcome of a particular action with regard to the self. That is, people typically ask, What will I get out of this action? The common aim in action, then, is a selfish one. Actions are generally performed to increase one's wealth or power. This is what Confucius means by action guided by profit. Even if a person does what is right, if the motivation is a nonmoral purpose—say, to gain rank—that person is still guided by profit. Confucius warns in the

Analects: "It is shameful to make salary your sole object" (XIV.1). Since he believed that morality should be the sole guide for all action, Confucius contended that action guided by profit leads to immoral circumstances and social disharmony wherein all people are selfishly looking out for themselves alone. Material benefits derived from invested labor are not in themselves bad, but the means by which they are obtained is of critical importance to Confucius. "Wealth and rank attained through immoral means have as much to do with me as passing clouds" (VII.16).

Selfish conduct motivated by personal profit implies a lack of true respect for others in a given society. For Confucius, this lack of respect reveals improper relationships within families, which in turn demonstrates a lack of self-discipline. This occurs because individuals have lost their grounding in morality, leading to problems in the family, which is the very basis of a good society. In this sense, Confucianism is very much a tradition of family values. A son who does not know how to treat his father will be a very poor citizen. Corrupt individuals, then, who have not cultivated the personal virtue necessary for proper familial relationships spread ill will throughout society. On the other hand, "It is rare for a man whose character is such that he is good as a son and obedient as a young man to have the inclination to transgress against his superiors" (I.2).

Another problem noted by Confucius is the fact that there is often a difference between what is said and what is done. Confucius said: "I used to take on trust a man's deeds after having listened to his words. Now having listened to a man's words I go on to observe his deeds" (V.10). Confucius recognizes that people are often untrustworthy. Without a direct connection between word and deed there is no basis for trust, since trust rests on the premise that what is said will be done. Without this basic trust, individuals lose the ability to represent themselves sincerely and to rely on others with any degree of confidence. Accordingly, society loses its footing.

Ignorance of the past is also a major cause of the troublesome human condition. What Confucius means specifically by this is an unfamiliarity with the Way of the sages. It was pointed out earlier that the sages model their lives on Heaven, thereby establishing a paradigm for the path to moral perfection. Without knowledge of the Way of the sages, people are cut off from the moral insight of the past. In such a state they become morally adrift and prone to wrong action. Confucius had so much faith in the Way of the sages that he remarked: "He has not lived in vain who dies the day he is told about the Way" (IV.8).

The most important virtue that a human being can possess for Confucius is benevolence (*jen*). To embody benevolence is to achieve moral perfection. This central Confucian idea is represented by a Chinese character that has been explained pictographically as consisting of two parts:

the component for "human" and the component for "two." That is, it represents two people standing together in harmony. Essentially, benevolence has to do with human relationships. Several scholars have argued that *jen* is better translated into English as "human-heartedness" or "humaneness." Regardless, *jen* is a wide-ranging moral term that represents the very pinnacle of human excellence for Confucius. And, according to him, it is definitely within the reach of human beings. "The Master said, 'Is benevolence really far away? No sooner do I desire it than it is here' " (VII.30). The core of a perfected human being, then, is a benevolent heart. Unfortunately, Confucius observes, this virtue is all too rare in the world: "I have never met a man who finds benevolence attractive" (IV.6). Consequently, potential social harmony is replaced with strife.

PRESCRIPTION

The Confucian prescription for the ills of human existence is based on self-discipline. When questioned about the perfect man, Confucius said: "He cultivates himself and thereby brings peace and security to the people" (XIV.42). The ideal ruler for Confucius rules by personal moral example. But just what does self-cultivation mean in this context? The answer to this question can be found by exploring the proposed solutions to the five ills outlined in the preceding section.

To overcome the human tendency to act out of a concern for profit, Confucius proposed "doing for nothing." Specifically, this involves doing what is right simply because it is morally right, and not for any other reason. For Confucius, the moral struggle is an end in itself; through it, one achieves a union of will with the Decree of Heaven. Acting in order to do what is right, rather than what is profitable, can serve also as a shield against life's disappointments. The state of benevolence is characterized by an inner serenity and equanimity and an indifference to matters of fortune and misfortune over which one has no direct control. Righteousness is its own reward, a joyous reward that transcends any particular social situation. Even if all one's efforts go unrecognized, by following the principle of "doing for nothing" one is never discontented. "Is it not gentlemanly not to take offence when others fail to appreciate your abilities?" (I.1). Furthermore, this principle motivates one to keep working for righteousness in a world that has little appreciation for it. Confucius himself is described as one "who keeps working towards a goal the realization of which he knows to be hopeless" (XIV.38). Faith in the Way of Heaven does not depend on results within the social world of rank and recognition. Remember that Confucius himself failed to secure a political position that would have provided him recognition and allowed him to put his ideas into practice. He says in the *Analects* that a man should strive to enter politics simply because he knows this to be right, even when he is well aware that his principles cannot prevail (XVIII.7). This relates to the notion of Destiny discussed in the first section of this chapter. Social success is a matter of Destiny; Confucius therefore concludes that it is futile to pursue it. Moral integrity, however, is within one's control, and in truth it is the only thing in life worth pursuing. One can struggle to understand the ways of Heaven, but it is clear that one should act humanely whatever Heaven sends. Again, it is the cultivation of self that is important, not social recognition. "The gentleman is troubled by his own lack of ability, not the failure of others to appreciate him" (XV.19).

The cultivation of self as a good family member is another of Confucius's prescriptions for a harmonious society. He believed that being a good family member had tremendous influence beyond the boundary of one's immediate family. "Simply by being a good son and friendly to his brothers a man can exert an influence upon government" (II.21). The transformation of society begins with the cultivation of the self within the environment of the family; it then spreads out like ripples caused from throwing a pebble in a still pond. The rules and relationships that govern the family are to be extended to include all of society. Benevolence toward people outside one's family should be an extension of the love one feels for members of one's own family. The most important relationship of all for Confucius is the one between a son and his father. When questioned about filial piety, Confucius advised: "Never fail to comply" (II.5). The manner in which a good son honors a father is by following his ways. "If [after his father's death], for three years, a man makes no changes to his father's ways, he can be said to be a good son" (I.11). This depends, of course, on the virtuous qualities of the father. Confucius is adamant that the father of the family, or by extension the emperor of the state, must rule by moral example. "If you set an example by being correct, who would dare to remain incorrect?" (XII.17).

Confucius was once asked what would be the first thing he would do if he were put in charge of the administration of a state. He replied: "If something has to be put first, it is, perhaps, the rectification of names" (XIII.3). The rectification of names means that there is an agreement between name and actuality. This correction is necessary, because without the agreement between name and actuality, or between word and deed, much is lost. For Confucius, a name carries certain implications that constitute the very essence of the named object. For example, when asked by a duke about good government, Confucius responded by saying: "Let the ruler be a ruler, the subject a subject, the father a father, the son a son" (XII.11). The concept of "son," for example, as we have just seen, is more than a biological designation. The name implies certain attitudes and responsibilities essential to harmonious existence. Moreover, without the connection between word and actuality there is no genuine trust. This is the definition of a lie. After hearing Confucius's remark on good government, the duke exclaimed: "Splendid! Truly, if the ruler be not a ruler, the subject not a subject, the father not a father, the son not a son, then even if there be grain, would I get to eat it?" That is, the word "grain" and the availability of grain are two different things. If there is no connection between them, then one may go hungry because of a locked, or perhaps even empty, granary. Words are easy to produce; if a person or government uses them to conceal the truth, then social chaos ensues. Trust is a critical ingredient of all dependable social interaction. Therefore, the self-cultivating gentleman is "trustworthy in what he says" (I.7) and "puts his words into actions" (II.13).

The antidote for the ignorance of the past referred to in the preceding section is study. Confucianism is a scholarly tradition. In China it is known as the Ju School—the term *ju* comes to mean "scholar"—and is recorded in Chinese sources as the school that delights in study of the Six Classics (*Lui Yi*). From this it is evident that Confucius placed great emphasis on learning. He advised: "Have the firm faith to devote yourself to learning, and abide to the death in the good way" (VII.13). But what is the content of this learning that allows one to abide in the good way? It is clear from the representation of Confucianism just mentioned that the content of Confucian learning is the Classics, a collection of books that constitutes the cultural legacy of the past. Most important for Confucius, the Classics give expression to the Way of the sages and thus grant access to the exemplary conduct that leads to moral perfection. Because of this, study of the Classics is understood to be a vital element in achieving excellence and a sacred enterprise that expands one's nature. It is also an important aspect of good government. "When a student finds that he can more than cope with his studies, then he takes office" (XIX.13).

Excellence is defined by the Confucian tradition primarily as the embodiment of benevolence. The manner in which one comes to embody benevolence constitutes the last of the five solutions being explored. This process really involves three elements: clinging to benevolence at all times while following the "golden rule" and observing the "rites."

Confucius said: "The gentleman never deserts benevolence, not even for as long as it takes to eat a meal" (IV.5). That is to say, one is to be ever mindful of benevolence in everything one does. The Confucian goal is to let benevolence determine all aspects of life, since it is the perfect virtue that denotes the Decree of Heaven. Confucius himself is described in the *Analects* as one who maintained correctness and benevolence at all times (VII.4). But how is one to know what constitutes benevolence?

The practice of benevolence consists in balanced consideration for others and oneself. One measure of the consideration for others is determined by the treatment one desires for oneself. Confucius says: "A benevolent man helps others to take their stand in so far as he himself wishes to take his stand" (VI.30). In other words, this is the golden rule: "Do unto others what you would have done to yourself." Confucius also states this rule in negative form. When asked to define benevolence, he said: "Do not impose on others what you yourself do not desire" (XII.2). In a general sense, then, one's own self becomes a measure of decent conduct. However, Confucius has more to say about the measure of excellent conduct than this. Even if a person's heart is in the right place, it is possible to offend others because of a lack of knowledge about what is appropriate conduct in a particular situation. Knowledge is a key component to ethical action. Specifically for Confucius, this means knowing ritually correct behavior, or the rites (*li*). These consist of regulations governing action in every aspect of life, as well as ceremonial propriety, such as in making offerings to the ancestors. The rites are designed to teach individuals how to act well and are therefore a critical component in moral education. Knowledge of the rites functions as a guide for action beyond the general decency derived from using one's own self as a measure of conduct. Self-interest must finally be harnessed to the rites in order to achieve moral perfection. "To return to the observance of the rites through overcoming the self constitutes benevolence" (XII.1). Observing these rules, a person transcends self-interest. The rites are a body of rules culled from past moral insights and guide action toward perfection. What are the rites based on, and how does one come to know about them? They are based on the Classics, and one comes to know of them through study. Thus, the interconnectedness of Confucius's ideas comes into focus. Moral perfection, or benevolence, is achieved by following the rites, which are known by studying the Classics, which give expression to the Way of Heaven as embodied by the sages.

Perhaps the most significant passage of all those recorded in the *Analects* is one that gives a summary indication of the path to perfection as it is understood in early Confucianism. "The Master said, 'At fifteen I set my heart on learning; at thirty I took my stand; at forty I came to be free from doubts; at fifty I understood the Decree of Heaven; at sixty my ear was atuned; at seventy I followed my heart's desire without overstepping the line' " (II.4). Here Confucius is saying that at fifteen he took up serious study of the Classics. This gave him access to a knowledge of the Way of the sages and, therefore, an awareness of the rites, the institutional form of their perfect

demeanor. At age thirty he was able to take a stand in the rites, or to put
the proper conduct of the rites into practice. By practicing the rites, he
moved at age forty from mere observation of the rites to true understanding of the rites. This led to a concomitant understanding of the Decree
of Heaven by age fifty. At sixty Confucius experienced a union of wills
with the Decree of Heaven, so that by age seventy he could follow his own
desire—now in harmony with the Decree of Heaven—with the result that
he spontaneously acted with perfect benevolence.

Indicated here is the salvific path of paradigmatic action. As perfect beings, the sages naturally act with benevolence. Their benevolence is the
external expression of a perfected inner state. As such, their benevolent
actions become models of and for perfection for Confucians who desire
to achieve the accomplished state of a sage. Again, the Way of the sages
is available in the Classics; thus the great attention paid to study in the
Confucian tradition. What the sages perform naturally becomes the model
for the conscious self-discipline that leads to moral perfection. Proper disciplined action is represented in the Confucian tradition as the rites (*li*).
From an outsider's perspective, the natural benevolent action of a sage and
of a self-disciplined person who follows the rites appear the same, but the
internal motive is different. The sage's behavior is the natural expression
of an inner perfected state, whereas the disciplined person's behavior consists of studied actions—the rites—that are modeled on the benevolence
of the sages. The goal of disciplined action, however, is to achieve a state
wherein perfect moral action becomes natural and spontaneous. This is the
state of the "gentleman," and this is what is said to have happened to
Confucius toward the end of his life. The sages express moral perfection
naturally, whereas the gentleman has achieved perfection by modeling his
life on the behavior of the sages. The actions of a gentleman and a disciplined Confucian student may also appear the same from the outside, just
as a master musician and a disciplined student appear to be making the
same moves. But once again, the motives are different in both cases. The
master musician has so internalized the fingering chart of the instrument
she is playing that she is no longer conscious of it, whereas the student is
still consciously following the fingering chart. Likewise, the gentleman
has so internalized the Way of the sages that he now acts spontaneously,
whereas the Confucian student who "stands in the rites" consciously follows the proper conduct that the rites represent. In either case, by following the rites, both the gentleman and the diligent student have embodied
benevolence, the very pinnacle of moral perfection.

As a paradigmatic tradition, Confucianism produces a chain of perfected moral action that makes the benevolent Way of the sages present
for the common people and creates moral examples for those who are not

involved in the elite tradition of textual study. It should be clear by now that moral perfection for the Confucian tradition is represented by the sages and that, as the ideal of human perfection, the gentleman has achieved moral perfection by studying the Classics and internalizing the Way of the sages. The Confucian practitioner is ideally moving along this same path. Direct observation of present-day human practitioners takes the place of textual study for those unable to read. To the degree that a practitioner can embody benevolence by following the Confucian rites, the Way of the sages is then present for all of society to observe and to follow. In this way, a line of moral perfection reaches back from the time of the sages and continues into the very present. If all people would follow this Way, Confucius believed, individuals would achieve perfection, society would be radically transformed, and benevolence would rule.

LATER DEVELOPMENTS

Because Confucius did not spell out his views on human nature in any detail, a major debate arose within the tradition soon after his death regarding this question: Is human nature originally good or evil? Opposing answers were supplied by two leading figures in the Confucian tradition. Representing the "idealistic wing," Mencius (371–289 B.C.E.) contended that human nature is originally good; representing the "realistic wing," Hsun-tzu (298–238 B.C.E.) argued that human nature is originally evil. Although we cannot possibly do justice to the entire Confucian tradition here, a brief examination of this debate gives further indication of the complexity of this tradition and adds to our overall consideration of human nature.

The writings and ideas of Mencius rank second in the tradition only to those of Confucius, and, above all, his name is associated with his theory of the original goodness of human nature. In a collection of his sayings recorded in a book that bears his name, Mencius articulates his position on the controversy over human nature that came to be regarded as orthodox for the Confucian tradition and normative for much of Chinese culture. In the *Mencius*, Mencius refutes a philosopher named Kao-tzu, who argues that human nature is intrinsically neither good nor bad and that morality therefore is something that has to be added artificially from the outside. "Human nature," Kao-tzu maintains, "is like whirling water. Give it an outlet in the east and it will flow east; give it an outlet in the west and it will flow west. Human nature does not show any preference for either good or bad just as water does not show any preference for either east or west." Mencius, however, is insistent that human nature is innately good. He counters Kao-tzu by explaining: "It certainly is the case that water does not show any preference for either east or west, but does it show the same indifference to high and low? Human nature is good just as water seeks low ground. There is no man who is not good; there is no water that does not flow downwards" (VI.A.2).

The core of Mencius's theory about innate human nature relates to his understanding of the human heart. For Mencius, the thinking, compassionate heart is a gift from Heaven (VI.A.15). This is what defines our essential humanness and sets us apart from animals. Specifically, the heart is a receptacle of four incipient tendencies or "seeds," as Mencius calls them. He maintains that "Man has these four germs just as he has four limbs" (II.A.6). If unobstructed and nurtured carefully, these seeds sprout into the four virtues so greatly prized by the Confucian tradition, as lofty trees grow naturally from small seeds. The four seeds of compassion, shame, courtesy, and sense of right and wrong develop respectively into the four virtues of benevolence, dutifulness, observance of the rites, and wisdom (II.A.6). And Mencius insists that these four seeds "are not welded on to me from the outside; they are in me originally" (VI.6). For Mencius, our original heart identifies us all as potential sages.

Mencius, however, agrees with many of the philosophers of his time that human beings are creatures of desire. Selfish desire in particular threatens to overwhelm the four seeds that define the source of our higher moral nature. The heavenly gift of the thinking heart is therefore recognized to be fragile and can be lost if not used and cultivated. This, of course, is the norm. Mencius says: "Heaven has not sent down men whose endowment differs so greatly. The difference is due to what ensnares their hearts" (VI.A.7). The ensnarement of the human heart, for Mencius, is the source of all evil; thus the great concern for carefully nurturing its innate qualities. "Given the right nourishment there is nothing that will not grow, and deprived of it there is nothing that will not wither away" (VI.8).

All hope for humanity, according to Mencius, lies in the human heart. Our desiring nature is something we share with all animals, but it is our thinking heart—that special gift from Heaven—that sets us up to be benevolent sages. Mencius offers a proof for the innate goodness of all people. "My reason for saying that no man is devoid of a heart sensitive to the suffering of others is this. Suppose a man were, all of a sudden, to see a young child on the verge of falling into a well. He would certainly be moved to compassion, not because he wanted to get in the good graces of the parents, nor because he wished to win the praise of his fellow villagers or friends, nor yet because he disliked the cry of the child" (II.A.6). What Mencius seems to be saying here is that every person in this situation would have an immediate, spontaneous, and unreflective urge to save the child. This reveals a pure impulse for righteousness over selfish profit. Mencius says nothing about the ensuing action. It may be the case that the man involved would, upon any reflection following the "all of a sudden," engage in calculating thoughts of self-interest. Regardless of what follows, however, the momentary urge indicated in this statement is all Mencius needs to demonstrate what he refers to as the seed of compassion. For him, this proves that human nature is intrinsically good.

Mencius's strongest opponent was Hsun-tzu, an important Confucian writer who was born toward the end of Mencius's life. Hsun-tzu held that our interior world is dominated by dynamic impulses of desire. The basic human problem for Hsun-tzu is that human libidinous urges have no clear limit. Nature has given us unlimited desires in a world with limited resources; hence, social strife arises among necessarily competitive human beings. In a text he composed himself, Hsun-tzu writes: "Man is born with desires. If desires are not satisfied for him, he cannot but seek some means to satisfy them himself. If there are no limits and degrees to his seeking, then he will inevitably fall to wrangling with other men" (section 19, p. 89). This view caused him to formulate a position on human nature diametrically opposed to that of Mencius: "Man's nature is evil; goodness is the result of conscious activity" (section 23, p. 157). Hsun-tzu was well aware of Mencius's ideas but insisted that they were wrong. "Mencius states that man's nature is good, and that evil arises because he loses his original nature. Such a view, I believe, is erroneous" (158). Hsun-tzu replaces Mencius's theory of the four seeds with his own theory of four incipient tendencies for profit, envy, hatred, and desire, which if left in their natural state give rise to the four evils of strife, violence, crime, and wantonness. These, he insists, are innate in all humans, so that the path that follows our own nature leads only to evil. "Any man who follows his nature and indulges his emotions will inevitably become involved in wrangling and strife, will violate the forms and rules of society, and will end as a criminal" (157).

Hsun-tzu goes on to compare the criminal-like human being to a warped piece of wood. "A warped piece of wood must wait until it has been laid against the straightening board, steamed, and forced into shape before it can become straight, because by nature it is warped" (164). Surprisingly, Hsun-tzu is rather optimistic about potential human accomplishments, for he too believed that with the proper education and training all people could become sages. "The man in the street can become a Yu [a sage]" (166). What is it, we might ask, that transforms the warped pieces of wood that are human beings into the straight boards of sages, or at least proper citizens? That is, what constitutes the straightening board for human beings? After his statement about warped wood, Hsun-tzu writes: "Similarly, since man's nature is evil, he must wait for the ordering power of the sage kings and the transforming power of ritual principles; only then can he achieve order and conform to goodness" (164). Hsun-tzu here confirms the absolute value of a fundamental Confucian idea; the straightening board consists of the rites, or what is here translated as "ritual principles." For him, the rites are the products of the sheer intellectual activity of the sages and were designed to curb and channel the boundless desires of human beings. When Hsun-tzu says that "goodness is the result of conscious activity," he means a conscious effort to transform oneself by diligently applying oneself to the rites, those guiding principles created and embodied by past sages. Hsun-tzu is clearly an advocate for culture over nature, for the rites are not an essential part of human nature. Everything that is good is a product of conscious human effort. The fact that we have two arms is natural, but virtue comes only with assiduous human effort. For him, the attentive application of the unnatural rites is the key to achieving human perfection. "In respect to human nature the sage is the same as all other men and does not surpass them; it is only in his conscious activity that he differs from and surpasses other men" (161). The sage, then, for Hsun-tzu, is a human being whose nature has been radically transformed by the Confucian rites.

The contrast between Mencius and Hsun-tzu is dramatic. Mencius believed that morality is naturally present in our hearts, whereas Hsun-tzu believed that it is something artificially instilled from the outside. Nevertheless, we observe an agreement in the ideas of Hsun-tzu and Mencius that identifies them both as Confucians. Both agree that the path to sagehood comprises the Confucian rites, those proper modes of action based on the paradigmatic behavior of past sages. For Hsun-tzu, the rites function as a straightening board to transform warped human beings into straight and benevolent citizens, whereas for Mencius, they function more like a racket press designed to keep a stored wooden tennis racket from warping; although innately present, the heart of compassion can become twisted if not reinforced with the constant observance of the rites. Although the two philosophers disagree sharply in theory, they are in complete agreement regarding practice. Human perfection is achieved through a process of following the paradigmatic actions and insights of past sages.

CRITICAL DISCUSSION

We may conclude this introduction to Confucianism with a few comments designed to bring into sharper focus some possible criticisms already hinted at in our discussion. Besides being a system that is rooted in the common decency of the golden rule, Confucianism is a tradition that teaches obedience to superiors. The relevant superiors are the father of the family, the ruler of the state, and the Confucian scholar who makes accessible the Way of the sages. If the heads of the family and state are just men, then all is well. But if such men are unjust, then the entire system is undermined. Confucius himself was aware of this problem and therefore insistent on the moral character of leaders. Nonetheless, his system gives a great deal of power to a few individuals and leaves the majority in a subordinate position.

Confucianism is also a fairly conservative tradition that looks to the past for guidance. This may be seen as an attitude that restricts the creativity of individuals in the present. This made Confucianism a primary target of attack during the Chinese cultural revolution of the late 1960s and early 1970s. Furthermore, it is a system dependent on an elite of literati, the Confucian scholars. We might ask, Do scholars have access to the past in a manner that is free of their own ideological agendas? Confucianism, it has been shown, is based largely on a transcendent view of morality. It may be argued that such a view is simply a way for a certain group to give special privilege to its own view of morality. We might then ask, Whose view of the past and whose view of morality is Confucianism based on? Most historians today contend that no view of the past is completely neutral or apolitical. All historical representations involve issues of power.

Many people seem to be excluded from the Confucian enterprise. The common people are represented as an undifferentiated and generally inept mass, another problem from the perspective of communist China. Women in particular do not seem to be included in Confucius's educational system. His view of human perfection is decidedly masculine, and all in all he has little to say about the potential of women for self-cultivation. When Confucius does speak about women, he does so in derogatory terms, suggesting that they are generally unruly and resistant to legitimate authority. Although the Confucian path to perfection may be expanded by its advocates to include both genders, the *Analects* poses a problem for readers who believe in the equality of the sexes.

Finally, the pragmatic nature of Confucianism has been criticized by other Chinese philosophers, such as the more metaphysically minded Taoists. The Taoist philosopher Chuang-tzu, for example, criticized the Confucians for their reduction of reality to only that which concerns human social affairs. Chuang-tzu reversed Hsun-tzu's assessment of what is valuable by advocating nature over culture. As a nature mystic aware of the immensity of life in all its forms, Chuang-tzu believed that the Confucians occupied a tragically small world. He also characterized Confucians as people overly concerned with utilitarian matters and countered this preoccupation with a celebration of the usefulness of uselessness. Over the course of time, however, Confucianism has proven to be a much more attractive system to Chinese thinkers for establishing virtuous human society than the more abstract metaphysical thought of Taoism.

Although Confucianism was discredited in China in the early twentieth century by the collapse of the imperial system and was a primary target of the cultural revolution (which identified it with everything that had been wrong with the older system), it has experienced somewhat of a revival, especially since the death of Mao Zedong in 1976. The revival, known as New Confucianism, has been carried out by a group of scholars who aim to modernize Confucianism rather than abandon it altogether. The modernization involves a process of weeding out those aspects of the older Confucian culture that are deemed problematic from a modern perspective, such as the subordination of women. An exemplary figure of this new movement is Tu Weiming, a professor currently at Harvard University who has explored Confucian thought for its application to the contemporary quest for more socially just and ecologically harmonious ways of living. He sees Confucianism as a positive resource for thinking about ways to overcome the destructive side of modernization that threatens both human communities and the natural world. In this new form, Confucianism is once again making significant contributions to considerations concerning the big questions of the day.

FOR FURTHER READING

Basic text: *The Analects* (many translations and editions). I have quoted from the excellent translation by D. C. Lau, *Confucius: The Analects* (London: Penguin, 1979). This is a very readable and reliable text that includes a valuable introduction. Another readily available translation is that by Arthur Waley, *The Analects of Confucius* (New York: Macmillan, 1938; New York: Vintage, 1989).

Mencius: I have quoted from the translation by D. C. Lau, *Mencius* (London: Penguin, 1970). This edition also includes an excellent introduction.

Hsun-tzu: I have quoted from the translation by Burton Watson, *Hsun Tzu: Basic Writings* (New York: Columbia University Press, 1963).

For more on Confucianism, see *Thinking through Confucius* by Roger T. Ames and David L. Hall (Albany: State University of New York Press, 1987).

To gain a better understanding of the place of Confucianism in Chinese philosophy, see *A Short History of Chinese Philosophy* by Fung Yu-lan (New York: Macmillan, 1948; New York: Free Press, 1966); *Disputers of the Tao* by A. C. Graham (Lasalle, Ill.: Open Court, 1989); and *The World of Thought in Ancient China* by Benjamin I. Schwartz (Cambridge, Mass.: Harvard University Press, 1985).

For more on New Confucianism and the writings of Tu Weiming, see *Confucian Thought: Selfhood As Creative Transformation* (Albany: State University of New York Press, 1985).

2

Upanishadic Hinduism: Quest for Ultimate Knowledge

An introductory examination of Hinduism can be very challenging, since there is no founder, no clear historical beginning point nor central text, as we find in most other religious traditions. Hinduism is an extremely diverse tradition that consists of a wide range of practices and beliefs, making the task of generalization nearly impossible. The term "Hinduism" itself is largely a Western construct designed simply to refer to the dominant religion of the majority of the people who inhabit the South Asian subcontinent. Therefore, in many ways, it is absurd to attempt to represent Hinduism with a single text, for no particular text is accepted as authoritative by all people who might identify themselves as Hindus, and many think of their religion as being grounded in a way of action, rather than a written text. Nevertheless, if one were to seek a "foundational text" to represent significant tenets of Hindu philosophy, a good selection would be one of the principal Upanishads. The group of texts known as Upanishads have played a decisive role throughout Hindu religious history; they have defined central philosophical issues in India for centuries and continue to be a major source of inspiration and guidance within the Hindu world today. One of the objectives of this chapter is to give a sense of the wide range of interpretive possibilities that emerge from early Hindu

texts, demonstrating specifically how practices as diverse as world renunciation and forms of worship that embrace the world itself as divine
are justified by the same texts.

The earliest Upanishads were composed in northern India in the seventh or eighth century B.C.E. The term "Upanishad" means literally to "sit
near" but has come to mean "esoteric teaching," for these texts represent
secret teachings passed on to groups of close disciples by forest-dwelling
meditation masters. The Upanishads, which contain highly speculative
thought about the ultimate nature of reality, are among the greatest intellectual creations of the world. Although the Upanishads do not present a
single philosophical system but rather give voice to exploratory and often
contradictory reflections, their overall theme is one of ontological unity,
the belief that everything is radically interconnected. The oldest and largest
of the Upanishads is the *Brihad Aranyaka Upanishad* ("The Great and
Secret Teachings of the Forest"). This text is not the product of a single
author but is a compilation of a number of conversations between teachers and students. The *Brihad Aranyaka Upanishad* has a great deal to say
about the ultimate nature of the world and the true identity of human beings, and thus provides a good starting point for exploring important issues within Hindu philosophy.

THEORY OF THE UNIVERSE

We observe in the *Brihad Aranyaka Upanishad* an ardent metaphysical
search for the absolute ground of all being. One of the central philosophical tenets of the Upanishads is that there is a single, unifying principle underlying the entire universe. At the level of ultimate realization, the world
of multiplicity is revealed to be one of interconnected unity. The attempt
to identify that unifying principle can be seen in a famous passage involving the philosopher Gargi Vacaknavi and the great sage Yajnavalkya (3.6).
Gargi opens an inquiry into the ultimate nature of the world, challenging
Yajnavalkya to identify the very foundation of all existence. She asks the
sage: "Since this whole world is woven back and forth on water, on what,
then, is water woven back and forth?" Yajnavalkya responds initially: "On
air, Gargi." But Gargi is not satisfied with this answer. "On what, then, is
air woven back and forth?" Yajnavalkya supplies another answer, and then
another, and still another as Gargi presses him to identify increasingly fundamental layers of reality. Finally, the sage reveals to her that the entire
universe is woven back and forth on what he calls "*brahman*." At this point
he claims that he can go no further; *brahman* is declared to be the end of
Gargi's search. Although other entities were suggested as the possible foundation of all being (e.g., space [4.1.1] and water [5.5.1]), these were re-

jected, as the one ultimate reality and absolute ground of all being came to be identified as *brahman*. *Brahman* was declared to be the highest aim of all metaphysical inquiry: "All the vedic learning that has been acquired is subsumed under '*brahman*' " (1.5.17).

The term *brahman* is derived from a Sanskrit root that means to "grow," "expand," or "increase." Although in early usage it was associated with sacred utterances, over the course of time it came to be identified with the very force that sustains the world. During the time of the Upanishads, it settled into its principal meaning of "ultimate reality," the primary cause of existence, or the absolute ground of being. Brahman was identified as the fine essence that pervades the entire universe. It is the totality of all reality, both manifest and unmanifest. Another famous passage from the *Brihad Aranyaka Upanishad* well portrays the metaphysical quest for the unitary ground of being that ends in *brahman* (3.9.). Since this passage yields keen insight into Hindu theology, I quote it in full.

The passage opens with the searcher Vidagdha Shakalya questioning the sage Yajnavalkya about the number of gods in existence. "How many gods are there?" he asks. Yajnavalkya responds first: "Three and three hundred, and three and three thousand." Not satisfied with this answer Vidagdha continues.

> "Yes, of course," he said, "but really, Yajnavalkya, how many gods are there?"
> "Thirty-three."
> "Yes, of course," he said, "but really, Yajnavalkya, how many gods are there?"
> "Six."
> "Yes, of course," he said, "but really, Yajnavalkya, how many gods are there?"
> "Three."
> "Yes, of course," he said, "but really, Yajnavalkya, how many gods are there?"
> "Two."
> "Yes, of course," he said, "but really, Yajnavalkya, how many gods are there?"
> "One and a half."
> "Yes, of course," he said, "but really, Yajnavalkya, how many gods are there?"
> "One."

When asked by Vidagdha to identify this "one god," Yajnavalkya concludes: "He is called '*brahman*'."

Although divinity expresses itself in multiple forms, ultimately it is One. Here again, we witness philosophical inquiry into the ultimate nature of reality that ends with the discovery of the single unifying principle called *brahman*. But if reality is one, how—and why—did it become many? Creation stories maintained by any tradition tell us much about that tradition. We find in the *Brihad Aranyaka Upanishad* an account of creation that provides answers to these questions and serves as a model for much Hindu thought.

"In the beginning there was nothing" (1.2.1). Yet a great deal can come from nothing, for much of the Hindu tradition holds that the entire universe came out of this original nothingness. Like the modern "Big Bang" theory, this text describes an expansion from an original dimensionless point of infinite unity; yet, unlike the Big Bang theory, this account of creation tells us *why* the expansion occurred.

In the beginning there was nothing but the single unitary principle, *brahman*. However, because it was alone, it was lonely and "found no pleasure at all" (1.4.2). In this state of loneliness, it desired another and so divided itself into two parts, a male and a female. Departing from the original state of abstract neutrality, the male and female pair began to interact sexually, and from this was born the entire universe of diverse forms. Thus, the original point of undifferentiated unity divided itself and, exploding outward, produced the phenomenal world of multiple forms. The *Brihad Aranyaka Upanishad* calls this *"brahman's* super-creation" (1.4.6). This account of creation expresses the true nature of reality and the ultimate aim of beings within that reality. We will have occasion to refer to this story later, but the important point is to realize that it accounts for the multiplicity of the world, while recognizing in a fundamental way the radical interconnectedness of the world. The original unity is never lost; it simply takes on the appearance of multiple forms.

This theory of the origin of the universe recognizes the simultaneity of unity and diversity. The One reality differentiates itself through what the text calls "name and visible appearance" (1.4.7). The world we experience with our senses, then, is a single reality, though it is clothed with a variety of names and appearances. This is aptly expressed in the following verse:

> The world there is full;
> The world here is full;
> Fullness from fullness proceeds.
> After taking fully from the full,
> It still remains completely full. (5.1.1)

Here we have a portrait of divinity that is simultaneously immanent and transcendent. *Brahman* is not only *in* the world, it *is* the world; there is also a dimension of *brahman* that is completely beyond the world of multiple forms. This is asserted in the *Brihad Aranyaka Upanishad* as a teaching about the two aspects (*rupa*) of *brahman* as the form and the formless: "the one has a fixed shape (*murta*), and the other is without a fixed shape (*amurta*)" (2.3.1). *Brahman* as all forms is everything that is solid and transitory, whereas *brahman* as the formless is ethereal and unchanging. A good way to approach this philosophy is to reflect on the double meaning of the phrase "Nothing ever remains the same." The world of concrete things is in constant flux and always changing; things never remain the same. On the other hand, the no-thingness from which all comes is eternal and unchanging; it ever remains the same. It is important to remember, however, that these are not two separate realities but the same reality seen from different perspectives. The world of forms is pervaded by the unified *brahman* as salt pervades the water in which it is dissolved: "It is like this. When a chunk of salt is thrown in water, it dissolves into that very water, and it cannot be picked up in any way. Yet, from whichever place one may take a sip, the salt is there! In the same way this Immense Being has no limit or boundary and is a single mass of perception" (2.4.12).

Before we move on to examine what the *Brihad Aranyaka Upanishad* has to say about human nature, one additional important point should be mentioned. Several passages insist that *brahman* is inexpressible and therefore impossible to define. We are told, for example, that "it is neither coarse nor fine; it is neither short nor long; it has neither blood nor fat; it is without shadow or darkness; it is without air or space; it is without contact; it has no taste or smell; it is without sight or hearing; it is without speech or mind; it is without energy, breath, or mouth, it is beyond measure; it has nothing within or outside of it; it does not eat anything; and no one eats it" (3.8.8). That is, *brahman* is completely beyond the world we experience with our senses. This is often expressed in the text by saying that *brahman* is "not this, not that (*neti neti*)."

On the other hand, there are passages that identify *brahman* with everything we experience with our senses: "Clearly, this self is *brahman*—this self that is made of perception, made of mind, made of sight, made of breath, made of hearing, made of earth, made of water, made of wind, made of space, made of light and the lightless, made of desire and the desireless, made of anger and the angerless, made of righteous and the unrighteous; this self is made of everything" (4.4.5). In direct contrast to the "not this, not that" view, this passage continues: "He's made of this. He's made of that." These two different ways of describing *brahman* led to divergent understandings of the world and the self, which in turn resulted in significant differences in religious practice. Two of the most important interpretations of the Upanishads are explored in the final section of this chapter.

THEORY OF HUMAN NATURE

The recognition that all of life is interconnected has clear implications for a theory of human nature. According to the *Brihad Aranyaka Upanishad*, our kin are not only fellow human beings but all other beings as well. This text teaches that the essential self of a human being is radically connected to all beings: "The self within all is this self of yours" (3.5.1). The ultimate self—referred to in the Upanishads by the term *"atman"*— is not, therefore, an autonomous unit operating independent of other beings but rather a part of this larger interrelated network of reality. "This very self [*atman*] is the lord and king of all beings. As all the spokes are fastened to the hub and the rim of a wheel, so to one's self are fastened all beings, all the gods, all the worlds, all the breaths, and all these bodies" (2.5.15). The text makes it very clear that the true self not only animates all beings but is inseparable from the whole of reality (2.5.1–14). The self is all, and all is the self.

The Upanishads certainly recognize a self that is transitory and separate from other selves. That is, the self as ego (*ahamkara*) is identified with the body and its social environment. This is the self we immediately think of when someone asks us who we are. This is also the self we ordinarily invest with great meaning and strive to preserve. This, however, is neither the ultimate self nor the true identity of a human being. The essential self is defined as the *atman*. Our ordinary self is simply a finite, conditioned mask covering our true and infinite nature.

Some passages in the *Brihad Aranyaka Upanishad* suggest that the *atman* is undefinable; it is not to be identified with anything: "About this self (*atman*), one can only say 'not—, not —.' He is ungraspable, for he cannot be grasped. He is undecaying, for he is not subject to decay. He has nothing sticking to him, for he does not stick to anything. He is not bound; yet he neither trembles in fear nor suffers injury" (3.9.28). Other passages, however, identify the *atman* with everything: "Clearly, this self is *brahman*—this self that is made of perception, made of mind, made of sight, made of breath, made of hearing, made of earth, made of water, made of wind, made of space, made of light and the lightless, made of desire and the desireless; this self is made of everything. Hence there is this saying: 'He's made of this. He's made of that'" (4.4.5). Note the seemingly contradictory nature of these two statements, which might be used to support very different notions of the self and the world. In either case, the text goes on to define the *atman* as the immortal, unchanging self; it "is beyond hunger and thirst, sorrow and delusion, old age and death" (3.5.1).

A central teaching of the Upanishads is that the true self is that eternal dimension of reality that is somehow not different from the highest reality of *brahman*: "And this is the immense and unborn self, unageing, undying, immortal, free from fear—the *brahman*" (4.4.24). Since the *atman* is identified with *brahman*, it too is defined as the very source of all life, the root of all existence: "As a spider sends forth its thread, and as tiny sparks spring forth from a fire, so indeed do all the vital functions, all the worlds, all the gods, and all beings spring from this self [*atman*]. Its hidden name is: 'The real behind the real,' for the real consists of the vital functions, and the self is the real behind the vital functions" (2.1.19). In sum, the *Brihad Aranyaka Upanishad* teaches that one's essential self transcends individuality, limitation, suffering, and death.

Another common designation we find for the *atman* is that it is the "inner controller" of all life (3.7.2–23). This designation is connected to perhaps the most notable characterization of the *atman* we find in the *Brihad Aranyaka Upanishad*. The *atman* is not an ordinary object of consciousness but rather the subject of consciousness, or the silent witness of consciousness. The *atman* is the knower of all knowledge, or the "perceiver of perception." "When, however, the Whole has become one's very self [*atman*], then who is there for one to smell and by what means? Who is there for one to see and by what means? Who is there for one to hear and by what means? Who is there for one to greet and by what means? Who is there for one to think of and by what means? Who is there for one to perceive and by what means? By what means can one perceive him by means of whom one perceives this whole world? Look—by what means can one perceive the perceiver?" (2.4.14). As the perceiver of perception, the *atman* is not an object of consciousness and therefore cannot be known in any ordinary way, for it is declared to be consciousness itself. Although there is a great deal of similarity between Upanishadic Hinduism and early Buddhism, many Buddhists tend to reject the idea that consciousness is identical to an essential self. Nonetheless, the Upanishads identified our true self as that which enables us to be conscious beings, namely all-pervasive consciousness. The primary aim of the Upanishads is to bring about a shift in identity from the transient ego self associated with the body to the eternal and infinite self that is not different from the All. In other words, the goal is to realize that the *atman* is *brahman*, although the task of delineating the details of this equation was left to later writers.

According to the Upanishads, our present life is just one in a long, long series of death and rebirth. When our present life ends, we are reborn in a new body. "It is like this. As a caterpillar, when it comes to the tip of a blade of grass, reaches out to a new foothold and draws itself onto it, so the self [*atman*], after it has knocked down this body and rendered it unconscious, reaches out to a new foothold and draws itself onto it" (4.3.3). That is, as a caterpillar moves from one blade of grass to another, so we move from one body to another. Although some later philosophers insisted that it is a different type of self that constitutes the individual self that undergoes reincarnation, reincarnation seems to have been assumed in the Upanishads.

Informed by this assumption, two paths are outlined in the *Brihad Aranyaka Upanishad* as possible postdeath experiences (6.2.15–16). The first option is the path of return to this life. After death, people's bodies are placed on the cremation fire. Those who performed religious sacrifices designed to enhance worldly life pass into the smoke. From the smoke, they pass into the night and eventually end up in the world of the ancestors. From there they pass into the moon, where they are turned into the rain, by which they return to the earth. Reaching the earth, they become food. The food is eaten by a man and then offered in the fire of a woman, where people take birth once again. This is the ongoing cycle of death and rebirth that defines life for most people. Enjoyment of the cycles of existence is presented here in a positive light.

There is another path, however, for the forest-dwelling meditation masters who have achieved the highest knowledge. After death, these are placed on the cremation fire and pass into the flames. From the flames, they pass into the day and eventually reach the world of the gods. From there they pass into the sun. The sun in much Hindu mythology represents the doorway out of this world, and, indeed, we are told that those who achieve the highest knowledge go on from the sun to reach the world of *brahman*, from which they never return to worldly life. This is one of the earliest representations of *moksha*, or "liberation" from the ongoing cycle of death and rebirth. Although these two paths are presented simply as the two postdeath possibilities in the *Brihad Aranyaka Upanishad*, some later Upanishads insist that the path of no return is far superior to the path of return. According to the more ascetic Upanishads, return to this world is an indication of one's failure to achieve ultimate knowledge of one's self. A very special kind of knowledge, then, is declared to be the culmination of a successful human life.

DIAGNOSIS

The main problem with human existence is that we are ignorant of the true nature of reality. "Pitiful is the man, Gargi, who departs from this world without knowing this imperishable" (3.8.10). We see from this statement that all success rests on knowing the imperishable *brahman*, of which we are a part. It is extremely difficult to know, however, since it is that "which sees but can't be seen; which hears but can't be heard; which thinks but can't be thought of; which perceives but can't be perceived. Besides this imperishable, there is no one that sees, no one that hears, no one that thinks, and no one that perceives" (3.8.11). Without knowledge of the unified and infinite *brahman*, one perceives only the ordinary objects of consciousness and therefore suffers the fate of identifying completely with the dying world of fragmentary and transitory forms. "With the mind alone must one behold it—there is here nothing diverse at all! From death to death he goes who sees here any kind of diversity" (4.4.19).

Ignorance of the true nature of reality is tantamount to ignorance of the true nature of our own selves. Or, stated in different terms, the human predicament consists of a severe identity problem: we don't know who we really are. We identify ourselves with the fragmented, seemingly disconnected phenomenal world of diversity, instead of with the One *brahman*. We are creatures of infinity stuck in highly conditioned and finite personalities. While in reality we are kin to the immense universe, we spend our lives overwhelmed and blinded by the limited projects of our own ego. The result of this is alienation: from others, from the very source of life, from the One, and even from our own true self. The human condition is thus an ongoing experience of fragmentation, isolation, and loneliness. Consequently, our social worlds are riddled with crime and hostile conflict, informed by belief in our own individuality, and we are plagued with existential anxiety, rooted in an investment in the disconnected, transitory self.

The life of the lone individual is anything but free, according to the Upanishads. Life grounded in the belief in a separate self is heavily conditioned and determined. The determining factors are identified as *karma* in the *Brihad Aranyaka Upanishad*, the first text to mention this concept so important to later Hindu thought. The sage Yajnavalkya talks about *karma* in this way: "What a man turns out to be depends on how he acts and on how he conducts himself. If his actions are good, he will turn into something good. If his actions are bad, he will turn into something bad. A man turns into something good by good action and into something bad by bad action" (4.4.5). Ordinary human life, informed by the belief in an autonomous self, is revealed to be highly contingent, conditioned by forces determined by previous actions. Yajnavalkya continues: "A man resolves in accordance with his desire, acts in accordance with his resolve, and turns out to be in accordance with his action." What this means is that we are psychologically programmed in such a way that under normal circumstances free action is impossible. We act out of desire, which itself is the result of some prior action recorded in the unconscious mind. That desire manifests itself as a resolve for action. The subsequent action leaves an impression in the mind, which then goes on to determine the nature of another desire, the root of future action. Here, then, is a picture of the human predicament as a cycle of psychological bondage. A great deal of Hindu yoga and meditation aims to free us from this limited and conditioned state.

PRESCRIPTION

The Upanishads are generally optimistic about the possibility of attaining ultimate freedom. The *Brihad Aranyaka Upanishad*, however, does not outline a single prescriptive path. A major task of later systematic writers was to articulate a coherent interpretation of this and other Upanishads and to delineate a specific path leading to the ultimate state that those texts describe. As we shall see, the divergent interpretations that emerged differed greatly about the nature of the world and the self.

Generally speaking, the Upanishadic path to freedom involves acquiring a special kind of knowledge. Ordinary knowledge will not cut the chains of our bondage. "Into blind darkness they enter, people who worship ignorance; And into still blinder darkness, people who delight in learning" (4.4.10). The Upanishadic texts do not disparage all learning but rather sound a note of caution about the limits of conventional knowledge. What this passage seems to be saying is that it is dangerous to rely too heavily on ordinary knowledge. Ordinary information is fine for operating in the conventional world of multiple forms; however, it is worthless for knowing the ultimate nature of reality and the self.

The *Brihad Aranyaka Upanishad* makes it clear that one must finally let go of any attachment to ordinary ways of knowing. The text tells us that one "should stop being a pundit and try to live like a child. When he has stopped living like a child or a pundit, he becomes a sage" (3.5.1). That is, after gaining significant exposure to the scriptures and becoming an expert in the scholarly sense, one should abandon any reliance on learning and try to return to the simple and spontaneous state of a child. This still, however, does not give clear indication of how one is to achieve ultimate knowledge and freedom. Only in very general terms does the *Brihad Aranyaka Upanishad* recommend a path of withdrawing from ordinary ways of being and meditating continually on the *atman*. This vagueness is characteristic not only of this text but of other Upanishads as well. It remained for later commentators to spell out in detail exactly what the final state involves and how it can be attained.

DIVERGENT INTERPRETATIONS

One of the greatest disagreements within Hinduism occurs between those who view ultimate reality as an impersonal absolute and those who emphasize a personal relationship with ultimate reality. (A concomitant question is: Is the world ultimately real or not?) Not surprisingly, these two radically different stances have led to widely divergent interpretations of the *Brihad Aranyaka Upanishad*. A complete introduction to later

Hinduism would involve a description of an expansive array of religious practices, including domestic rites, temple rituals, pilgrimages, yogic discipline, and so forth, as well as the beliefs that inform these diverse practices. Although such a task is impossible within the limitations of this chapter, the ideas of two leading figures from the Hindu tradition— Shankara and Ramanuja—are examined to indicate the wide range of practices and beliefs that are included under the rubric of Hinduism. Both are identified as Vedanta philosophers, where "Vedanta" means literally the "end of the Vedas," that is, the culmination of the revealed books of wisdom known as the Vedas. This term is taken primarily to refer to the teachings of the Upanishads but also includes the *Bhagavad Gita* and the *Brahma Sutra*. Although there are also schools of Hindu philosophy that are not Vedanta, Shankara and Ramanuja represent two of the most influential schools of Hindu thought and practice. Since both Shankara and Ramanuja wrote commentaries on the *Brahma Sutra*, a text that further investigates the concept of *brahman* introduced in the Upanishads, we can use these two works to explore this fundamental divergence in interpretation.

Shankara's Advaita Vedanta

Shankara (788–820) is one of the best-known Hindu philosophers in India and in the West. Although his philosophical system of Advaita ("Non Dualism") informs the activities of only a small minority of Hindus and has tended to overly dominate Western understandings of Hinduism, it represents an important philosophical position within the Hindu world and constitutes one of the most popular rationalizations for the act of religious renunciation.

What does it mean to know *brahman*? Perhaps the most pressing question that remained from Upanishadic speculation was: What is the relationship between the ultimate reality of *brahman* and the world of multiplicity we experience with our senses? A concomitant question arose: What is the status of a personal God and the individual soul? Shankara was one of the first Indian philosophers to formulate a consistent and singular viewpoint based on the Upanishads that addressed these important questions. His is a philosophy of unity that ultimately devalues all diversity. For Shankara, *brahman* is the only truth, the world is ultimately unreal, and the distinction between God and the individual soul is only an illusion.

Brahman, for Shankara, is the sole reality. It is the absolute undifferentiated reality, one without a second (*advaita*) and devoid of any specific qualities (*nirguna*). Since he understands the highest realization of *brahman* to be a state in which all distinctions between subject and object are obliterated, he concludes that the world of diversity must finally be false. Shankara recognizes that the Upanishads speak of two aspects of *brahman*, one with qualities (*saguna*) and one without (*nirguna*), but he maintains that the former is simply the result of perception conditioned by limiting factors. "Brahman is known in two aspects—one as possessed of the limiting adjunct constituted by the diversities of the universe which is a modification of name and form, and the other devoid of all conditioning factors and opposed to the earlier" (1.1.12). In fact, Shankara claims that all apparent distinctions within *brahman* are the result of the superimposition of the frames of reference of the viewer. This brings us to one of the most important concepts in his philosophy: the theory of illusion, or "*maya*." *Maya* is the process by which the world of multiplicity comes into being; it is the force by which the formless takes form. *Maya* both conceals and distorts the true reality of *brahman* and is manifest epistemologically as ignorance (*avidya*). Its workings cannot be explained in words, since language itself is a product of *maya*. Since all diversity is finally false for Shankara, *maya* is the major obstacle to the highest realization of ultimate knowledge.

What this means is that the world we experience with our senses is not *brahman* and therefore not ultimately real: "The senses naturally comprehend objects, and not Brahman" (1.1.2). By this Shankara certainly does not mean that the world is a figment of our imagination. He was a staunch opponent of subjective idealism. For him the world has an apparent reality; that is, it is existentially real. He writes: "It cannot be asserted that external things do not exist. Why? Because they are perceived. As a matter of fact such things as a pillar, a wall, a pot, a cloth, are perceived along with each act of cognition. And it cannot be that the very thing perceived is non-existent" (2.2.28). Shankara does recognize the category of the nonexistent and gives as a stock example "the son of a barren woman." Our world, on the other hand, has an apparent reality, and in this sense it "exists." However, since the experience of the world is devalued by the ultimate experience of *brahman* in which all distinctions are obliterated, it cannot be the absolute reality. Just as the contents of a dream are devalued upon waking, so too the experience of the world is devalued upon the waking of ultimate enlightenment. The stock example used to explain this is the snake and the rope. A person erroneously perceives a rope to be a snake in dim light. The fear that the person subsequently feels is real enough, existentially. However, when the light of knowledge illuminates the "snake," it is discovered to be a rope all along. The snake was merely superimposed onto the rope, giving the snake an apparent reality. So too—as the illustration is applied—the world and *brahman*. The world of multiplicity is ordinarily superimposed onto the nondual *brahman*, with the result that we live in an illusory world. The experience of the world, however, is revealed to be false in the ultimate knowledge of *brahman*. This theory allows philosophers to disassociate the problematic world from the true reality, just as reflections of the moon in various pots of water are finally disassociated from the moon.

The same argument is applied to two other important differentiated entities: the personal God and the individual soul. Shankara defines the personal God as *brahman* with attributes. But since all attributes are the product of the limiting factors of ignorance, God, too, is finally declared to be an illusion. Worship of the personal God, however, is highly beneficial, for although God is not the highest reality, it is the highest reality conceivable for creatures still enmeshed in the cosmic illusion of *maya*. That is, the personal God is a necessary component of spiritual experience, since it provides a transition between the world and *brahman* for those who are still attached to the world. In the end, however, one must give up this sense of separateness and reintegrate all gods back into one's self.

A related concept for Shankara is the individual soul (*jiva*). By now it should be clear that all diversity for Shankara is considered to be the result of illusory perception, so it will come as no surprise to learn that he ultimately rejects the individual soul as illusory. Although the *jiva*, or individual soul, involves a higher level of realization than the ego-identity associated with the body, in the final analysis it, too, is unreal. The true self for Shankara is the *atman*, defined as pure consciousness. Like the world and God, the individual soul is merely an apparent reality, whose appearance is the result of viewing the self through the limiting factors of ignorance. He writes that the self "is endowed with eternal consciousness, . . . it is only the supreme Brahman Itself, which while remaining immutable, appears to exist as an individual soul owing to association with limiting adjuncts" (2.3.18). Though in everyday experiences we feel ourselves to be agents of our own actions, this, too, is an illusion. This means that the true self is eternally free from the conditioning effects of *karma*; to be free one needs only to realize that bondage is a mental construct. Shankara also maintains that the self is beyond all experience, since this involves a difference between the experiencer and that which is experienced. Therefore, at the highest level of realization, the individual soul, the subject of all experience, disappears as an illusion; the true self is declared to be identical with *brahman*, the absolute unified ground of being.

The goal of all spiritual endeavor for Shankara is the realization of this ultimate fact. The highest level of the knowledge of *brahman* involves the obliteration of all distinctions between the knowing subject and all known objects in the state of absolute identity. A favored metaphor for the ultimate experience so conceived is the reemergence of all drops of water back into the single undifferentiated ocean. This is how Shankara interprets the Upanishadic quest for ultimate knowledge.

But what are the essential components of a path designed to accomplish this ultimate feat? In the first section of this chapter we encountered the *Brihad Aranyaka Upanishad*'s creation myth, which recounts how the world of multiple forms came into being out of desire, a desire for another. The essential element in the story for Shankara is the unity that preceeds the diversity produced by desire. Since desire is associated with the creative force that divides the original oneness, eradicating desire is a necessary step toward the process of reunification. This brings us to the idea of renunciation. The highest spiritual path, according to Shankara, consists of a meditative practice designed to lead one to the insightful realization that "I am *brahman*." He calls the practice of meditating on and realizing the true self "*samadhi*." An important prerequisite to this practice, however, is a withdrawal from ordinary social and domestic activities and a retreat from our ordinary investment in the data of the senses. That is, one of the most prominent consequences of Shankara's theory is the move toward the practice of world renunciation. Shankara is credited with founding an important order of renouncers (*sannyasis*) known as the Dashanamis. These are men who embark on the path by performing their own funeral rite, thereby indicating the end of their former identity and the beginning of full-time participation in a celibate religious community and meditation on *brahman* as the impersonal absolute.

Ramanuja's Vishishta Advaita Vedanta

Diametrically opposed to the views of Shankara is the perspective of those Hindus—especially the Vaishnavas (worshippers of God in the form of Lord Vishnu)—for whom the personal nature of the divine is an ultimate attitude and not an illusion to be transcended. One of Shankara's most determined and well-known opponents was Ramanuja (1017–1137), an important theologian and chief interpreter of Vedanta for the southern Indian devotional movement known as Shri Vaishnavism. His philosophical system is designated Vishishta Advaita ("Nondualism of the Differentiated"), since it takes differentiated things to be real, and understands them to be attributes of a nondual reality. Ramanuja's philosophy values both unity and multiplicity, a stance that results in a very different view of the nature of God, the world, and the self.

In his commentary on the *Brahma Sutra*, Ramanuja criticizes Shankara for his refusal to acknowledge any qualities or distinctions in the nondual reality of *brahman*. Like Shankara, Ramanuja accepts the Upanishadic assertion that *brahman* is the sole reality; however, for him, *brahman* means God, who is endowed with innumerable excellent qualities. "The word 'Brahman' primarily denotes that supreme Person who is the abode of all auspicious qualities to an infinite degree and is free from all worldly taint. This supreme Person is the only Being the knowledge of whose real nature results in liberation" (1.1.1, p. 1). Thus Ramanuja does not make a distinction between *brahman* and God, as does Shankara. Rather, Ramanuja interprets Upanishadic descriptions of *brahman* as "without qualities" to mean the absence of certain kinds of qualities: qualities that are negative or binding. In effect, he reverses Shankara's privileging of *brahman* without qualities (*nirguna*), arguing that *brahman* with qualities (*saguna*) is the higher form. Specifically, Ramanuja resists Shankara's conceptualization of *brahman* as pure undifferentiated consciousness, contending that if this were true, any knowledge of *brahman* would be impossible, since all knowledge depends on a differentiated "object." "Brahman cannot be, as the Advaitins say, non-differentiated pure Consciousness, for no proof can be adduced to establish non-differentiated objects" (1.1.1, pp. 19–20).

The particular kind of experience for which we should aim, according to Ramanuja, is a blissful knowledge of *brahman* as the Lord with infinite and amazing qualities or, stated more simply, the love of God. But for this relationship to be possible, there must be a distinction between the knowing subject or the one who loves (the individual soul), and the known object or the beloved (the Lord). Many of the devotional theologians within Hinduism remark that they do not want to become sugar (Shankara's goal); instead, they want the blissful experience of tasting sugar (Ramanuja's goal). This means that difference must be taken seriously, and this implies a very different picture of the world of sense experience than the one we encountered in Shankara's Advaita system.

The world is real, for Ramanuja, and was created out of God's desire to become manifold. That is, the world is the result of a real transformation of *brahman*. The stock example used to explain this viewpoint is the transformation of curds from milk. Curds that are produced from processing milk are both different and nondifferent from their source. This view is more widely accepted by Hindus than is Shankara's view that the world is ultimately an illusion. It implies that the creative process that resulted in multiplicity is not finally to be overcome but rather is to be appreciated for what it truly is, the product of God's creative activity. Like Shankara, Ramanuja connects the desire of the one to become many with the concept of *maya*, but instead of conceptualizing *maya* as "illusion," as does Shankara, Ramanuja takes it to be the "creative power" of God. "The word Maya does not mean unreal or false but that power which is capable of producing wonderful effects" (1.1.1, p. 73). The world, then, is viewed in a much more positive light, and in fact Ramanuja goes on to characterize it as the "body of God." He maintains that *brahman* "is the creator, preserver, and destroyer of this universe, which It pervades and of which It is the inner Ruler. The entire world, sentient and insentient, forms its body" (1.1.1, p. 55). That is, the conditioned and transitory world is an attribute of the unconditioned and eternal God, as the transitory body is an attribute of the eternal soul. The world is therefore different from God, yet it is also inseparably connected to God, as an attribute is connected to its substance.

This is also the case with the individual soul (*jiva*). It, too, is considered to be part of the body of God, and it is in this manner that Ramanuja interprets the Upanishadic identity of *brahman* and the true self. Whereas Shankara ultimately characterized the individual soul as a false illusion, for in his view all distinction is obliterated in the final experience of *brahman*, Ramanuja maintains that it is real and eternal. As a part of *brahman*, the soul is both different and nondifferent from the whole (2.3.42, p. 298). The world of matter and individual souls enters into God at the time of dissolution and separates from God at the time of creation. Rejecting Shankara's claim that the true self is pure consciousness beyond all experience, Ramanuja maintains that the true self is a special enjoyer of experience (2.3.20, p. 285). In its highest state, it is the eternal, blissful knower of *brahman*.

The path to freedom and the blissful experience of *brahman* is well represented in the following passage. "This bondage can be destroyed only through Knowledge, i.e., through the Knowledge that Brahman is the inner ruler different from souls and matter. This Knowledge is attained through the Grace of the Lord pleased by the due performance of the daily duties prescribed for different castes and stages of life, duties performed not with the idea of attaining any results but with the idea of propitiating the Lord" (1.1.1, p. 80). Far from renouncing the world of action, a very particular way of acting is indicated here that is linked to the *karma-yoga* of the *Bhagavad Gita*, the other major Vedanta text. *Bhagavad Gita* 2.47 states that one in pursuit of ultimate liberation should act in a manner that avoids both an attachment to the results of action and the abandonment of action. That is, as a path of action, *karma-yoga* is situated between two modes of behavior current in Hindu religion. On the one hand, the path of Vedic sacrifice—and ordinary action, for that matter—is a mode of action wherein the act is performed with a controlling concern for the outcome of the action. Why, after all, do we do anything if it is not for the result we expect to achieve by performing the act? Much religious activity follows the same logic; a religious act such as Vedic sacrifice is performed to obtain some desired result. In accord with the *Bhagavad Gita*, however, Ramanuja holds that such action reveals a fundamental ignorance and serves only to bind us further. Life, according to Ramanuja, is a cosmic play (*lila*), wherein God is the ultimate Playwright (2.1.33, p. 237). The ordinary human urge to control the outcome of all our actions is tantamount to an effort to usurp the role of the Playwright. Moreover, insisting on a particular outcome of action in a world everabundant as *brahman* is like walking into an extraordinary store filled with an amazing assortment of candies with a fixed desire for a certain kind of candy bar, one that, as it turns out, happens not to be there. The result is suffering and bondage in a potentially wonderful situation. What, then, to do? The answer certainly does not lie in abandoning all action, for that is the other mode of behavior to be avoided. Following the *Bhagavad Gita*, Ramanuja insists that one should engage in the action that comes to one according to one's own life situation. World renunciation is simply another attempt to establish control and cannot lead us to the state of blissful enjoyment. Instead, Ramanuja advises us to surrender completely to God, for only then are we free to enjoy the marvelous show that is the world. Whereas Shankara renounces the world, Ramanuja demonstrates how to live in it freely.

Although Ramanuja has little to say about the worship of concrete forms of God in his commentary on the *Brahma Sutra*, he belongs to a devotional community in which this type of meditation is the central religious practice. Acts directed to pleasing the Lord instead of one's egoistic self are often enacted in the context of worship of concrete forms or bodies of God, either in a temple or at a home shrine. Informed by such texts as the *Brihad Aranyaka Upanishad*'s conversation wherein Vidagdha asked Yajnavalkya how many gods there are, these concrete forms are considered to be multiple forms of a single, nondual divinity. *Brahman* is understood to be fully present in these special bodies, which are limited forms of the infinite that God compassionately assumes for the purpose of granting accessibility to embodied human beings with ordinary senses. The limited forms are like the defining frame placed around certain works of art that serve to allow focused perception of something that might have otherwise been missed. A great deal of Hindu practice involves the loving service of such concrete forms of God. Whereas Shankara saw these acts as preliminary to the higher business of *samadhi* meditation, for Ramanuja, loving acts directed toward God are supreme. Loving devotion implies a very different attitude toward human emotions than we observe in Shankara. Since the world is real for Ramanuja, everything in it—including human emotions—can be used as fuel for the spiritual life.

The goal of such devotional acts is a kind of union with God, wherein the liberated soul lives in the loving presence of the Lord but does not dissolve into undifferentiated oneness with Him. This is often conceived of in Vaishnavism as an eternal and blissful existence in God's heavenly abode of Vaikuntha. Here "the released self abides as an enjoyer of the supreme Brahman" (4.4.20, p. 493).

We observe, then, two radically different religious sensibilities arising from—or at least being justified by—the same Upanishadic texts. For Shankara the nondualism of the *Brihad Aranyaka Upanishad* means that the world of multiplicity and everything connected with it is, in the final analysis, an illusion. With the dawn of true consciousness, the world, the individual self, and even God are revealed to be unreal. Participation in the ordinary world, then, is viewed as a hindrance to the highest spiritual life. The consequence of this view is a religious life that values world renunciation and is suspicious of anything based on ordinary human senses. Ramanuja, on the other hand, interpreted the nondualism of the *Brihad Aranyaka Upanishad* to mean that there is a single cause to everything but that the multiple effects of that single cause are real. Ultimate reality is understood to be God as the Inner Controller of the manifold world and the individual soul. The consequence of this position is a religious life of devotional activity that views the world positively and uses the ordinary senses to pursue a blissful experience of the differentiated *brahman*. Although world-renouncers can still be found in almost all religious centers in India today, devotional practices in temples and home shrines dominate the Hindu tradition.

CRITICAL DISCUSSION

The Vedanta philosophy represented by Shankara and Ramanuja is a textual tradition. What this means specifically is that Vedanta philosophers—though they insist that the final proof of anything must be experience—rely heavily on scriptures such as the *Brihad Aranyaka Upanishad*, which they take to be authoritative. Many philosophers today would not accept scripture as a reliable source of truth. Moreover, Vedanta philosophy rests on the transcendental claims of the Upanishads, represented by the concept of *brahman*. Obviously, this too makes it suspect for secular philosophers, for whom the idea of transcendence is highly problematic. This is, after all, what makes Vedanta a "religious" philosophy. The philosophical traditions of India differ from many of those in the West on this exact point, for much of Hindu philosophy is intended to be of practical assistance to spiritual experience.

In contrast to many of the other theories represented in this book, Vedanta philosophy appears to have little to say about social and political struggles and reforms or about practical morality. Although some recent defenders of Vedanta philosophy have denied this accusation, it holds a certain amount of truth. The writings of Vedanta philosophers are preoccupied with achieving a higher knowledge and freedom and with metaphysical concerns regarding the nature of ultimate reality, the world, and the self. *Brahman* for Shankara, for example, has little to do with the ordinary world and transcends all normative distinctions, and the true self is beyond the categories of good and evil. It should be pointed out, however, that Shankara insists that there are moral consequences of all actions for people living in the conditioned world of *maya*. Selfless, compassionate acts erode false boundaries and lead to higher realization, whereas egoistic, violent acts reinforce false boundaries and lead to further bondage. Moreover, although in theory Ramanuja's system values the world, sometimes in practice it is the case that worldly particulars are valued only so far as they lead to the knowledge of God, and not in themselves.

Although women participate actively in the metaphysical discussions of the *Brihad Aranyaka Upanishad*, and although there is no textual evidence to suggest that they were in any way excluded from the higher goals expressed in that text, women are excluded from Shankara's order of renouncers and are never allowed to serve as temple priests in Ramanuja's tradition of Shri Vaishnavism. Although Ramanuja opened his tradition to women and the lower classes, Vedanta philosophy in general, and Shankara's school in particular, tends to be very elitist. It requires a knowledgeable religious practitioner who is well educated in scripture, at least in its expectations for the highest realization. In classical Indian society, this deters all but those who occupy the upper classes. Those denied such preparation by birth are likewise often denied the opportunity for the highest achievement—at least in this lifetime.

FOR FURTHER READING

Basic Text: *Brihad Aranyaka Upanishad* (many translations and editions). All quotations are from the translation by Patrick Olivelle, *Upanisads* (New York: Oxford University Press, 1996). This is a very readable and reliable text that includes a valuable introduction. Other readily available translations are those by Robert E. Hume, *The Thirteen Principal Upanishads* (New York: Oxford University Press, 1971), and by R. C. Zaehner in *Hindu Scriptures* (New York: Knopf, 1966).

Shankara's commentary on the *Brahma Sutra*: Few reliable translations exist. I have quoted from one of the most available English translations: Swami Gambhirananda, *Brahma-Sutra-Bhasya of Sri Shankaracarya* (Calcutta: Advaita Ashrama, 1977).

Ramanuja's commentary on the *Brahma Sutra*: Few reliable translations exist. I have quoted from one of the most available English translations: Swami Vireswarananda and Swami Adidevananda, *Brahma-Sutras, Sri Bhasya* (Calcutta: Advaita Ashrama, 1978).

For an overall introduction to Indian philosophy, see M. Hiriyanna, *Outlines of Indian Philosophy* (Bombay: George Allen & Unwin, 1973).

For more on the philosophy of the Upanishads, see Paul Deussen, *The Philosophy of the Upanishads* (New York: Dover, 1966).

For more on the *Brahma Sutra*, see S. Radhakrishnan, *The Brahma Sutra: The Philosophy of Spiritual Life* (London: George Allen & Unwin, 1960).

For more on Shankara's Advaita Vedanta, see Eliot Deutsch, *Advaita Vedanta: A Philosophical Reconstruction* (Honolulu: University Press of Hawaii, 1969).

For more on Ramanuja's Vishishta Advaita Vedanta, see John Carman, *The Theology of Ramanuja* (New Haven: Yale University Press, 1974).

For more on the worship of concrete forms of divinity within Hinduism, see Diana Eck, *Darsan: Seeing the Divine Image in India* (New York: Columbia University Press, 1996).

C H A P T E R

3

Buddhism: In the Footsteps of the Buddha

Buddhism is a multifaceted religious tradition that includes a variety of teachings and conceptions of the Buddha, as well as many different pathways to the ultimate goal. Most Buddhists, however, regard their tradition as a way of following the Buddha to the goal of Nirvana or Buddhahood. Although Buddhism arose on the Gangetic plain of northern India in the fifth century B.C.E., it soon spread to become a very prominent form of religion throughout most of Asia. Sometime after its establishment, Buddhism split into two major divisions. One branch eventually developed into Theravada, or the "Way of the Elders," which became the dominate type of Buddhism in Southeast Asia, and the other developed into Mahayana, or the "Great Vehicle," which became the dominant type of Buddhism in Central and East Asia. A third offshoot, the Vajrayana or "Diamond Vehicle," developed further into a distinctive form of Mahayana and became prominent in Tibet. Although there is much variety within the Buddhisms of the world, for the limited purposes of this chapter we will focus on some of the main teachings of and differences between Theravada and Mahayana Buddhism. This will be achieved primarily by comparing several aspects of South and Southeast Asian Theravada Buddhism as represented in the Pali Canon with aspects

of Mahayana Buddhism as represented in the Lotus Sutra, a text of enormous importance in East Asian Buddhism.

The Pali scripture of Theravada Buddhism has much to say about how
we are to understand Buddhist teachings. Imagine that you find yourself
before a great being, a master, a being who knows it all. This is a chance
of a lifetime, your opportunity to ask any questions for which you ever
wanted an answer. What might you ask? Is the world eternal or does it
have an end? Does a person continue to exist after death or not? Is there
a soul separate from the body or not? What might the answers be? There
is a story of such an experience found in the Pali Canon. Here we meet
a monk by the name of Malunkyaputta who comes before the Buddha
asking for answers to these very questions. Furthermore, he tells the
Buddha that if he receives satisfactory answers to these questions he will
continue to live a religious life under the guidance of the Buddha. But if
he does not receive acceptable answers to these questions he will abandon the monastic life. The Buddha informs him that he does not intend
to answer his questions, for he reminds Malunkyaputta that he never promised to answer such questions, and insists that "the religious life does not
depend on dogma" (PC 121). He says that anyone waiting for such answers from the Buddha will die before he ever receives them all. "It is
as if, Malunkyaputta, a man had been wounded by an arrow thickly
smeared with poison, and his friends and companions, his relatives and
kinsfolk, were to procure for him a physician or surgeon; and the sick
man were to say, 'I will not have this arrow taken out until I have learnt
whether the man who wounded me belonged to the warrior caste, or to
the Brahman caste, or to the agricultural caste, or to the menial caste. . . .
I will not have this arrow taken out until I have learnt whether the bow
which wounded me was a cupa, or a kodanda. . . . I will not have this
arrow taken out until I have learnt whether the shaft which wounded me
was feathered from the wings of a vulture, or of a heron, or of a falcon,
or of a peacock, or of a sithalahanu. . . . (The man's long list of questions goes on and on).' That man would die, Malunkyaputta, without ever
having learnt this" (PC 120-21).

What is the problem with the kinds of questions Malunkyaputta puts
before the Buddha? If we examine them closely, we see that they take
something for granted that the Buddha did not share; they assume something about the nature of reality not held by the Buddha. Any answer,
therefore, would result in affirming something that the Buddha did not
want to affirm. In a sense, such metaphysical questions establish their own
parameter and limit the range of possibilities. Moreover, the kinds of questions Malunkyaputta brought to the Buddha lock one into a dualistic, two-
value logic. In effect they are inquiring: Is reality this or that? They are

like the problematic question: Did you stop beating your wife; yes or no? Such questions make clear assumptions that may not fit the case. Built into the metaphysical questions Malunkyaputta put to the Buddha were ideas and a whole baggage of presuppositions that the Buddha did not care to confirm. Thus he refuses to answer such questions. In effect, the Buddha of the Pali Canon is saying: If you come to me with a load of presuppositions we cannot hope to communicate. In a sense you have already answered your question. And has it gotten you anywhere? Is reality really such that it can grasped with two-value logic? The Buddha as a practical physician also seems to be asking: And what good does a rational picture of reality do for you? If I told you, for example, that the world is eternal would it alleviate your suffering and enable you to achieve peace? The Buddha of the Pali scriptures avoids metaphysical sidetracks and establishes a direct path to teachings that are designed to achieve ultimate goals. He says: "And why, Mulunkyaputta, have I not elucidated this? Because, Malunkyaputta, this profits not, nor has to do with the fundamentals of religion, nor tends to aversion, absence of passion, cessation, quiescence, the supernatural faculties, supreme wisdom, and Nirvana; therefore have I not elucidated it" (PC 122).

The pointlessness of metaphysical inquiry is illustrated with the story of the poisoned arrow; surely this man will die without ever knowing the answers to his many questions. What difference do the answers make anyway? "The Tathagata [a title for the Buddha]," the Buddha informs another questioner, "is free from all theories" (PC 125). Rather than constructing yet more seductive theories, the Buddha clears the way of distracting speculations in order to remove the very arrow causing all suffering and to cure all illness. Early Buddhist teachings, then, are often said to be regarded as a raft that is to be discarded once one has crossed over the ocean of suffering, or like medicine that is to be dispensed with once one has gained full health. The Buddha of the Pali Canon proceeds as a wise physician by dispensing the medicine of the Dharma, practical teachings designed to remove the arrow of human suffering; these concern the nature of suffering, the origin of suffering, the cessation of suffering, and the path leading to the cessation of suffering. This is what the Buddhist tradition calls the Four Noble Truths. Before examining these, let us look briefly at the life of the remarkable figure who set forth these truths about the nature of human existence.

LIFE OF BUDDHA

The story of the life of the Buddha is a major cornerstone of Buddhism. But how are we to read this story? An attempt was made in much of the

scholarship of the nineteenth and twentieth centuries to separate mythology from history in the story of the life of the Buddha, and to expunge
the story of the former in an attempt to bring the real facts of the story
to light. Presumably this effort would result in a clearer picture of who
the Buddha really was. This approach, however, totally compromises the
authors of the texts that portray the life of the Buddha and undermines
their sense of reality. The only accounts we have of life of the Buddha
are the stories as they are told. What we today find incredible, may have
been completely believable to Buddhist authors, and *vice versa*. Our aim
should not be to fit these stories into our contemporary sense of reality,
but rather to strive to understand the meaning expressed in the stories
themselves. I suggest that we read the story of the life of the Buddha as
the sacred property of the Buddhist community that accounts for how the
Buddhist spiritual path came into being and establishes an ideal pattern
for life. Furthermore, it is a story that expresses an existential message
concerning the nature of human life. Many have claimed that an understanding of Buddhism depends upon comprehending this existential
message.

The story of the life of the Buddha does not begin with a single birth,
for Buddhism shares a belief in reincarnation with other South Asian religious traditions. Buddhists trace a long sequence of virtuous past lives
of the Buddha in a series of texts known as the Jatakas ("Birth Stories")
as he gradually advances toward the culmination of awakening in his last
life. In this final life, the Buddha was born of royal parents as a privileged prince. His name was Siddhartha, and his birth was not an ordinary
one. His mother, Maya, conceived him while dreaming of a white elephant, and he was born immaculate without pain from his mother's side
in the wooded grove of Lumbini in the vicinity of the town of Kapilavastu
located in the Himalayan foothills near modern Nepal. Upon birth the infant Siddhartha took seven steps, declaring that he would be enlightened
in this very life. The unusual birth of the Buddha identifies him as a special, even superhuman being, making him a worthy exemplary figure. But
if the future Buddha were too superhuman, it would not be possible for
humans to emulate him. Accordingly, the humanness of Prince Siddhartha
must be established, and the story is explicit in making the struggles of
the future Buddha very human.

After his birth a prophetic seer predicted that if he took constant pleasure in household affairs he would become a universal monarch, but if he
renounced worldly pleasures he would become instead a great religious
leader. Prince Siddhartha grew up in a social context perfect by conventional standards, a world of great wealth in which all his physical desires
were more than fulfilled. Furthermore, no signs of suffering or unpleas-

antries were allowed within the palace walls. The prince's seductively comfortable world was created and carefully controlled by his father, King Suddhodana, who feared that any exposure to suffering would cause his young son to question a future as a powerful, wealthy political leader. And yet, even in this seemingly perfect world something was amiss – and this something forced Prince Siddhartha to seek a goal higher than that of conventional definition. What was it that shattered the ideal world of the palace? Is it really possible to avoid suffering in human life?

One day Prince Siddhartha desired to go for a chariot ride in a nearby royal park. During this outing he came upon something that he had never previously seen: an old man. Never having encountered such a being before, he assumed that this man was a unique individual and asked his chariot driver what kind of person this was. His driver stunned him by revealing to him that the condition of old age is the future of everyone – the young prince included. Greatly agitated by this realization, Prince Siddhartha hurried back to the palace. King Suddhodana was informed about what had happened and immediately set about trying to take his son's mind away from the inevitability of aging by arranging sensual entertainment for him. Although the king redoubled his efforts to protect his son from any exposure to suffering, on another day Prince Siddhartha ventured again into the park in his stately chariot. This time he encountered a man who was gravely ill. Once more he asked his chariot driver whether this was a particular kind of man or whether sickness could strike anyone, and again the driver disturbed the prince's world of childlike innocence by telling him the truth. The prince returned to the palace even more distraught. Even though the king once more tried his best to distract his son and keep him busy with sensual enjoyment, the prince journeyed to the park again. This time he saw a sight that disturbed him even more and shattered the last shred of his youthful ignorance: he saw a dead man. The words of his chariot driver made it clear to him that death would be the end of him too. Though his father tried his best, there was no consoling Prince Siddhartha. On his final excursion to the park, the privileged prince saw a simple monk who had renounced the world, and sensed that this man showed a possible way out of the world of suffering. From this moment on, although he was married to a beautiful princess who had just given birth to their son, Prince Siddhartha was determined to renounce the life of the palace.

Pressing through the resistance of his father and the heavy gates of the palace, Siddhartha left the royal city to take up a life of ascetic practice in the forest to search for a way out of suffering. Once free of the city he cut off his majestic top of hair and sent all his jewelry and fine clothes back to the palace with his favorite horseman. He then embarked on a six-year experimentation with ascetic practices, going from teacher to teacher to learn and master the different meditative techniques each had to offer. None of these, however, satisfied him. He then met five ascetics with whom he practiced severe types of austerities, and nearly starved himself to death by extreme fasting. This too he found unsatisfactory.

Realizing that the austere practices of the forest were just as fruitless as the life in the palace, the former prince left this way of life too by accepting a bowl of sweet milk-rice pudding from a cowherd woman. With this action he discovered the "middle way," situated between the decadently opulent life of the palace and the harshly ascetic life of the forest. His five companions were so scandalized by his behavior that they abandoned him, assuming that he had fallen from the true path. Soon after, the future Buddha sat beneath a Bodhi Tree determined not to rise until he had pierced through the problem of suffering. Fearing he was slipping beyond control, Mara, the god of egoistic desire, attacked him with great force, horrific demons, and seductive nymphs to drive him from his power spot previously occupied by preceding Buddhas. Mara's efforts, however, were in vain, for Siddhartha would not budge. Mara then demanded of the former prince: "Who is witness to your great merit?" In a gesture that is celebrated in much Buddhist sculpture, Siddhartha reached down with his right hand to touch the Earth, who quaked an affirmative response. At this point Siddhartha's success was assured; entering into deep meditation, he contemplated the nature of existence and achieved enlightenment that very night. He became the Buddha, "the Awakened One."

The Buddha passed seven days sitting under the Bodhi Tree experiencing the bliss of profound freedom or Nirvana. Then, after deciding to teach others what he had realized, he got up and traveled to a deer park located near the famous holy city of Banaras where he found the five ascetics he had practiced with formerly. Here he turned the "Wheel of Dharma" for the first time, and taught them the core of his realization in the form of the Four Noble Truths. Laying out the basic principles of his teachings, he established through his own life the rules for a monastic existence and a model of discipline for future monks to follow. After a long teaching career and upon reaching the age of eighty, the Buddha traveled to a grove of trees near the city of Kusinagara. There he lay down on his right side, and after urging his followers to recognize the transitory nature of everything and work toward enlightenment with diligence, he remained completely mindful and passed into what is called Maha-Pari-Nirvana, "the Great and Complete Emancipation." The Pali Canon of Theravada Buddhism suggests strongly that the only lasting influence of the Buddha is the Dharma – his teachings – and the Vinaya – the monastic discipline. Buddha himself passes beyond all influence, leaving only a model for how one can achieve supreme enlightenment and Nirvana oneself.

A very different view of the Buddha, however, is presented in the Lotus Sutra. Without actually denying the more personal and historical view of the Buddha expressed in the Pali scriptures, the Mahayana view of the Lotus Sutra states that the Buddha who lived on Earth in a particular span of time appeared in a "phantom body," or in a body self-created by a being who is cosmic and eternal. That is, his human form was a particular skillful means (*upaya*) to assist those who needed the Buddha in this form. Mahayana Buddhism later developed the notion of the three bodies of the Buddha. The historical Buddha is regarded as the Nirmana-kaya, or "Emanation Body" manifested for the spiritual development of certain kinds of people. The Sambhoga-kaya, or "Enjoyment Body," is a celestial body in which Buddha appears to bodhisattvas, followers of Mahayana, in pure celestial Buddha worlds and also is enjoyed in visions. But the most important of the three bodies is the Dharma-kaya, which is a cosmic body encompassing the totality of all reality. It is paradoxically nonexistent and yet all existence depends on it. It is unconditioned because it is not conditioned by karma and desire, but not unconditioned because it has the capacity to manifest itself as something conditioned. It is infinite, immutable, simultaneously immanent and transcendent, eternally present, and spread throughout all places in the universe. Furthermore, the teachings of the Buddha are not limited to a particular time and place, but rather are on-going, infinite, and multifaceted. In the Mahayana language of the Lotus Sutra, Buddhists are not orphans after the passing away of the historical Buddha, but rather the children of a compassionate father who is directly involved in the world, working tirelessly to edify human beings and develop them toward the ultimate realization of their own Buddhahood. The Buddha of the Lotus Sutra is a powerful and actively engaged savior who thinks: "I am the father of all creatures and I must snatch them from suffering and give them the bliss of the infinite, boundless Buddha-wisdom" (LS 88). This unified cosmic Buddha is able to take many different forms in the world appropriate for saving particular types of people. "The present buddhas in the universe, whose number is as the sands of the Ganges, . . . appear in the world for the relief of all creatures" (LS 71). As we will see, this perspective on the Buddha opens up the possibility for many other expressions of religiosity besides monastic discipline. In this context, for example, worship of the Buddha and other devotional practices find a welcome home.

THEORY OF EXISTENCE

What was it that the Buddha taught about existence? Answers to this question are varied, but almost all Buddhists recognize a core of the Buddha's teaching that include an articulation of the three marks or characteristics of existence. That is, the Buddha explained that human reality is characterized by impermanence (*anitya*), lack of a solid self (*anatma*), and unsatisfactoriness (*dukkha*). A major Buddhist insight – well represented in the story of the four signs Prince Siddhartha encountered in the royal park – is that all things are subject to change. *Anitya*, the first of the three marks of existence, tells us much about the nature of the world in which we live; namely, that it is transitory or fleeting. There is nothing solid or autonomous in the world. Everything that is born dies; no thing, being, idea, plan or state of mind endures. This leads to a great deal of anxiety for human beings, who are always striving after something lasting and secure. But nothing is permanent in the world. Theravada Buddhists do not normally recognize any creator god, ground of being, or Unmoved Mover behind the continual movement of the world. The distinctive way Buddhists express insight into the nature of existence is to say that everything that arises does so in a manner that is dependent upon something else. Moreover, not only are all things continually changing, but their changes also effect subsequent changes in other things.

That nothing is solid or autonomous is best understood by the teaching of dependent origination, which illustrates the radical interconnectedness of all things and beings by demonstrating that everything that exists is contingent on something else. Theravada tradition maintains that while he was meditating under the Bodhi Tree the future Buddha comprehended the interdependent nature of states of being in terms of a twelve-fold chain of causation. Human ignorance leads to mental formations, which lead to individual consciousness, which leads to the formation of a personal mind and body, which leads to the six senses, which lead to sensorial contact, which leads to sensations, which lead to cravings, which lead to clinging, which leads to the desire for further becoming, which leads to re-birth, which leads to aging and dying, which in turn leads to more ignorance. The twelve-fold chain of causation explains the arising of all things, beings and states. In effect, it functions like a creation myth in other religious traditions. Since the twelve-fold chain of dependent origination has no clear beginning, it is often depicted in Buddhist art as a twelve-spoked wheel. Tibetan Buddhist artists, for example, portray the twelve-fold chain of dependent origination as the Wheel of Existence, wherein each of the twelve conditions is illustrated with a picture. The hub of the wheel is driven by hatred, delusion, and desire, usually depicted as a snake, pig, and cock respectively, and the entire wheel is held in the jaws and claws of Mara, the demonic ruler of conditioned existence who fights to keep all from achieving liberation. Buddhist teachings aim to dissolve this chain of radically conditioned existence by freeing one from the snare of ignorance (particularly through the Four Noble Truths), for once this link is broken the entire chain unravels.

According to Buddhist notions of reincarnation, our present life is but one in a long successive series of lives. One's place in the current world is determined by one's own karma. That is, one's birth in the world is not the result of an accident, nor is it decided by a rewarding or punishing god, rather is the consequence of one's own intentional past actions, good and bad. Again, there is no creator god in Buddhism; karma alone is understood to be sufficient to propel the universe along its course. Buddhists conceive of many different realms that one might be born into as a result of the quality of one's karmic action. The Tibetan Wheel of Life just referred to often depicts the many possible worlds one can be reborn into; besides the human realm, these include both heavenly and hellish realms.

A somewhat different view of the world than is found in the Pali Canon of Theravada Buddhism is suggested in the Mahayana Buddhism of East Asia. Although it is difficult to make general statements about Mahayana Buddhist conceptions of the nature of the world, the notion of the Dharmakaya of the Buddha, a form that is cosmic, eternal, omnipresent, and intensely involved in the world, implies that there may be something unconditioned and unchanging in or behind the world. The Buddha of the Lotus Sutra certainly is a powerful and substantial presence who is very much in charge of the world. Nonetheless, even this text stops short of defining the Buddha as a creator god, and in the end, Mahayana Buddhism affirms the insubstantiality of the world.

THEORY OF HUMAN NATURE

The teaching that there is nothing solid in the world also applies to the self. The second mark of existence teaches that there is no self (*anatma*). A story in the Pali Canon about an encounter between one king, Milinda, and a wise monk by the name of Nagasena expresses Buddhist notions of human nature. After establishing that he is free from political retribution for any comment he might make, Nagasena inquires about the mode of transportation by which the king has arrived at their meeting. Upon learning that the king has come in a chariot, the wise monk questions him about the nature of his chariot (PC 131-32). He asks: "Is the axle the chariot?" The king answers that it is not. "Are the wheels the chariot?" Again the king denies this is so. The conversation continues with Nagasena moving through the entire chariot, identifying the individual parts of which it is made and asking whether any particular part is the chariot. The king persists in rejecting the idea that any of the individual constituents of the chariot are the chariot itself. The monk comes to his main point: "Your majesty, although I question you very closely, I fail to discover any chariot. Verily now, your majesty, the word chariot is a mere empty sound. What chariot is there here? Your majesty, you speak a falsehood, a lie: there is no chariot. . . . Just as the word 'chariot' is but a mode of expression for axle, wheels, chariot-body, pole, and other constituent members, placed in a certain relation to each other . . . in exactly the same way the words 'living entity' and 'Ego' (autonomous self) are but a mode of expression for the presence of the five attachment groups, but when we come to examine the elements of being one by one, we discover that in the absolute sense there is no living entity there to form a basis for such figments as 'I am,' or 'I'" (PC 132-34). Nagasena insists that a person's name is "but a way of counting, a term, an appellation, a convenient designation, a mere name; for there is no Ego (autonomous self) here to be found" (PC 129). His point is that the claim that a person consists of a permanent, unchanging, autonomous self is false. No basis can be found for its reality.

The "five attachment groups" mentioned in the quotation above refer to the five *skandha*s, alternatively translated as the five "aggregates" or "components" that make up a person. Before examining these five components of a person, we need to understand that for Buddhists just as there is no chariot separate from its individual parts, likewise, there is no "person" apart from these five components. The teaching of the five aggregates is a way of accounting for an entire person without resorting to the idea of a "self." Once the five aggregates are examined and analyzed, one discovers that there is nothing behind them that can be taken as a substantial center or permanent "I". Buddhist practice aims to dismantle the unexamined (and false) belief in separate individuality or the idea of the self. Any concept of an ego, self, or soul as an ever-lasting, independent, and absolute entity, an unchanging substance behind the changing phenomenal world, is strongly denied any authentic existence. According to the teachings of the Buddha, the idea of a self is an imaginary belief corresponding to no veracity.

This does not mean that there is no sense of self-reference, continuity of memory, or relative individuality, but that there is no permanence underlying being. Rather than a permanent being, the human is a mind, body, and sense of self that consist of sequences of passing moments. In this sense, a human "being" is really more of a human "becoming." Furthermore, the idea of a separate self, which leads to selfishness and egoism, is not only false, but produces many harmful effects; it is the root of all existential suffering (especially regarding death) and social problems, such as theft, poverty, and violence – all of which assume separate selves in competition with one another. The realization of the absence of a separate self, on the other hand, can lead to a state of selfless loving kindness and compassion for others. Thus, great effort is made in Buddhist teachings to erode and eventually eliminate the idea of one's own permanent individuality.

The first of the five *skandhas*, "components" or "aggregates" of a person, is "form" (*rupa*), the material aspect of a thing or person. It is matter or the stuff of the world, itself made up of ever-changing atoms. In the context of a person, the first aggregate of "form" is the body, including the six sense organs (the mind is included in the list of senses in Buddhism), as well as their corresponding objects in the external world. The second *skandha* is the aggregate of "sensations" (*vedana*), the physiological process resulting from contact of form with form, of the senses with their corresponding objects. Sensations are the feelings produced as the eye comes in contact with visible forms, the ear with sounds, the tongue with tastes, the nose with odor, the body with tangible objects, and the mind with mental objects, such as thoughts. These are said to be of three kinds: pleasant, unpleasant, and neutral. The third aggregate is "perception" (*samjna*). When the six sense organs come in contact with their corresponding objects, sensations are produced that then lead to recognition of objects. When one touches a table with the hands and eyes, for example, not only are sensations produced, but the result is a detection of the object as "table." Perception also occurs in contact with mental objects. Perceptions, then, are the six types of mental discriminations resulting from the six types of sensations. The fourth *skandha* is the aggregate of "mental formations" (*sanskara*). The mental formations include our predispositions, impulses, attitudes, and tendencies that make up the unique character of our own personality. What is known as karma is also included in the aggregate of mental formations. Sensations and perceptions alone do not produce karmic effects, but mental formations are tied to volitional activities in thought, word or deed, both good and bad, such as wisdom or conceit. Mental formations play a key role in the creation of our ongoing conditioned existence, and need to be looked at again after examining the fifth aggregate, which is "consciousness" (*vijnana*). Consciousness is comprised of moments of awareness: not only does one sense and perceive a table, to return to the example above, but one is now aware of the table. Although some Asian schools of religious thought look to consciousness itself as being the core of a permanent self, the Buddha of the Pali Canon taught that consciousness only arises when one of the six sense organs experience a sense object. Consciousness is dependent upon the conditions in which it arises, and therefore is neither independent nor permanent, but is as conditioned as the other four aggregates.

A second look at the fourth *skandha* is instructive for better understanding the way the five aggregates relate to one another. When the arising and passing moments of form, sensations, perceptions, and consciousness interact they create karmic residue or latent impressions called *sanskaras* or mental formations. These in turn are the predispositions that generate and condition the continual arising and passing away of additional combinations of the four other aggregates. One's consciousness, then, is deeply conditioned by mental formations. A romantic affair that goes sour, for example, very often affects one's next love affair, even though in theory the two are completely separate relationships. Something is carried over that shapes and influences the next experience. Driven and conditioned by unconscious latent impressions, the combinations of form, sensations, perceptions, and consciousness are both ongoing and self-perpetuating. Again, there is no unmoved mover behind the movement; there is only movement, only change. One thing disappears, conditioning the appearance of the next in a series of cause and effects. The mental formations, however, which include both conscious and unconscious memory, provide a connection between the arising and passing moments of the unique combinations of the aggregates.

What this means is that a human life is, in effect, very short. "Strictly speaking, the duration of the life of a living being is exceedingly brief, lasting only while a thought lasts. Just as a chariot-wheel in rolling rolls only at one point of the tire, and in resting rests only at one point; in exactly the same way, the life of a living being lasts only for the period of one thought" (PC 150). Rebirth or reincarnation, then, is happening rapidly and constantly each moment of our lives. As contemporary biology, psychology and physics confirm, our bodies and minds are changing incessantly. Buddhists explain the concept of the simultaneity of continuity and discontinuity in the process of reincarnation with the aid of a candle. During further conversations, the wise monk Nagasena asks king Milinda whether he is the same person he was as a young boy. "Nay, verily bhante. The young, tender, weakly infant lying on its back was one person, and my present grown-up self is another person" (PC 148). Here discontinuity is emphasized. But Nagasena presses the king on this point and gets him to see also that in the case of a person "It was I, your majesty, who was a young, tender, weakly infant lying on my back, and it is I who am now grown up" (PC 148-49). Now continuity is stressed. How can both of these statements be true? Buddhists use the metaphor of a flame to illustrate this point. If you were to light a candle and then come back an hour later, would you see a different flame or the same flame? Nagasena questions the king:

"It is as if, your majesty, a man were to light a light; would it shine all night?"

"Assuredly, bhante, it would shine all night."

"Pray, your majesty, is the flame of the first watch the same as the flame of the middle watch?"

"Nay, verily, bhante."

"Is the flame of the middle watch the same as the flame of the last watch?"

"Nay, verily, bhante."

"Pray, then, your majesty, was there one light in the first watch, another light in the middle watch, and a third light in the last watch?"

"Nay, verily, bhante. Through connection with that first light there was light all night."

"In exactly the same way, your majesty, do the elements of being join one another in serial succession: one element perishes, another arises, succeeding each other as it were instantaneously. Therefore, neither as the same nor as a different person do you arrive at your latest aggregation of consciousness" (PC 149).

Nagasena's point is that just as the flame one witnesses upon lighting a candle and the flame one witnesses upon returning an hour later are both a different flame and the same flame, so too a person now and that person ten years earlier are both a different person and the same person. The difference is due to the fact that a person is continually changing (the aggregates of form, sensations, perceptions, and consciousness comprise moments that arise and pass away) and the sameness is due to the connecting memories, predispositions, unconscious impressions, and karmic links of the aggregate of the mental formations. By extending the metaphor of the candle to include the fresh lighting of one candle with another candle – just as the latter is about to go out – an explanatory illustration is provided for rebirth or reincarnation following the death of the physical body with the persisting karmic connections that determine and condition the next life.

So what are we to conclude about Buddhist conceptions of human nature? Clearly the Buddha labored hard to dismantle the idea of a permanent, autonomous self. But are we to understand the teaching of no self as a firm and absolute doctrine? When the Buddha was asked directly whether a soul does or does not exist, he remained silent. Let me close this section with a statement from the Pali Canon that complicates any simplistic view of the Buddhist notion of the self. After a section that lays out the teaching of the five aggregates and confirms that there is no basis of an "I" here, we read: "He, however, who abandons this knowledge of the truth and believes in a living entity must assume either that this living entity will perish or that it will not perish. If he assumes that it will not perish, he falls into the heresy of the persistence of existences; or if he assume that it will perish, he falls into that of the annihilation of existences. . . . To say: 'The living entity persists,' is to fall short of the truth; to say, 'It is annihilated,' is to outrun the truth" (134). This statement, to say the least, challenges one to think deeply about the very nature of existence.

DIAGNOSIS

What is the basic problem of human existence according to Buddhist teachings? This question brings us to the Four Noble Truths, the very core of Buddhist Dharma, the subject of Buddha's first sermon delivered to the five ascetics in the deer park near Banaras, and the key to shattering the twelve-fold chain of causation at the point of ignorance. The First Noble Truth states that life is *dukkha*; this is also the third mark of existence. The word *dukkha* is often translated as "suffering," but is perhaps more accurately translated as "dissatisfactory." As we saw in the story of the life of the Buddha, this is also true for a privileged prince who has it all. *Dukkha* includes feelings such as insecurity, uncertainty, lack, and loss. It refers to a state of basic existential anxiety about life, that things are imperfect, always flawed. It is also a response to impermanence; good things never last. Human beings are uneasy, anxious, vulnerable, frustrated, and disappointed in a world in which everything – including ones own self – is constantly changing. As with other Buddhist teachings, the claim that life is suffering is not to be taken as an ultimate doctrinal statement about the nature of reality, but rather as a statement about the experiential reality of human beings. The Buddha did not claim that life is ultimately *dukkha* and nothing but *dukkha*, but rather that we experience it as *dukkha*. In the role of a wise physician (rather than a metaphysician) the Buddha diagnoses the human predicament as *dukkha* and proceeds from there.

Three kinds of *dukkha* are recognized in Buddhist literature. First, there is ordinary suffering, such as aging, sickness and death. Ordinary suffering also includes such experiences as encountering unpleasant conditions, separation from loved ones, not getting what one wants, and sadness. The second type of suffering is *dukkha* produced by change. Even the experience of ordinary happiness eventually yields a form of suffering produced by change. The Buddha is not saying that there is no happiness in human life, but rather he highlights the fact that happiness — like everything else — does not last, and therefore is not fully satisfactory. When happiness disappears unhappiness arises. The last type of suffering is *dukkha* as conditioned states, primary among them being the troublous state created by a false sense of self. The emphasis on *dukkha* does not make Buddhism a pessimistic religion; Buddhism simply stresses the necessity of first facing a realistic assessment of the ordinary human condition as characterized by suffering in an effort to move beyond it.

After diagnosing the human condition as *dukkha*, the Buddha as an effective physician moves on to identify the cause of our disease. The Second Noble Truth asserts that the cause of our suffering is "craving" or "grasping" (*tanha*). Our problem is that we try to hold onto things and experiences which by nature cannot be held onto. *Dukkha* is caused by an ever-changing self trying desperately to cling to a world in continual flux; it is the result of a non-existent self trying to possess things that by definition cannot permanently be possessed. The essence of life is change, while the essence of grasping is to prevent change. Importantly, this grasping must be seen as a selfish kind of craving. Craving is a willful act that is motivated by the idea of a separate and permanent self. It is the expression of an intense desire to perpetuate the self. It is a thirst for the will to be, to exist, to become more and more, to grow more and more, to accumulate more and more, to have more and more. And all of this leads to continual and conditioned suffering.

PRESCRIPTION

What then are we to do about the human condition of suffering according to Buddhist thought? Is it possible to escape from the experience of *dukkha*, and if so what is the means to do so? These questions lead us to the Third and Fourth Noble Truths. The Buddha does not leave his followers in a hopeless state. Far from it: he claims that there is a healthy state beyond the existential anxiety of *dukkha*. The Third Noble Truth asserts that there is a cessation of *dukkha*, which, of course, involves the end of craving. The Third Noble Truth, in effect, negates the First Noble Truth; thus the importance of seeing Buddhist teachings as useful only so long as they are applicable.

The ultimate state in Buddhism is referred to as Nirvana. The word Nirvana literally means "blowing out" or "extinguishing," as in the blowing out of a fire. In the present context, the reference is to the blowing out of *dukkha* by means of extinguishing the fire of craving (*tanha*). This leads to the blessed state of Nirvana. When craving becomes extinct, then *dukkha* is gone, and the result is Nirvana. This is the highest goal of Buddhist practice, and perhaps this is all that can be said about Nirvana. Buddhist scriptures warn again and again that Nirvana can never be completely defined by words. Describing Nirvana to one who has not experienced it is said to be like a turtle trying to describe to a fish what it is like to walk on dry land. There is nothing in the fish's experience that enables it to understand land conceptually. So too with Nirvana, which is wholly beyond ordinary experience. Despite the warnings, however, attempts have been made to define Nirvana. It is perhaps best defined as absolute freedom, but has also been referred to as the "Unconditioned," "Truth," "Bliss," or "Ultimate Reality." It is the freedom to see things as they really are, emancipated from the limiting distortions of self-projections. It is a tranquil liberation from the tormenting existential anxieties of life, such as those that drove young Prince Siddhartha out of his palace. Far from the pessimistic self-annihilation of nihilism, Nirvana is said to be a blissful and dynamic state in which all hatred, delusion, and desire has been annihilated. Nirvana is a sublime religious state that can be experienced in this very life, as is demonstrated in the sacred biographies of the Buddha by the fact that the Buddha lived for more than forty years after achieving the awakening of Nirvana under the Bodhi tree.

We now come to the Fourth Noble Truth, the prescription to end the disease of *dukkha,* the medicine that allows one to achieve the supremely healthy state of Nirvana: the Eightfold Path. This path is also known as the "Middle Way," since it is situated between the two extremes of a life dedicated to satisfying ordinary pleasures, as exemplified by the palace in the story of the life of the Buddha, and the excessive asceticism exemplified by the harsh routine the future Buddha practiced with the five ascetics in the forest. Some spiritual paths that originate in India – such as the eight-limbed practices of classical yoga – are meant to be followed successively, as one climbs a ladder rung by rung; but the Eightfold Path is comprised of eight practices that are to be followed simultaneously, as one might follow the spokes of an eight-spoked wheel concurrently to its central hub. The Eightfold Path addresses three major concerns: ethical conduct (*sila*), which is based on the concept of universal love and compassion for all living beings, mental discipline (*samadhi*), which culminates in the meditative realization of the true nature of the self and the world, and wisdom (*prajna*), which has to do with establishing correct knowledge about reality and is fulfiled in Enlightenment. In general, it may be said that the Eightfold Path aims at cultivating behavior not motivated by the idea of the self.

Ethical conduct includes three practices of the path: Right Speech means that one should speak in a manner that benefits all beings. One should speak at the right time and place, and abstain from lying, harsh or harmful speech, and useless speech. If one has nothing worthy to say, one should maintain a "noble silence." Right Action involves the cultivation of moral, honorable and peaceful conduct in oneself and others. It avoids killing, stealing, cheating, engaging in illicit sex, and consuming intoxicants. Right Livelihood denotes making a living or profit that does not involve harming other beings or come at the expense of the welfare of others. Examples of wrong livelihood are the manufacture and sales of weapons, the slaughter of animals, and the production of intoxicants and poisons.

Mental discipline is comprised of the following three practices: Right Effort entails applying oneself energetically to the generation and cultivation of wholesome states of mind. Overcoming unwholesome states, one should channel one's energy to the development of all aspects of the Buddhist life. Right Mindfulness is a meditative practice in which one aspires to be diligently aware of one's body, feelings, mind, and thoughts. It is often considered to be the most critical aspect of the path. Mindfulness meditation usually involves giving attention to breathing as one seeks deeper and deeper insight into the nature of reality as marked by dissatisfaction, impermanence, and lack of a solid self. All of Buddhist practice might be summed up as: Be ever mindful! Right Concentration differs from mindfulness meditative practices in that it involves the cultivation of meditative states through the technique of calming the mind and concentrating it on a single point. There are, then, two types of meditative practice referred to in Buddhist scripture. One involves withdrawing the senses from ordinary sensory experience and narrowing awareness from its usual wide spectrum in order to achieve one-pointed concentration. Rather than narrowing awareness or shutting down awareness, the other aims to open awareness completely so that one becomes fully aware of reality as it really is and achieves deep insight into the nature of the world and self. If a balloon were popped behind a person in an ordinary state of being, that person would most likely jump. If a series of balloons were popped the person would typically react less and less as the series went on until that person became used to the sound. If a balloon were popped behind a person in deep concentrative meditation, there would presumably be no reaction since that person's senses and awareness are withdrawn. If, however, a balloon were popped behind a person engaged in mindfulness meditation, the person would react, and not only that, but would go on reacting to the entire series of poppings, experiencing each as a new and unique event.

Wisdom includes Right Thought and Right Understanding. Right Thought involves thoughts of selfless detachment, thoughts that transcend the idea of the self, or simply, loving thoughts. Right Understanding means understanding things as they really are. It connotes harmonizing one's mind with the ultimate nature of reality characterized by the three marks of existence. Most importantly, this means understanding the Four Noble Truths, for it is this teaching that explains things as they really are. Thus, there is something wonderfully circular about Buddhist teachings: the Fourth Noble Truth is the Eightfold Path, and the eighth aspect of this path consists of understanding the Four Noble Truths, the main subject of the Buddha's first sermon.

DIFFERENT PATHS

In addition to understanding the complexity of Buddhist practice in terms of the Eightfold Path, it is important to appreciate the great variety found within Buddhism. Within Theravada Buddhism alone there exist two very different ways of being Buddhist: one for the monks and another for the laity. Buddhist monastic discipline is defined primarily by the Vinaya, namely 227 rules that govern the monk's life. Although the word discipline may have negative connotations in some contexts, here it comes to mean a way of acting that is not motivated by personal desire or self-concern. Discipline is concerned with volition and volitional acts, that is, with karma. Whereas ordinary action is self-directed and produces conditioning karma, disciplined action – action performed without the burden of self – will not produce further conditioned action or karma. Detached actions that are not motivated by personal desire do not produce further attachments or bondage; they are thus a path to freedom. Put simply, the studied actions of monastic discipline lead to selfless action – action minus the self. Buddhist monks are not so concerned with acting in a pragmatic way, but in a way that is in harmony with the highest reality. Moreover, Buddhist monks do not just strive for freedom, but for a particular experience represented by the Buddha's enlightenment. This means that Buddhist discipline aims to follow in the footsteps of the Buddha as carefully as possible, for the perfected way of life expressed spontaneously by the awakened Buddha is understood to be the very model for monastic discipline. That is, the Buddha's way of being and the monastic way of life are the two sides of the same coin; the difference is in the motivation. The Buddha's actions are the natural expression of a disciplined mind, whereas the monk's actions are intentional means to create a disciplined mind; but in either case, the actions are ideally the same.

Pursuit of a perfected way of being, however, requires the controlled environment of the monastery and the support of a non-monastic laity. The Buddhist laity is comprised of those who have accepted the five Buddhist precepts but do not aim for the higher goal of Nirvana in this lifetime; rather, they strive to improve their karmic lot in this life and the next by generating good karmic merit. There are, then, really two goals in Buddhist society: Nirvana is actively pursued by the monks, while the laity occupy themselves with laying the foundation for its attainment in a future life by amassing beneficial merit. The relationship between the monks and the laity is one that is to be mutually supportive. The laity supply the monks with food and clothing in exchange for at least three important returns: the monks teach the Buddha's Dharma, exemplify a model life, and provide a productive field for merit-making. Buddhist monasteries in Sri Lanka and Southeast Asia are often located near settlements to facilitate the daily round of the monk's begging for food. The monastery is regularly opened to the laity so that they can listen to the monks chant Buddhist texts, hear a sermon on the life and teachings of the Buddha, and receive the five precepts: not to kill, steal, lie, consume intoxicants, nor engage in illicit sex. In this way the monks actively influence the life-style of the lay Buddhist society in their role as active teachers. In addition to this, to the degree that the Buddhist monks maintain the Vinaya or monastic discipline, they lay claim to being the legitimate bearers of the spiritual path articulated by the Buddha. As they express this publicly through a range of rituals, the monks formally declare the eternal presence of the Buddha's Dharma and affirm their role as the successors to the Buddha's authority in matters of spirituality. The result is that the monks provide a model of perfection for their greater society and establish themselves as legitimate fields for merit. As the monks follow in the footsteps of the Buddha and imitate his way of being in the world, they establish a concrete and empirically available model for the laity who interact with them. The devout laity in turn provide another kind of model for those members of their society who have not taken the five precepts. In this way a paradigmatic line can be observed that stretches back to the Buddha through the monks, and to a lesser extent through the laity. Furthermore, giving gifts of food, clothing, and shelter to the monastic community, which is considered to be a rich and fruitful field for making good karmic merit, becomes a promising occasion for the laity to develop themselves spiritually as they prepare to better themselves in this life and the next.

The considerable variety within Buddhism can be even better appreciated when we examine a Mahayana text such as the Lotus Sutra. Mahayana Buddhists consider their approach "Greater" for several reasons. It is open to all, involves an all-embracing compassion, and has a greater goal. The Mahayana Buddhism of the Lotus Sutra differs greatly from Theravada Buddhism. We have already seen that Mahayana Buddhists have a different view of the Buddha: whereas Theravada Buddhism is oriented to a historical understanding of the Buddha, without actually denying this understanding the Lotus Sutra asserts that if the Buddha had lived on earth in a particular span of time it was in an "emanation body" by a being who is cosmic and eternal, but can manifest in numerous forms. There are further differences. The Theravada ideal of human perfection is the accomplished monk, or *arhat*, who worked diligently for his own enlightenment, while the Mahayana ideal of human perfection is the bodhisattva, literally an "enlightenment-being." The bodhisattva is one who takes a double vow: to realize Buddhahood, but not to enter final Nirvana before all beings have been liberated. Rather than disappearing from worldly existence at the end of life as do the *arhats*, bodhisattvas pursue various perfections (*paramitas*) and dedicate their bodhisattva lifetimes and subsequent lives as Buddhas to the compassionate act of helping others attain the liberation of enlightenment.

Important among the perfections pursued by a bodhisattva is the perfection of wisdom. Specifically this refers to achieving insight into the "emptiness" (*sunyata*) of all factors of existence. Mahayana Buddhists claim that all aspects of existence are "empty of own-being" (*svabhava*); this is another way of saying that all things are radically interdependent and interconnected. The Heart Sutra claims that the aggregate of "form is emptiness and emptiness is form." This is true for all of the five aggregates that make up a person. In a sense, the bodhisattva looks simultaneously through two seemingly contradictory lenses: through the lens of wisdom the bodhisattva sees that there are no independent beings; through the lens of compassion the bodhisattva resolves to save all beings. The teaching that form is emptiness does not mean that matter does not exist, but rather it tells us something about the nature of matter. Emptiness is not an ultimate reality that transcends all forms of existence, but rather all forms of existence are themselves empty. Emptiness regarded in this nondualistic way, ultimately affirms the value of this world and all beings. This is the insightful wisdom of the bodhisattva that supports magnificent compassion for all beings. The greatly compassionate and vastly wise bodhisattva is often contrasted in Mahayana literature with the *arhat*, who is characterized in this context as a haughty, cold, and self-centered monk.

Furthermore, the concept of the Dharma, or the Buddha's teachings, is expanded. If the Buddha existed only in northern India during the sixth century B.C.E., then his teachings would be finite and complete upon his death. On the other hand, if the Buddha exists at all times, his teachings are infinite in form and continue at all times. Consequently, Dharma would be the ongoing teachings of an Omnipresent Being. Many Mahayana sutras claim to present a teaching that is given only when the time and place is right for the revelation of advanced wisdom. The Lotus Sutra regards the Dharma as "infinite, boundless, unprecedented" (LS 52), and considerably varied in a manner suitable to the great variety of human dispositions. Additionally, whereas the highest goal of Theravada Buddhism is a final passing out of this world, Mahayana Buddhist texts often speak of realizing "Buddha nature." But even when the term Nirvana is used, it is understood quite differently.

One of the astounding claims of Mahayana Buddhism is that the supreme goal of Nirvana and ordinary existence (Samsara) are the same.

The Lotus Sutra puts it this way: "All existence, from the beginning, is ever of the nirvana-nature" (LS 66). Some schools of Mahayana Buddhism, consequently, hold a view of consciousness somewhat different from that presented in Theravada scriptures. These schools maintain that prior to being affected by the conditioning and distorting influences of mental formations and defilements, consciousness exists in its true essence as a pure and enlightened luminosity that is the basis for Buddhahood. The aim, then, is to uncover what is already there. Nirvana is said to be unattainable for at least two reasons. First, it is unattainable because it is not some objective thing or concrete goal that can be attained. Second, it cannot be attained because it already is. Striving for Nirvana or Buddha nature elsewhere is compared in East Asian Buddhism to the process of searching for an ox while riding an ox. The implications of this for Buddhist practice are immense.

A story is told in the Lotus Sutra about a man who went to visit a friend, and while with him got so drunk that he fell asleep. The man's friend had to leave on official business, but before he left he sewed a priceless jewel inside the man's jacket as a gift. When the man awoke he set out on a journey to a foreign land seeking his livelihood by working extremely hard just to make ends meet. Sometime later he once again met his friend, who was horrified to learn that the man had been laboring so hard when all the while he had a priceless jewel sewn in his jacket. "Tut! Sir, how is it you have come to this for the sake of food and clothing? Wishing you to be in comfort and able to satisfy all your five senses, I formerly in such a year and month and on such a day tied a priceless jewel within your garment. Now as of old it is present there and you in ignorance are slaving and worrying to keep yourself alive. How very stupid! Go you now and exchange that jewel for what you need and do whatever you will, free from all poverty and shortage" (LS 177). The text makes it clear that the priceless jewel is eligibility for Buddhahood, and that the pittance the man had earned from his hard labor is the lesser goal achieved through short-sided monastic discipline. If he had only known the truth, the man would not have had to work for a daily wage, as he had an infinitely precious and free gift with him all the time. In fact, his labors kept him from realizing what was there with him all along. A similar story is found in the Lotus Sutra about a king and his young son, who ran away, forgot his origins, and fell into a life of poverty. The wayward son too labored hard for a meager wage (i.e., *arhat's* nirvana) until the day he found his way back home and realized that as son of the king he already possessed infinite wealth (i.e., Buddha nature) (LS 110-15). Both of these stories make the same point: that one does not have to work to achieve Buddha nature, but rather one merely needs to realize what already is. The *arhats* of the Lotus

Sutra come to understand: "From of old we are really sons of the Buddha, but only have taken pleasure in minor matters" (LS 115). From a Mahayana perspective, the goal-oriented activity of monastic discipline that seeks Nirvana elsewhere steals attention away from the here and now and blocks acceptance of what truly is. To the degree that a conception of Nirvana posits a perfect world outside of the present one, it creates dissatisfaction with present existence, and therefore, can in its most radical form be seen as a cause of *dukkha*. A motto of Theravada Buddhism might be "Be on constant guard," while a motto of Mahayana Buddhism might be "Be on friendly terms with whatever comes."

Whereas the path to perfection within Theravada Buddhism is understood to be singular, as defined by the Vinaya, the Mahayana Buddhism of the Lotus Stura recognizes countless ways to realize Buddha nature. In addition to strict monastic practice, this opens up a world of devotional surrender to Buddha as a savior and to various forms of temple worship. Included among the countless ways to achieve the ultimate, the Lotus Sutra claims: "Even anyone who, with distracted mind, with but a single flower has paid homage to the painted images shall gradually see countless buddhas. Or those who have offered worship, were it by merely folding the hands, or even raising a hand, or by slightly bending the head, by paying homage to the images gradually see innumerable buddhas, attain the supreme Way. . . If any, even with distracted mind, enter a stupa or temple and cry but once 'Namah Buddha,' they have attained the Buddha-way" (LS 69). Along side of those forms of Buddhism that rely on self-effort in realizing enlightenment, then, we find various forms of Buddhism that understand the spiritual path to be one of reliance on an all-powerful and saving Buddha. Within Japanese Buddhism, these two approaches are called respectively *jiriki* – by the power of oneself — and *tariki* – by the power of another.

WOMEN IN BUDDHISM

Buddhism, like all the great world religions, is comprised of enormous variety. It would, therefore, be difficult to marshal a critique of Buddhism as a whole, since any remark made would most likely be contradicted by some form of Buddhism. Instead, I will end this chapter with a few comments on the position of women in Buddhism as represented in the Pali Canon and the Lotus Sutra. Overall, Western feminists have pointed out that in traditional forms of monastic Buddhism women have been viewed as spiritually inferior to and as a temptress for male monks. Women in monastic literature have been depicted as being sensually unrestrained and having animalistic tendencies not found in men. The Buddha of the Pali scriptures advises men to avoid women as much as possible. A segment of the Pali Canon well illustrates the somewhat ambiguous view of women situated with a monastic perspective. In a section of the text that addresses the admission of women into the monastic order, a maternal aunt of the Buddha named Gotamid asked the Awakened One if she could retire from the household life to pursue a monastic life. The Buddha replied: "Enough, O Gotamid, do not ask that women retire from household life to the house-less one, under the Doctrine and Discipline announced by The Tathagata" (PC 441). Seeing her in a sad and dejected state, the Buddha's close disciple Ananda intervened on Gotamid's behalf and approached the Buddha himself. At first the Buddha repeated his refusal to let women into the order, but Ananda changed his tactic and inquired about the competency of women for achieving the higher states, including the ultimate state of an *arhat* (here translated as "saintship"). To this the Buddha replied: "Women are competent, Ananda, if they retire from household life to the houseless one, under the Doctrine and Discipline announced by The Tathagata, to attain to the fruit of conversion, to attain to the fruit of once returning, to attain to the fruit of never returning, to attain to saintship" (PC 444). After admitting this, the Buddha agrees to allow women into the monastic order under the condition that they accept eight additional rules, all designed to keep them distant from and subordinate to men. We learn from this, then, that women were allowed into the monastic order according to the Pali scriptures, and furthermore, were considered to be capable of achieving the highest spiritual goal. However, this comes at a cost. The Buddha explains to Ananda that if women had never been allowed into the order, Buddhist Dharma would have lasted fully intact for one thousand years, but since they were allowed into the order, Buddhist Dharma would last for only five hundred years. "Just as Ananda, when the disease called mildew falls upon a flourishing field of rice, that field of rice does not long endure, in exactly the same way, Ananda, when women retire from household life to the houseless one, under doctrine and discipline, that religion does not long endure" (PC 447). Although we must be careful not to conflate the representation of women in Buddhist literature with any on-the-ground social reality, there is obviously much that is problematic from a modern perspective about the viewpoint expressed above. Much of it appears to be male projectionism. On the other hand, many Theravada Buddhists point out that the Buddha created the women's order in a way that kept them independent of the men's order to assure their freedom from male domination, and the texts refer to many holy women and good daughters of the Buddha.

The Lotus Sutra fairs somewhat better in its attitudes toward women. This text advocates an all-inclusive universal salvation, which clearly includes women. Virtuous women are recognized in the Lotus Sutra as "good daughters," and are regarded as skilled teachers and potential bodhisattvas, although there may still be a residual sense that they do best under the guidance of a male "good son." Nonetheless, the Buddha of the Lotus Sutra acknowledges the place of virtuous women along side virtuous men: "If there be any people who ask what sort of living being will become Buddhas in the future, you should show them . . . If good sons and good daughters receive and keep, read and recite, expound, copy even a single word of the Law-Flower Sutra . . . these people will be looked up to by all the worlds; and as you pay homage to tathagathas, so should you pay homage to them" (LS 187). Today, as Buddhism continues to establish itself in new countries and cultures around the world, women are carving out novel places for themselves in a tradition that has been largely dominated by men.

FOR FURTHER READING

The Pali Canon (PC) is available in different forms and translations. All quotations and references are from the selections in Henry Clarke Warren, *Buddhism in Translations* (New York: Antheneum, 1974), since this paperback edition is still readily available through a number of publishers.

Several translations of the *Lotus Sutra* (LS) exist. Quotations and references are from *The Threefold Lotus Sutra*, translated by Bunno Kato, Yoshiro Tamura, and Kojiro Miyasaka (New York: Weatherhill, 1984).

For an overview of Buddhism, see Donald W. Mitchell, *Buddhism: Introducing the Buddhist Experience* (New York: Oxford University Press, 2008); Richard H. Robinson, Willard L. Johnson, and Thanissaro Bhikkhu, *Buddhist Religions: A Historical Introduction*, 5th ed. (Wadsworth/Thomson, 2004); and Peter Harvey, *An Introduction to Buddhism: Teachings, History and Practices* (Cambridge: Cambridge University Press, 1990).

For more on Theravada Buddhism, see Robert C. Lester, *Theravada Buddhism in Southeast Asia* (Ann Arbor: University of Michigan Press, 1973), and Walpola Rahula, *What the Buddha Taught* (New York: Grove Press, 1974; many other editions are available, including an online edition).

For more on Mahayana Buddhism see Paul Williams, *Mahayana Buddhism: The Doctrinal Foundations* (London: Routledge & Kegan Paul, 1989).

For more on women in Buddhist literature see: Diana Y. Paul, *Women in Buddhism* Berkeley: University of California Press, 1985); and Jose Ignacio Cabezon, ed., *Buddhism, Sexuality, and Gender* (Albany: State University of New York Press, 1992).

4

Plato: The Rule of Reason

Let us start our examination of nonreligious (or not explicitly religious) theories of human nature by considering the philosophy of Plato (427–347 B.C.E.). Although it dates back nearly two and a half millennia, Plato's pioneering thought is still of great contemporary relevance. He was one of the first to argue that the systematic use of our reason can show us the best way to live. A clear conception of human virtue and fulfilment, based on a true understanding of human nature and its problems, is in Plato's view the only way to individual happiness and social stability.

PLATO'S LIFE AND WORK

A short sketch of Plato's background will help us understand the origin of his ideas. He was born into an influential family in the Greek city-state of Athens, which enjoyed economic prosperity through its empire and trade, and at one stage developed a remarkably democratic system of government, which we now honor as the first experiment in democracy. We remember Athens above all as a center of unprecedented advances in the arts and intellectual inquiries, including sculpture, drama, history, mathematics, science, and philosophy. One of its greatest figures was the ethical philosopher Socrates, whose teaching deeply impressed Plato. But these thinkers lived in a politically disturbed period in Athens: the war with Sparta ended in disastrous defeat, and a period of tyranny ensued. When a new faction came to power, Socrates came under suspicion because of his association with certain people. He was brought to trial and condemned to death in 399 B.C.E. on a charge of subverting the state religion and corrupting the young.

Socrates' method of arguing and teaching was akin in some ways to that of the "Sophists" of his day. These self-styled experts offered, for a fee, to impart certain kinds of skill; in particular the art of rhetoric (i.e., persuasion by public speaking), which was important for political advancement in Athens. (The Sophists could be described as the public relations consultants of their time!) They also discussed ethics and politics. Athenians were aware of the variety of beliefs and practices in various cultures around the Mediterranean, so they were confronted with the question of whether there is any criterion of truth in these matters. The Sophists often expressed skepticism about whether moral and political values were anything more than arbitrary conventions. What we now call "cultural relativism" was thus a tempting option at this early stage of thought.

Unlike the Sophists, Socrates charged no fees for his teaching, and he concerned himself with fundamental philosophical and ethical questions. His great inspiring idea was that we can come to know the right way to live, if only we will use our reason properly. He has been called "the founder of philosophy," not so much for any conclusions he reached, but for pioneering the use of rational argument and inquiry in an open-minded, nondogmatic way. Famously, Socrates claimed superiority to unthinking people only in that he was *aware* of his own ignorance about so many difficult matters, whereas they thought they knew. He was adept at showing by persistent questioning that they did not know what they claimed to know. Plato's early dialogues (especially the *Apology*) portray Socrates as believing that "the unexamined life is not worth living," and as making his fellow Athenians think about their lives in ways they would not otherwise have done. Socrates felt called with a kind of religious intensity to disturb people's mental complacency; so it is not surprising that he found himself a focus of hostility, even to the point of death.

In all this, Socrates deeply influenced Plato, who was shocked at the execution of his inspirational teacher. Although disillusioned with contemporary politics, Plato retained Socrates' faith in rational inquiry; he was convinced that it was possible to attain knowledge of deep-lying truths about the world and about human nature, and to apply this knowledge for the benefit of human society. Socrates did not leave any writings—his influence was entirely oral. Plato himself expressed some skepticism about the value of books, tending to agree with Socrates that actual dialogue was the best way to get people to think for themselves and perhaps change their approach to life. However, Plato did write extensively, often with great literary skill, and his works are amongst the first major treatises in the history of philosophy. They are in conversational form, typically with Socrates taking the leading part in the argument. Most scholars think that in the early dialogues such as *Apology, Crito, Euthyphro,* and *Meno,* Plato was mainly expounding Socrates' ideas, whereas in later works (which tend to be longer and more technical) he was expressing his own distinctive theories. Plato founded the Academy in Athens, which can be described as the world's first university.

One of the most famous and widely studied of Plato's texts is the *Republic,* a lengthy, complex, and closely argued dialogue between several characters; it is traditionally divided into ten books (which do not always make natural divisions of the argument). As the title suggests, one main theme is an outline of an ideal human society, but the central argument concerns the problems and fulfilment of individual human beings. In this work, Plato touches on many topics, including metaphysics, theory of knowledge, human psychology, morals, politics, social classes, the family, education, and the arts. I will concentrate on the *Republic* here, with occasional reference to other dialogues. I will incorporate some critical points along with my exposition. (There is a traditional page-numbering system for Plato's texts: my references are to the *Republic* unless otherwise stated.)

METAPHYSICAL BACKGROUND: THE THEORY OF FORMS

Although Plato mentions God, or the gods, at various places, it is not clear how seriously he takes such talk (he was hardly a believer in the polytheism of Greek popular religion). When he does talk of "God" in the singular, he does *not* mean the biblical conception of a personal Being who appears to or communicates with individual people and intervenes in human history. Plato has in mind a rather more abstract ideal: in the *Philebus* and *Laws,* God or the divine is identified with reason (*logos*) in the universe. (The prologue of the Gospel of John, "In the beginning was the word (*logos*) . . . " shows the influence of this Platonic idea.) In the *Timaeus,* Plato gives a creation story that differs from the biblical doctrine of God's creation out of nothing in that Plato's "divine wisdom" organizes the world out of preexisting matter and can only do the best he can with this somewhat recalcitrant material.

What is most distinctive of Plato's metaphysics, however, is his theory of "Forms" (the Greek word is *eidos*). But it is a matter of difficult philosophical interpretation to say what exactly this amounts to, for Plato hardly ever presents it as an explicit theory, nor does he argue for it in any very systematic way. It is mentioned or assumed at crucial points in various dialogues, though to Plato's credit we also find him wrestling with difficulties in it, in the *Parmenides*. We have to remember that he was a pioneer in philosophy, struggling to express and clarify fundamental ideas for the first time in human thought.

Plato realizes that human knowledge is not simply a matter of mere passive observation of things and events in the world around us. As he argues in the *Theaetetus*, our knowledge involves understanding, in that we actively interpret the stimulations we receive through our sense organs, we apply concepts to organize and classify what we perceive, using our mental powers as well as our sense organs (see the related remarks on Kant's epistemology in Chapter 7). Plato's Forms can be identified with concepts, at least as a first approximation. I will present four main aspects of the Forms here: logical or semantic (to do with meanings and concepts), metaphysical (to do with what is ultimately real), epistemological (to do with what we can know), and moral or political (to do with how we ought to live).

The logical or semantic aspect of the Forms is their role as concepts or principles of classification that constitute the meaning of general terms. What justifies our application of one word or concept such as "bed" or "table" to many particular beds or tables? These are Plato's own examples at *Republic* 596, where part of his point is that craftsmen making things must have a concept of what they are trying to make. But the "one over many" structure applies to any general concept. We recognize things in the world as falling under natural kinds: species of animal and plant; kinds of metal, rock, and liquid. Even with simple sensory qualities, such as redness or heat, there are many things that are red, and many others that are hot, but one concept of each quality. And, at 507, Plato distinguishes the many different good things and beautiful things from the single Forms of Goodness and Beauty.

The "nominalist" view about concepts or universals is that there is nothing that all instances of a concept literally have in common—at best, there may be some similarities between them. The view traditionally labelled "Platonic realism" is that what makes particular things count as Fs is their resemblance to, or "participation in," the Form or Idea of F, understood as an abstract entity, something existing in its own right, and different from all the individual instances of it. At *Republic* 596, Plato's view seems to be that for each general word there is one Form. But elsewhere he suggests that only some special kinds of words or concepts, those that pick out genuine unities (including what we would now call "natural kinds") express what he would call a Form. He is reluctant to accept, for example, that there are Forms corresponding to the terms "mud," "dirt," or "barbarian" (the latter was used for all non-Greeks, like our word "foreigner").

An important metaphysical aspect of the Forms is that Plato thinks of them as more real than material things, in that they do not change, decay, or cease to exist. Material objects get damaged and destroyed, but the Forms are not in space or time, and they are not knowable by the senses, only by the human intellect or reason (485, 507, 526–27). Plato's grand metaphysical theory is that beyond the world of changeable and destructible things there is another world containing these unchanging eternal Forms. The things we can perceive are only distantly related to these ultimate realities, as he suggested by his haunting image of the typical human condition as people chained like prisoners, facing the inner wall of a cave in which all they can see are mere shadows cast on the wall, knowing nothing of the real world outside (515–17). If Plato were alive today, he might be quick to point out how well his image applies to so many of us who rely for our (supposed) knowledge of the real world on watching television, movies, and computer screens!

Most people may be concerned only with shadows, and ignorant of ultimate reality, but Plato thought that by a process of education it is possible for human minds—or, at least, the more able of them—to attain knowledge of the world of Forms. The epistemological aspect of his theory is that only this intellectual acquaintance with the Forms properly counts as knowledge. Plato discusses the nature of knowledge in several dialogues, but in the *Republic* we find the thesis that only what fully and really exists can be fully or really known: perception of impermanent objects and events in the physical world is only "belief" or "opinion," not knowledge (476–80). (Plato elaborates on the mechanics of his cave story to make it fit the more detailed structure of his theory of knowledge: his prisoners see the shadows cast from a fire by artifacts carried about within the cave, whereas outside there are more real objects, which themselves cast shadows by the light of the sun.)

One of the clearest illustrations of the theory of Forms comes from the geometrical reasoning with which Plato was familiar, and which Euclid was to systematize later. Consider how in doing geometry we think about lines, circles, and squares, although no physical object or diagram is *perfectly* straight, circular, or equal-sided. What we count as straight or equal for practical purposes, to some degree of approximation, will not be so by a more precise standard—irregularities or differences can always be found if things are examined closely enough, perhaps by a microscope. Yet we can prove theorems concerning geometrical concepts—straight lines without thickness, perfect circles, exact squares—with complete certainty, by deductive arguments. Similarly, we know truths of arithmetic that are quite independent of the vagueness or impermanence of the material things we count. ("1 + 1 = 2" is not disproved by the merging of two water droplets!) We thus seem to attain knowledge of exactly defined, unchangeable mathematical objects, namely patterns or Forms that material things imperfectly resemble. Like many other philosophers since, Plato was deeply impressed by the certainty and precision of mathematical knowledge, and he took this as an ideal to which all human knowledge should approximate. He therefore recommended the teaching of mathematics as a vital means toward detaching our minds from mere perceptible objects.

It is the moral application of the theory of Forms that plays the most important role in Plato's conception of human nature and society. We can distinguish many particular courageous actions or just dealings from the general concepts or Forms of Courage and Justice. In the early dialogues Plato depicts Socrates seeking an adequate general definition of such virtues and never being satisfied with mere examples or subclasses of them. We have to distinguish these ideals from the (often complicated and messy) reality of particular human beings in real-life situations. Often an action or a person may be right, just, or admirable in one way but not in others (e.g., doing the best thing for one friend or relation may involve neglecting another). But Plato holds that the ethical Forms set absolute standards of value for us (472–73). Just as no material object is perfectly square, perhaps no human being or society is perfectly good.

For Plato, the Form of Goodness is preeminent in the world of Forms: it plays an almost God-like role in his system, being described as the source of all reality, truth, and goodness. He compares its role in the world of the Forms to that of the sun as the source of all light in the world of material things (508–9). Plato's twin images of sun and cave—concerned with the source of light and the notion of coming to "see the light"—give us a memorable pictorial presentation of the theory of Forms.

It is crucial to Plato's whole philosophy that we can, by the proper use of our faculty of reason, both come to know what is good and actually become good. In this he was following the lead of his role model Socrates. In some of the early dialogues (*Protagoras* and *Meno*), Plato portrays Socrates arguing for what seems to have been the historical Socrates' own doctrine, that to *be* virtuous, to be a good human being, it is enough to *know* what human virtue is. All the virtues are said to be identical at root, in that one cannot possess any one of them without having the others; and this unique human goodness is identified with knowledge in the wide sense of wisdom, not mere store of information, or intellectual virtuosity.

Socrates was thus committed to the doctrine that nobody knowingly or willingly does what he or she thinks to be wrong. But this seems to conflict with obvious facts about human nature: we often know quite well what we ought to do, and yet somehow or other we don't get around to doing it—indeed, we sometimes find ourselves unwilling to do it. We shall see later how Plato attempts to cope with this difficulty.

The theory of Forms is Plato's answer to the intellectual and moral skepticism or relativism of his time. It is one of the first and greatest expressions of the hope that we can attain reliable knowledge both about the world as a whole and about the proper conduct of human life and society. Yet we may well suspect that Plato has overintellectualized the role of reason and knowledge. He makes a good case that we all need to use our reason in exercising prudent self-control, moderating our emotions and desires, their expressions and fulfillments. But in the central metaphysical sections of the *Republic* (Books V–VII) Plato insists on a highly theoretical conception of reason as consisting in a special kind of knowledge of the Forms which is open only to a trained intellectual elite. It is not very plausible that such specialized philosophical thinking is either necessary or sufficient for human goodness.

THEORY OF HUMAN NATURE: THE TRIPARTITE STRUCTURE OF THE SOUL

Plato is one of the main sources for the dualist view, according to which the human soul or mind (these terms are here used synonymously) is a nonmaterial entity that can exist apart from the body. According to Plato, the soul exists before birth, it is indestructible, and will exist eternally after death. His main arguments for these doctrines are in the early dialogues. In the *Meno,* Plato tries to prove the preexistence of the soul, arguing that what we call learning is really a kind of "recollection" of an acquaintance our souls supposedly had with the Forms before birth (a version of the Eastern doctrine of reincarnation). People of average intelligence like a slaveboy, can be brought to understand mathematical propositions (the simpler ones, anyway!) and to realize why they must be true, by having their attention called to the steps of a proof. Plato says, plausibly enough, that the mental ability to recognize the validity of the inferential steps and the necessity of the conclusion must be innate. But then he makes the much more disputable claim that such innate abilities can only be explained by the human soul's knowledge of the Forms in a previous life. We might now offer evolutionary explanations of innate human abilities (see Chapter 10).

In the *Phaedo,* Plato presents a number of other arguments that the human soul must persist after the death of the body. He tries to disprove the materialist theory of the earlier Greek atomists (such as Democritus) that the human soul is composed of tiny particles that dissipate into the air at death. He also argues against the conception (which Aristotle later developed in more detail, see Chapter 5) that the soul is a kind of "harmony" of the living human body and brain, like the music made by an instrument when properly tuned and played. Plato's arguments are sometimes intricate and apparently playful, but they repay careful study: we can learn a lot by trying to specify exactly where they go wrong.

Plato held, with the intensity of a religious belief, that it is the immaterial soul, not the bodily senses, that attains knowledge of the Forms: he compares the soul to the divine, the rational, the immortal, indissoluble and unchangeable. The soul is the higher element in human nature, the body the lower. The preoccupation of the philosopher or wise person should be the care of his or her soul; and since the soul is immortal, this is also a preparation for death and the life after death. In the famous scene at the end of the *Phaedo*, in Socrates' last conversations in prison before drinking the hemlock, Plato presents his hero as looking forward to the release of his soul from all bodily cares and limitations. The doctrines of the immateriality and immortality of the soul also appear at the end of the *Republic* in "the myth of Er" in Book X (608–20). This has seemed to many commentators to be an ill-fitting appendix to a philosophical work, but Plato seems to have found it appropriate at certain points to resort to more literary, less argumentative, means of communication. This is ironic, given his suspicion of the rhetorical power of the arts such as poetry.

What is really central to Plato's main moral discussion in the *Republic* is his theory of the three parts of the soul (435–41). Although this is expressed in terms of "the soul," we need not interpret it as involving metaphysical dualism: we can take it as a distinction between three different aspects of our mental nature. We can recognize the existence of internal conflicting tendencies in ourselves, even if we take a materialist, evolutionary view of human beings as one kind of animal with a well-developed brain. (I will concentrate here on Plato's tripartite theory, but we should note that in the *Philebus* and *Laws* he presents human nature as divided *two* ways between reason and pleasure; and he says more about pleasure in the *Gorgias* and *Protagoras*.) Echoes of Plato's threefold distinction can be found in many thinkers since (e.g., in Freud).

At this point in Plato's thought we can see him acknowledging the implausibility of the Socratic doctrine that nobody willingly (or clear-sightedly, or wholeheartedly) does what he or she believes to be wrong. He wrestles with both the theoretical question of how such inner conflict is possible and the practical problem of how one can achieve inner harmony. Let us first examine his arguments for the tripartite structure.

Consider an example of mental conflict or inhibition, such as when someone is thirsty but does not drink the available water because he believes it is poisoned, or because of some religious asceticism—quite often we do not (or not immediately) gratify our bodily urges. But conversely, we sometimes find ourselves giving way to the temptations of the proffered cigarette, the second cream cake, the third glass of wine, or the seductive charmer, even though we know that the consequences are likely to be bad for us. Bad habits can notoriously become addictive: gluttony (or, these days, anorexia), alcoholism, drug dependence, habitual search for new sexual partners. Plato argues that where there is any kind of internal conflict, there must be two different elements with contradictory tendencies. In the case of the thirsty man, there must be one part that makes him want to drink and a second that forbids him; the first Plato calls "Appetite" (under which he intends to include all the physical urges, such as hunger, thirst, and sexual desire), and the second he calls "Reason."

So far, Plato is on familiar ground. But he argues for the existence of a third element in our nature by examining different cases of mental conflict. His first example may seem rather weird: a story of someone who felt a fascinated desire to look at a pile of corpses and yet was disgusted with himself for having such a desire (440). Plato claims that to explain cases like this we need to recognize the existence in ourselves of a third element that he calls "Spirit" or passion. His argument for this is not very explicit, but it seems to be that because there is an *emotion* of self-disgust involved, not just an intellectual recognition of the irrationality or undesirability of the desire, Spirit must be distinct from Reason.

We surely have to agree that emotion is different both from bodily desires and from rational or moral judgment. Love is not the same as lust, but on the other hand it is more than a mere intellectual judgment about the admirable qualities of the beloved. Anger, indignation, ambition, aggression, and the desire for power are not *bodily* desires, nor are they mere judgments about the value or disvalue of things, although they involve such judgments. Plato goes on to remark that children (and even animals) show Spirit before they display Reason; and anyone who has dealt with children can confirm this from experience of their high spirits, delights and frustrations, stubbornness, and (sometimes) aggression and bullying.

Plato asserts that Spirit is usually on the side of Reason when inner conflict occurs. But if it is a genuinely distinct element in the mind, there must presumably be cases where it can conflict with Reason. Plato quotes a line of Homer "He smote his breast, and thus rebuked his heart" in brief confirmation of this. And we can surely add examples from our own experience—occasions when we have felt emotions of anger, jealousy, or love that we judge unreasonable, undesirable, or even immoral. Perhaps there can even be cases in which one is pulled in *three* directions by the different elements—for example, by lust, romantic love, and reasoned judgment about who would be the best partner!

Plato presents his threefold theory in vivid, even crude, images. In the *Phaedrus* at 253–54 (a dialogue mainly about love) he compares the soul to a chariot, pulled by a white horse (Spirit) and a dark horse (Appetite), driven by a charioteer (Reason) who struggles to keep control. At *Republic* 588 Plato describes a person as composed of a little man, a lion, and a many-headed beast. This obviously involves an infinite regress—a person within a person, and so on—but Plato was too good a philosopher not to notice this and he must have been offering the picture only as an image.

Is Plato's tripartite anatomy of the soul adequate? It can be seen as an interesting first approximation, distinguishing some elements in human nature that can conflict with each other. But it is hardly a rigorous or exhaustive division, even if one redescribes the parts in modern terms as intellect, emotion, and bodily desire. In particular, it is not very clear what Plato's middle element of Spirit amounts to. Emotions are part of our human nature, of course, but Plato seems also to have had in mind human desires or drives that are not *bodily* appetites but not exactly emotions either, such as self-assertion, ambition, and desire for money, status, or power. And where does the will come into the story? Doesn't Plato still have to accept that it is one thing to recognize or judge (with one's reason) what one ought to do, and another to do it, or try to do it? A different tripartite distinction of mental faculties that has become standard, especially since the advent of Christianity, is as follows: reason, emotion, and *will*. Perhaps we need to distinguish at least five factors in human nature: reason, will, nonbodily motivations or drives, emotions, and bodily appetites.

Much of Plato's discussion seems to be conducted with men rather than women in mind, but he had views about the sexes that were strikingly original in his time. In Greek society, women played almost no part in public life and were usually confined to their reproductive role and household duties. The philosophical discussions of love in the Platonic dialogues are all about male homosexual love, which was socially accepted then. In the *Republic* (449 ff.), however, Plato argues that there is no role in society that need be restricted to either sex. He allows that some women are athletic, musical, philosophical, and even "high-spirited." (The mind boggles! —he meant courageous, and therefore suitable for military service.) Plato still patronizingly assumes that men are on average better than women at everything, but he thinks that the only absolute distinction is the biological one (that males beget children and females bear them) and that any other differences are only matters of degree. He was therefore prepared to admit women of appropriate talent to the ruling class.

One other main feature of Plato's theory of human nature should be emphasized: we are social creatures (i.e., to live in society is natural to human beings). Human individuals are not self-sufficient, we each have many needs that we cannot meet by ourselves. Even food, shelter, and clothing can hardly be obtained without the help of others. A desert island individual would struggle for survival and would miss out on the distinctively human activities of friendship, play, art, politics, learning, and reasoning. Manifestly, different people have different aptitudes and interests; there are farmers, craftsmen, soldiers, administrators and so on, each fitted by nature, training, and experience to specialize in one kind of task; division of labor is therefore essential in society (369–70).

DIAGNOSIS: DISHARMONY IN SOUL AND SOCIETY

Reason, Spirit, and Appetite are present to some degree in every person. Depending on which element is dominant, three kinds of people exist. The main desire of each type is, respectively: knowledge, reputation, or material gain. Plato describes them as, philosophic, victory loving, and profit loving (581). He has a very clear view about which of the three elements should rule: it is Reason that ought to control both Spirit and Appetite (590). But each has its proper role to play, and there should ideally be harmonious agreement between the three aspects of our nature, with Reason in overall command. Plato expresses this in an eloquent passage at 443:

> Justice . . . isn't concerned with external actions, but with a man's inward self. The just man will not allow the three elements which make up his inward self to trespass on each other's functions or interfere with each other, but by keeping all three in tune, like the notes of a scale . . . will in the truest sense set his house in order, and be his own lord and master, and at peace with himself. When he has bound these elements into a single controlled and orderly whole, and so unified himself, he will be ready for action of any kind . . .

And just as the reasoning part of the soul ought to direct and control the other parts, so those people with the most highly developed "reason" (which includes moral wisdom, as we have seen) ought to rule society in the interests of everyone. A well-ordered, "just" society will be one in which each class of person plays their distinctive role, in harmony with each other (434).

Plato describes this ideal condition of human beings and society by the Greek word *dikaiosune,* which has traditionally been translated as "justice." But, when applied to individuals, the word does not have its modern legal or political connotations. There can be no exact English translation: "virtue," "morality," "proper functioning," "well-being," or even "mental health" may help to convey what Plato had in mind. At 444, he says that virtue is a kind of mental health or beauty or fitness, and vice a sort of illness or deformity or weakness. His fundamental point is that what is good or bad for us depends on our human nature, the complex of factors in our psychological makeup.

The theory of the parts of the soul (with the background theory of Forms as objects of knowledge) thus defines Plato's ideals for individual and social well-being; and when he looked at the facts of his own day he found that they were very far from ideal. One wonders whether his judgment of our present condition would be any less harsh. Many people still do not show much "inward harmony" or controlled coordination of their desires and mental powers. And many human societies do not manifest the orderliness and stability that Plato sought.

The problems of human individuals that Plato diagnoses are intimately related to the defects in human societies. One cannot simply attribute to him either the conservative or right-wing view that social problems are due to individual wrongdoing, or the liberal or left-wing view that individual vices can be blamed on faults in the social order. Plato would say, I think, that the two are interdependent: an imperfect society tends to produce flawed individuals, and troubled or badly brought-up individuals contribute to social problems.

Plato devotes Book VIII of the *Republic* (543–76) to a systematic classification of five kinds of society, beginning with the ideal outlined earlier that he calls an "aristocracy" (meaning a meritocracy, an aristocracy of talent rather than birth), and going on to diagnose four types of imperfect society, which he calls "timarchy," "oligarchy," "democracy," and "tyranny." Plato also describes a kind of defective individual supposedly typical of each society. He offers an account of how each political stage can arise by degeneration from its predecessor, and how each individual character may be formed as a result of problems in the previous generation (concentrating on relations between fathers and sons).

In a "timarchic" society such as that of ancient Sparta, honor and fame—e.g. in warfare and hunting—are valued above all. Reason and philosophical understanding are neglected, and Spirit plays the dominant role in society and in members of the ruling class (545–49). Perhaps something similar was true of feudal society in premodern Europe.

In an "oligarchy," the older class divisions break down, money making becomes the dominant activity, and political power comes to lie with the wealthy. Plato expresses disgust for the resulting type of character, who

> . . . establishes his appetitive and money-making part on the throne, setting it up as a king within himself, . . . and makes the rational and spirited parts sit on the ground beneath appetite, one on either side, reducing them to slaves. . . . He won't allow the first to reason about or examine anything except how a little money can be made into great wealth. And he won't allow the second to value or admire anything but wealth and wealthy people or to have any ambition other than the acquisition of wealth or whatever might contribute to getting it. (553)

(Plato would obviously not be too keen on the free-for-all competition of contemporary capitalism!)

"Democracy" may arise by the poor majority seizing power. In the *Republic,* Plato took a very jaundiced view of democracy as he understood it, influenced no doubt by his experience of the arbitrariness and instability of Athenian democracy, in which every adult male citizen (but not women or slaves) could vote in the meetings that decided policy, and government positions were often filled by lot (555–57). Plato thought it absurd to give every person an equal say, when most people—in his view—do not know what is best. He criticizes what he labels the "democratic" type of person as lacking in discipline, pursuing mere pleasures of the moment, indulging "unnecessary, spendthrift" desires (whereas the *successful* money maker, for all his faults, at least has to exert some self-control):

> A young man . . . associates with wild and dangerous creatures who can provide every variety of multicolored pleasure in every sort of way.
> . . . seeing the citadel of the young man's soul empty of knowledge, fine ways of living, and words of truth . . . [these desires] finally occupy that citadel themselves.
> . . . and he doesn't admit any word of truth into the guardhouse, for if someone tells him that some pleasures belong to fine and good desires and others to evil ones and that he must pursue and value the former and restrain and enslave the latter, he denies all this and declares that all pleasures are equal and must be valued equally. (559–61)

Anarchy, Plato thinks, is the sequel to the chaotic and unbridled liberty of democracy: permissiveness spreads, fathers and teachers lose authority. (He is horrified at the idea of liberating women and slaves!) There then arises a desire for restoration of some sort of order, and usually some forceful, unscrupulous individual emerges, wins absolute power, and becomes a tyrant (565–69). The tyrannical character, as Plato diagnoses it, is not so much the tyrant himself (who has to exercise some intelligence and self-control to gain and maintain his power), but the person who is completely dominated by his own appetites, especially sexual desires. He will stop at nothing, he will sacrifice possessions and money, family relations and friends in the frenzied pursuit of his lusts (572–76).

In this series of social diagnoses and character sketches, one may feel that the analogies between individual and society are sometimes overstretched. But each sketch shows notable sociological and psychological insight, and their contemporary applications are obvious. Plato concludes that each type of person and society departs further from the ideal, reaching a deeper level of degradation and unhappiness. He is very clear that the money-making, pleasure-seeking, and lust-dominated people are far from happy, and this is part of his case why "justice" or "morality" is in the interests of the individual.

PRESCRIPTION: HARMONY OF SOUL THROUGH EDUCATION, AND GOVERNMENT BY THE PHILOSOPHER-KINGS

Plato has said that "justice" or well-being is essentially the same thing in both individual and society—a smooth working together of the parts within the soul or the classes in the state (435); and the lack of such harmony is injustice. But there is some ambiguity in the *Republic* about whether individuals can change themselves independently of institutional reforms, or whether social change must precede individual improvement and make it possible. (This is a problem that is still with us.) One main purpose of Plato's argument is to answer the challenge put in the mouth of the cynical Thrasymachus (in Book I) by showing that it is, after all, in the long-term interest of the individual to be just or moral. Plato does this by reconceptualizing what justice is, insisting that, since it is a harmony of the three elements in our souls (Book IV), it is bound to make each one of us a happier, more fulfilled human being (Book IX).

But how can such harmony be attained? Plato remarks at 444 that virtue and vice are the result of one's actions: so it seems that what we make of ourselves is, at least to some extent, up to us (an existentialist theme, see Chapter 9). In the famous speech of Socrates in the *Symposium* (200–212) Plato outlines a route by which our love (*eros*) can be gradually transformed from erotic desire for beautiful bodies, through admiration for beauty of soul, and eventually to love of "absolute" or divine beauty, the Form of beauty itself. But this presupposes "instruction in the things of love"—and who is qualified to provide that?

Here the social element comes into Plato's story: he lays great stress on appropriate education as the most important way to produce virtuous, harmonious, well-balanced, "just" people (376–412, 521–41). Plato was one of the first to see education as the key to constructing a better society. And by "education" he does not mean just formal schooling, but upbringing, including all the social influences on someone's development. In some places (377, 424–25) he anticipates Freud's emphasis on the importance of early childhood. Plato goes into considerable detail about the kind of education he envisages, and formal academic study is by no means at the center but is reserved for an elite subgroup at an appropriately mature age. What Plato sees as vital for everyone is a training of the whole person— Reason, Spirit, and Appetite together. He therefore recommends gymnastics, poetry, and music as elements of the common curriculum. We may find the details of his educational scheme amusingly archaic, but the idea that the "character-forming" foundations are more important than academic superstructures remains as realistic as ever.

But how is education to be instituted? It requires a clear conception of what is being aimed at, a whole theory of human nature and human knowledge, in fact. Moreover, it needs elaborate social organization and resources. This is one main reason why in the *Republic* Plato offers a prescription that is radically political:

> There will be no end to the troubles of states, or of humanity itself, till philosophers become kings in this world, or till those we now call kings and rulers really and truly become philosophers, and political power and philosophy thus come into the same hands. (473)

Plato is well aware that this sounds absurdly unrealistic, but given his understanding of the Forms, human knowledge, and human nature, we can see his rationale for it. If there is such a thing as the truth about how we ought to live, then those who have such knowledge are the only people who are properly qualified to govern society. Philosophers are, in Plato's conception, those who have come to know the ultimate realities, including the true standards of all value, so if *they* were to govern society, the problems of human nature could be solved.

To produce lovers of wisdom, fit to be philosopher-kings or "Guardians," the higher stages of education will be open only to those with sufficient mental ability. At an appropriate age, they will study mathematics and then philosophy, the disciplines that lead the mind toward knowledge of the Forms and a love of truth for its own sake. The elite thus produced would prefer to continue with their intellectual studies, but Plato expects them to respond to the call of social duty and apply their expertise to the running of society. After experience in subordinate offices, some of them will be ready for supreme power. Only such lovers of wisdom and truth will be impervious to the temptations to misuse power, for they will value the happiness of a right and rational life more than material riches (521).

The way of life of these Guardians is to be spartan, in something like the modern sense of the word (Plato seems to have derived some of his ideas from the Greek state of Sparta). They are to have no personal property and no family life. The state is to select which Guardians are suitable for breeding, and organize "mating festivals." The resulting children are to be brought up communally by nurses and precautions are to be taken to ensure that no parent recognizes his or her own child (457–61). Here Plato goes flatly against the psychological need for strong emotional bonds between children and the adults who bring them up (normally their parents). As a high-born Greek male, he obviously had no experience of child care and children's needs.

Plato's view that his trained Guardians will be such lovers of truth and goodness that they can be trusted never to misuse their power seems naively optimistic. He ignores the wisdom of the adage that power corrupts—and absolute power corrupts absolutely. There is surely a need for constitutional checks and balances to guard against exploitation or tyranny. Plato asks "Who is qualified to wield absolute power?" But should we not rather ask "How can we ensure that nobody has absolute power?"

What if well-educated, supposedly knowledgeable people disagree about questions of morals and politics—as we know they often do. Is there any way of showing who is right? Plato hopes to use rational argument, and he is one of the great philosophical pioneers in doing so. But when someone thinks they know the ultimate truth about such questions of value and policy, they may be intolerant of anyone who disagrees, and may feel justified in forcing their view on others (as the history of religious and political controversies bears witness).

What of the rest of society—the nonelite? There are many different economic and social functions that need to be performed, and a division of labor is the natural and efficient way of organizing this. Plato makes a threefold division of society (412–27), parallel to his theory of the soul. Besides the Guardians, there is to be a class traditionally called the "Auxiliaries," who play the roles of soldiers, police, and civil servants: they will put the directions of the Guardians into effect. The third class would contain the workers—farmers, craftsmen, traders, and all those who produce and distribute the material necessities of life. The division between these three classes will be very strict; Plato says that the "justice" or well-being of the society depends on each person performing his own proper function and not interfering with others (432–34).

> The object of our legislation is not the welfare of any particular class, but of the whole community. It uses persuasion or force to unite all citizens and make them share together the benefits which each individually can confer on the community; and its purpose in fostering the attitude is not to enable everyone to please himself, but to make each man a link in the unity of the whole. (519–20)

Plato seems more concerned with the harmony and stability of the whole society than with the well-being of the individuals in it. We may be in favor of "community spirit," and of each person contributing something to the well-being of society, but Plato seems to envisage rather more than this in his strict class division and his insistence that each person fulfill his allotted function and that alone. This is what he calls "justice" in the state, but it is plainly not what *we* mean by the term, which implies equality before the law and some degree of social justice, or fair shares for all. If a worker is not content to be a worker, to accept a strictly limited share of economic goods and have no say in politics, then Plato's state would forcibly compel him to remain in his station. But what is the point of such a rigidly organized society unless it serves the interests of the individuals in it?

Plato's republic has an authoritarian, even totalitarian, character. He has no compunction about censorship—he proposes to exclude poets and other artists from his ideal society, on the grounds that they appeal to the lower, nonrational parts of our nature (605). His hostility to poetry may be more understandable when we realize that until his time it was almost the only source of common conceptions of ethics, and he was fighting for the socratic appeal to reason. He would surely be horrified at the pervasive and almost unregulated influence of the media and the entertainment and advertising industries on everyone in contemporary society from early childhood onward. We may not like Plato's solution of state censorship, but he calls our attention to the continuing problem of how truth and goodness can be presented and inculcated amid a welter of competing cultural and economic interests and influences.

In the *Republic,* Plato dismisses democratic constitutions rather quickly, and we may think, unfairly. He was thinking of Athenian-type democracy in which every citizen had a vote on major decisions. Even if electronic voting systems might make this technically feasible nowadays, it would surely result in unstable government, subject to the changing whims of an enormous population easily influenced by collective emotion and "rhetoric" or clever advertising, which was Plato's criticism of Athenian democracy. However, the most crucial feature of modern democracies—that a government must submit itself for reelection within a fixed period of time—provides a means for peaceful change that is absent from the *Republic*. It should be noted that in later work, the *Statesman* and the *Laws*, Plato advocated the rule of law and endorsed democracy, for all its imperfections, as the best kind of constitution given human nature as it is.

The *Republic* is one of the most influential books of all time. I have concentrated on this one work; the reader should remember that Plato wrote much else, developing and changing his views over time. Socrates and Plato started a tradition of rational inquiry into how we should live. Nothing, I suspect, would please them more than to know that some of us still carry this on.

FOR FURTHER READING

Basic text: Plato's *Republic.* There are many translations, but the one that has recently earned most praise for readability and liveliness is by G. M. A. Grube, revised by C. D. C. Reeve (Indianapolis: Hackett, 1992).

The *Republic* is a lengthy and complex work; some readers may prefer to approach Plato via his shorter dialogues, such as the *Euthyphro, Apology, Crito, Phaedo, Meno,* or *Protagoras*.

There is an excellent thematic introduction to ancient philosophy in Julia Annas's volume in the Very Short Introduction (series Oxford University Press, 2000).

For an introduction to Plato's thought see, in the Past Masters series, R. M. Hare, *Plato* (Oxford University Press, 1982). This is available as the first part of a trilogy entitled *Founders of Thought* (series Oxford University Press, 1991), which also contains introductions to Aristotle and Augustine.

There is a deeper philosophical discussion of the *Republic* in Julia Annas, *An Introduction to Plato's Republic* (series Oxford University Press, 1981). This combines scholarship with clear-sighted attention to the main moral argument, its foundation in claims about human nature, and its continuing contemporary relevance (see especially the summing up in Ch. 13).

For a classic attack on Plato's political program, see K. R. Popper, *The Open Society and Its Enemies,* 4th ed. (London: Routledge, 1962).

For a very full scholarly treatment of Plato's moral philosophy, see Terence Irwin, *Plato's Ethics* (series Oxford University Press, 1995).

C H A P T E R

5

Aristotle: The Ideal of Human Fulfilment

ARISTOTLE'S LIFE AND WORK

Aristotle (384–322 B.C.E.) lived in the next generation after Plato, and also spent much of his life in Athens, so the brief historical background sketched in Chapter 4 applies here too. He joined Plato's Academy at the age of seventeen, and the influence of Plato on his thought is obvious. Although Aristotle was deeply impressed by the views of his mentor, he was capable of criticizing them on important points (which is the ideal relationship between philosophical teacher and pupil).

Aristotle left Athens in 347, probably for political reasons, and for a few years he became a tutor to the Greek warlord who became famous as Alexander the Great, the world conqueror (but who demonstrated little sign of having learned from his academic mentor!). Aristotle came from a medical family and he did extensive research on the structure of animals and plants. This experience of empirical scientific work shows in his writings, which, despite their abstractness, display a more this-wordly spirit compared with Plato's yearning for transcendence. Aristotle returned to Athens in 335 and founded the Lyceum, which continued the tradition of systematic intellectual inquiry started by Plato's Academy. In the last year of Aristotle's life, political infighting forced him out of Athens once again.

The corpus of Aristotelean texts that have come down to us cover an amazing range—logic, metaphysics, epistemology, astronomy, physics, meteorology, biology, psychology, ethics, politics, law, "poetics" (theory of the arts)—and in many of these subjects Aristotle was a pioneer. There was no clear distinction between philosophy and science in those days: Aristotle was interested in formulating the fundamental concepts and principles in every area. He studied what we now recognize as the sciences of astronomy, physics, biology, and psychology, laying down foundations that remained largely unquestioned until the seventeenth century. Apparently, many more of his writings have not survived: the talents and energy of the man were prodigious. The texts that we do have tend to be abbreviated and allusive lecture notes rather than polished, elegant literary works like Plato's dialogues. Aristotle's writing is abstract, technical, and systematic: he is a philosophers' philosopher.

However, the *Nicomachean Ethics*, the main work in which Aristotle discusses human life, its ideals and its vicissitudes, is relatively accessible. My references will be to this text (using the standard numbering, prefaced by "NE"), unless otherwise indicated. It is not easy reading (no substantial philosophy is), but like Plato's *Republic*, it deals with profound issues of how to live; it is not overly lengthy, and is reasonably well organized, in some passages it rises to a sort of eloquence. The *de Anima*, a shorter and more technical work, is also important for Aristotle's view of human nature.

METAPHYSICAL BACKGROUND: FORMS AS PROPERTIES, AND THE FOUR KINDS OF QUESTION

Aristotle sometimes talks of gods, but he does *not* mean the biblical concept of a personal Being who has a plan for human history and reveals Himself to particular people. Though he may have paid outward respect to popular Greek polytheism (Zeus, Hera, Athena, et al.) at *Metaphysics* XII.8, 1074b1 ff., Aristotle says these are anthropomorphic myths for the common people. He did have a concept of a single supreme god, for in the *Physics* Book VII, he argues that there must be an unmoved mover, a changeless cause of all the processes of change in the universe. (St. Thomas Aquinas turned this into one of his "Five Ways" of proving the existence of the Christian God.) Moreover Aristotle held that "it is the function of what is divine to think and use its intellect" (*Parts of Animals* IV. 10, 686a29), but the kind of thought attributed to the Aristotelean god is intellectual contemplation, not any sort of *care* about human affairs.

The unmoved mover is more a concept of scientific theory than an object of worship or obedience.

Aristotle was influenced by Plato's theory of Forms, but severely critical of it. We saw in Chapter 4 how Plato proposed that what makes particular things count as Fs is their "participation in" the Form of F, understood as an abstract entity existing apart from all the instances of it. Aristotle opposes this separation of the Forms, and rejects Plato's metaphysical picture of another world containing the eternal Forms, beyond the world of changeable material things. His own view (standardly labeled "Aristotelian realism") is that there really is something common to all things to which a general concept F can correctly be applied, namely the property (or Aristotelian Form) F—but this common property exists *in the things that have it*, not separately in some other world. This makes Plato's image of the cave dwellers inappropriate: for in Aristotle's understanding of our human situation, our need is not to find a way out of the cave into a different world, but to discern more clearly what is already before our eyes.

Talk of Forms as properties in things rather than as separate entities seems to bring us back to robust common sense, but when such talk is probed philosophically, it becomes problematic. And Aristotle sees this. In what sense is it the *same* property (e.g., of catness, or being a cat) that is found in all cats? If we use a noun like "property" (or "Form"), a word with a singular and a plural, we seem to commit ourselves to thinking of the property as a mysterious kind of *thing*, which can be wholly and completely present in many different things at the same time. Aristotle realizes that we need to distinguish different *categories*—for example, things or substances are fundamentally different from properties or qualities, and we have to say different sorts of things about each.

Do we find the same one-many structure in the use of all general terms, or is the detail different in other cases? Aristotle notices that we often use words in extended ways that do not carry exactly the same meaning in every case. One of his standard examples is the adjective "healthy": we talk of healthy people, food, exercise, climate, a healthy complexion, having a healthy respect for something, and so on, and it is obvious that we do not mean to say that all these are healthy in the primary sense (applicable to people) of having well-functioning bodies that are likely to live long.

Aristotle applied this lesson to value terms, and especially to the most general value term "good." He was aware that different subjects require various methods of study and degrees of precision, so that ethics differs from mathematics in the sorts of results that are possible (NE1094b12–29). Accordingly, he questioned whether all good things are good in some unitary sense, involving a separate Platonic Form of the Good. In NE I.6 (1096a12–1097a14), Aristotle gives a rapid salvo of technical arguments against the Platonic view (introduced by a declaration that friendship with Plato is dear, but the truth is even dearer!). One of his basic points is that we recognize *several* things as good in themselves, that is, as worth having or pursuing for their own sake, not for the sake of anything else (e.g., pleasure, honor, wisdom), but when we ask what makes such different things all good, there seems to be no general answer we can give, for wisdom surely is good in an irreducibly different way from the way in which honor (or pleasure) is good. (This would seem to rule out even a single Aristotelian Form of goodness, a property that all good things possess.)

Another methodological and metaphysical lesson that Aristotle bequeathed to us is traditionally called "the doctrine of the four causes." In the *Physics*, II.3, 194b16, he distinguishes four questions we can ask about anything, with their corresponding answers or explanations:

1. What is it made of? Its matter ("the material cause")
2. What is it? Its form; the sort of thing it is ("the formal cause")
3. What brought it into existence? Its cause in the modern sense ("the efficient cause")
4. What is it for? Its purpose or function ("the final cause")

Aristotle seems to have assumed that all four questions always have an answer. With respect to the fourth, this commits him to a "teleological" view of the whole universe, according to which everything has a definite purpose or function, a goal that it serves or somehow strives toward. Human artifacts like beds, knives, and telephones have purposes for which they were constructed; and the organs of plants and animals, such as roots, hearts, and eyes, have functions, as Aristotle well understood from his biological studies. As for *whole* animals and plants, although it is odd to speak of them existing "for" some purpose, we have an idea of what counts as a mature, flourishing specimen of each species. (More controversially, Aristotle tries to do something like this for the human species.) But we do not think of inanimate natural objects—rocks, mountains, rivers, glaciers, beaches, clouds, sun and moon, planets, stars, and galaxies—as existing for a purpose (unless, of course, you believe that God created each of them with a particular end in view). And we do not think there is some "natural," mature, or best state of these things that they tend to grow toward in favorable conditions. Aristotle seems to have overextended the scope of teleology, then, but otherwise his distinction of four sorts of questions is a useful clarification of our thought.

In such ways, Aristotle repeatedly teaches us not just to latch onto the first idea that occurs to us or the first theory we hear of (which is the lazy way in philosophizing), but to think more carefully, to examine a suitably varied set of cases, to take the trouble to recognize the complexity of the world and of our ways of thinking and talking about it, and to be open-minded, without factional spirit, in our consideration of general theories. He can be honored as a founding father of the kind of "analytical" philosophy exemplified in the thought of Ludwig Wittgenstein in the mid-twentieth century.

THEORY OF HUMAN NATURE: THE SOUL AS A SET OF FACULTIES, INCLUDING RATIONALITY

As we have seen, Plato defended the dualist view, according to which the human soul is an immaterial substance that can exist apart from the body after death. Aristotle radically undermines this whole way of thinking in a subtle way that I will now try to explain.

On this topic it is Aristotle the biologist who makes a vital contribution to philosophy. He sees human beings as one kind of animal, albeit a very special kind, uniquely capable of rational thought. And he sees animals (by which we mean not just mammals, but reptiles, birds, insects, crustaceans, etc.) as one main class of living things, plants being the other. All life thus forms an enormous hierarchy of orders, genera, and species, each with its own distinguishing features. The main outline of this tree-like branching structure was recognized long ago from empirical observation by early biologists such as Aristotle himself and was further refined by Linnaeus in the eighteenth century, before Darwin came up with the theory of evolution, to explain how the hierarchy relates to a historical lineage of descent (see Chapter 10).

Aristotle outlines his approach in his groundbreaking short treatise traditionally known by its Latin name, *de Anima* ("Of the soul"), and which is the first book on psychology. Straight away we should be aware of the problems in using the word "soul" to translate the Greek *psyche*. One danger is that "soul" has strong religious connotations of piety and immortality, deriving from both Christianity and Plato. But Aristotle lived four centuries before Christianity and he offers an entirely different conception of *psyche* from Plato. We can substitute "mind" for "soul," but that only replaces one four-letter noun by another. The crucial difference in the Aristotelian conception is that the soul or mind is not thought of as a thing or substance at all (not even an *immaterial* substance). Aristotle's view might be best expressed by not using *any* noun to translate *psyche*, but to say instead that living things are "ensouled"; that is, they have certain distinctive ways of existing and functioning.

Technically, Aristotle applies his general distinction of matter and form to this case, and says that the soul is the "form" of a living thing. But

"form" here does not mean Platonic Form, nor does it have the more ordinary meaning of shape; rather it means what makes something the *fundamental sort* of thing it is (the second "formal cause" in the four
questions). What, then, makes something alive? This question is not meant
in the sense of what brought it into being (which would be the third, "efficient" cause), but, rather, what is it for something to be alive, what criteria does anything have to satisfy to count as a living thing?
Remembering that plants as well as animals are alive, we can say that the
criteria are metabolism and reproduction. The first is what Aristotle called
"self-nourishment, growth, and decay" or "the nutritive faculty" (*de
Anima* 412a13, 414a32), and he also mentions reproduction (415a22).
What then distinguishes plants from animals? (Or to put it dangerously,
what is distinctive of the animal kind of soul?) Animals have the faculties of sense-perception, desire (412a33), and self-movement (414b18).
That is, animals, unlike plants, perceive through their sense organs and
move themselves around to fulfill their desires.

What then do human beings do or have that is extra to all this? Aristotle
says: the faculty of "thought and intellect" (414b19), but it may not be
immediately clear what he means: it must be a kind of thought that other
animals do not have—presumably thoughts that can be expressed in language, in claims that such-and-such is the case, and for which reasons for
and against can be given. The human soul or mind should thus be understood not as a thing, but as *a distinctive cluster of faculties, including
reasoning*, that are fundamental to the human way of living and functioning. Aristotle himself writes (*de Anima* 408b15) "it is surely better
not to say that the soul pities, learns, or thinks, but that the man does
these with his soul," and we can suggest that it is better still to say that
the *man* pities, learns, and thinks (using his mental faculties or abilities).

So the soul of any living thing X is not a substance, an entity, an extra
(separable) thing; it is rather the way that X lives, operates, functions—
and that "way" may itself be analyzable as a set of faculties or ways of
functioning that normally go together. (But in special cases some can be
absent; e.g., somebody who loses their memory, or an infant who has not
yet learned to speak). On this conception, it makes no sense to talk of a
soul or mind existing without a body, for if there is no body (or, at least,
no *living* body), then there can be no *way* that the body is functioning,
for it is not functioning at all. Aristotle draws this conclusion at 414a19:
the soul cannot exist without a body (contrary to Plato), not because it is
itself a kind of body (contrary to the Greek materialists, who had suggested that the soul is a whiff of gas, composed of very fine particles or
atoms), but because the soul is not a thing of any kind, rather it is a complex property of living bodies.

Aristotle makes a significant, but puzzling, qualification to this trenchant conclusion. He suggests that there is something specially different about the human intellect, namely our faculty for purely theoretical thought (which he calls "contemplation," though he has mathematics and physics in mind, rather than aesthetic contemplation, meditation or prayer). And he seems to say that this faculty, or this kind of soul, can exist separately from the body, "as the everlasting can from the perishable" (*de Anima*, 413b26). Perhaps what he meant is that in gods, though not in us, there could be intellectual functioning without a body.

It looks as if Aristotle could not bring himself completely to reject his Platonic heritage, yet it is hard for us to see how he could consistently go back on the logic of his own general argument. How can we conceive of mathematical thought going on without there being a living, embodied mathematician? These days it will be suggested that a computer can do mathematics, but even if we allow that what it does can count as "thought," the fact remains that for it to happen there has to be a complex arrangement of wires and electrodes with currents pulsing through them—a complex material object, if not a *living* body. The notion of totally disembodied thought remains conceptually problematic. As we will see in the Historical Interlude, some of Aristotle's Islamic and Christian successors were happy to exploit this bit of backtracking in his philosophy of mind.

In Chapter 4 we have examined Plato's tripartite theory of the soul. Aristotle must have been aware of this theory, but he reconceptualizes it. Insofar as he talks of "parts" or "elements" of the soul, Aristotle cannot mean this literally as spatial parts or bits, because for him the soul is not a body, but a set of capacities of the living body. A *part* of an Aristotelean soul obviously has to be understood as one such capacity, distinct from others in the set. One might expect Aristotle, then, to follow Plato's lead by distinguishing the capacities for reasoning, for emotion, and for bodily desire, but he does not exactly follow this tripartite division. He usually contrasts *two* elements, one possessing reason (the bit that does the thinking) and the other possessing reason only in the weaker sense that it can obey reason, though it can also be disobedient (NE1098a5). Elsewhere he talks of rational and nonrational aspects of the soul (NE1192a28 ff.). It seems that Aristotle sees the most important distinction as between Plato's Reason on one hand and Spirit and Appetite on the other: both emotion and desire being potentially obedient to reason, in the sense that how one feels and what one wants can be affected by one's considered judgment about what is best, although notoriously this does not always happen.

Later, Aristotle finds occasion to make a distinction *within* the rational part, between our capacity for reasoning about necessary propositions (in mathematics, and, in his view, in natural science), and our ability to deliberate about what to do (NE1139a5). This is the distinction between theoretical and practical reason, which is taken up by Kant (see Chapter 7).

Another crucial aspect of Aristotle's theory of human nature, like Plato's, is that we are ineradicably social beings. In the traditional translation, "man is a political animal" (NE1097b11, and *Politics*, I.2, 1252a24; his word *politikon* has also been rendered as "civic" or "social"). Elsewhere, he wrote that "social animals are those which have some single activity common to them all (which is not true of all gregarious animals); such are men, bees, wasps, ants, cranes" (*History of Animals* I.1, 488a8). This is a striking anticipation of the sociobiological approach of E. O. Wilson, which we will mention in Chapter 10. But Aristotle recognized that what is distinctive of human social life is our awareness of justice and injustice (*Politics*, I.1, 1253a15). He believed that our human nature reaches its full development only when we live as members of an organized society, of which his paradigm was the *polis*, the Greek city-state, with a population of less than 100,000 or so.

But who exactly count as rational beings, qualified to take part in public life and politics? Aristotle's use of the masculine gender is no accident, for like most ancient Greeks he assumes without argument that women, although human, are innately different in mental capacity from men and less fitted for rational thought, so they should stick to their reproductive and domestic roles. He writes: "the relation of male to female is naturally that of the superior to the inferior—of the ruling to the ruled" (*Politics* I.V.7), and "the male is naturally fitter to command than the female, except where there is some departure from nature" (I.XII.1). These appeals to "nature" do not seem to be based on any empirical study of the abilities of women; rather, like many other uses of the very slippery term "nature" through history, they are the "common sense" of the time, which may be nothing more than the expression of prejudice and perceived self-interest. With respect to women, Aristotle was conservative where Plato was ahead of his time.

Aristotle also assumed that there are innate differences between individuals in their ability to think and reason. He frequently talks of "good birth" and (like Plato) takes it for granted that there will be social classes based on the division of labor, with large numbers of workers (farmers, traders, craftsmen, and soldiers) who will not, for the most part, be capable of the higher forms of thought. He also displays some prejudice against the old and the young.

Moreover, like others of his time, Aristotle sees no general objection to slavery, for he believes that some people are slaves by nature:

> . . . all men who differ from others much as the body differs from the soul, or an animal from a man (and this is the case with all whose function is

bodily service, and who produce their best when they supply such service)—all such are by nature slaves, and it is better for them . . . to be ruled
by a master. (*Politics* I.V.8)

However, Aristotle admits that "the contrary of nature's intention often
happens," so that slaves sometimes have the bodies (and upright carriage)
of freemen (I.V.10); and if he were more open to an unprejudiced examination of the empirical facts, he would have to allow that some slaves
have mental capacities at least equal to those of their masters. (Surely
there are no humans, except perhaps the severely mentally disabled, who
differ from other humans as much as a nonhuman animal from a human.)
Aristotle's discussion of slavery is somewhat nuanced, for he makes a
distinction between *just* slaveholding—in cases where (he claims!) there
is a "natural" mental difference between master and slave, yet a community of interest and a relation of friendship between them—and *unjust* enslavement based only on legal sanction and superior power (I.VI.10).

Like other Greeks of his time, Aristotle also assumes without argument a "natural" distinction between Greeks and "barbarians." At *Politics*
I.II.4, he implies that all barbarians are slaves by nature, and quotes with
approval the saying of a Greek poet that the barbarous people should be
governed by the Greeks. At NE1154a30 he lets slip the racist remark
that, although the "brutish" (animal-like) type of human being is rare, it
is more common among non-Greeks.

Aristotle's assumptions of patriarchy, slavery, and imperialism are
shocking to our contemporary sensibilities. One can imagine empire
builders (such as the British colonial administrators of a century ago, with
their classical education) finding him sympathetic. But this should not
prejudice us against the rest of his thinking: for there is nothing to prevent us from accepting an Aristotelian analysis of mind as a set of capacities of the living body and an Aristotelian idea of human fulfilment,
while insisting that the distinctively human rational capacities are, on average, equally present in every person, irrespective of sex, class, race, and
nationality, and that human needs and aspirations—and rights—are cor-
respondingly universal.

IDEAL AND DIAGNOSIS: HUMAN
FULFILMENT, VIRTUES, AND VICES

Aristotle accentuates the positive. Rather than diagnosing some fundamental fault in the human condition and prescribing a remedy for it—
which is what many religions do—Aristotle first gives us an account of
the end or purpose or meaning of human life, then suggests how it can

be put into practice, and how failures to live up to the ideal might be avoided or remedied. This is connected with the fact that where religions (and Plato, to some extent) tend to offer an otherworldly kind of salvation or solution, Aristotle offers a thoroughly this-worldly account of human fulfilment. In that respect his approach is more like Confucianism (Chapter 1) than the other theories we have considered so far.

(Whether one presents a theory in terms of its diagnosis and prescription—the framework we have chosen to use in this book—or in terms of ideal and realization—more in keeping with Aristotle's approach—is only a matter of emphasis and style of presentation. A diagnosis of what is wrong in human beings presupposes some value judgment about how we should ideally be; conversely, an ideal sets a standard that many human beings will be found not to achieve.)

Aristotle begins the *Nicomachean Ethics* by asking whether there is one end or aim that we seek, for its own sake, in all our actions and projects (NE1094a1–b12). He says that we can all agree that there is such an end, and that we call it "happiness," but we may disagree about what happiness actually is (NE1095a17). A word of caution is needed here about the use of "happiness" to translate Aristotle's *eudaimonia*. The etymology of the Greek word connects it with the notion of having a good guardian spirit or "genius" (*daimon*). In Aristotle's usage it does not carry any such supernatural connotation, but it does imply meeting an objective ethical standard—whereas "happiness" in contemporary English does not. We can say of a mentally disabled adult that he is happy with his toys, or of a drug addict that she is happy when she has a source of supply and no side effects, or of a rapist or pedophile that he is happy as long as he can find victims and not get caught out—but Aristotle would emphatically reject the notion that any of these people enjoy *eudaimonia*, for on his conception that is to imply that a person is leading an *admirably* fulfilled life. "Fulfilment" might indeed be a better translation; "flourishing" is another word that has been used to express the Aristotelian ideal; "felicity" or "perfection" also suggest it; "blessedness" might do, if divested of Christian connotations. (The latter has been used for the ideal recommended by Spinoza, which is a rationally contemplative state of mind, as Aristotle's own favored ideal turns out to be.)

Can we say anything more substantial about this state of ideal human fulfilment, which is the meaning or purpose of life? Aristotle applies his theory of human nature as having a uniquely rational capacity and comes up with a formula that puts a bit more content into his so far very abstract notion of *eudaimonia*:

. . . if all this is so, and a human being's function we posit as being a kind of life, and this life as being activity of soul and actions accompanied by reason, and it belongs to a good man to perform these well and finely, and each thing is completed well when it possesses its proper excellence; if all this is so, the human good turns out to be activity of soul in accordance with excellence (and if there are more excellences than one, in accordance with the best and most complete). But furthermore it will be this in a complete life. For a single swallow does not make spring, nor does a single day; in the same way, neither does a single day, or a short time, make a man blessed and happy. (NE1098a1 ff.)

The reader may be aghast to be told that this is one of the more eloquent passages in Aristotle! He is a very sober and serious philosopher, always careful to put in all the qualifications that he sees as needed, however much they clog up his sentences. The message that emerges is a valuable one, however: (a) that human fulfilment consists in *activity*, namely the exercise of our faculties, not in mere passive enjoyment; (b) that it must involve the use of our distinctively human *rational* capacity; (c) that this activity should be conducted "well and finely," displaying the best, most complete kind of "excellence" or *virtue*; and (d) that it should last over an extended *lifetime*.

This formula obviously invites further inquiry into the nature of human excellences (the Greek word *arete* has often been translated as "virtue," but it has to be realized that, for Aristotle, inanimate things can have *arete*; for example, an axe has it if it functions well in chopping (in English, we can say it is a *good* axe, but not a *virtuous* one!). Corresponding to the reason-giving and reason-obeying parts of the soul, mentioned earlier, Aristotle distinguishes excellences of intellect and excellences of character (NE1103a15). The former divide into theoretical and practical. Two theoretical excellences are *sophia*, or intellectual accomplishment (what we would now call academic excellence), and *techne*, or technical expertise (Aristotle displays his prejudice by not valuing this so highly). Practical excellence is *phronesis*, practical wisdom; that is, being good at deliberating about what to do in real-life situations and reaching wise decisions about them.

Plato made no such distinction between *sophia* and *phronesis*, holding as he did that theoretical knowledge of the Forms was necessary for correct practice; Aristotle makes an important new contribution by emphasizing the independence of practical wisdom. As he puts it at 1139a21 ff.:

What affirmation and denial are in the case of thought, pursuit and avoidance are with desire; so that, since excellence of character is a disposition issuing in decisions, and decision is a desire informed by deliberation, in consequence both what issues from reason must be true and the desire must be correct for the decision to be a good one, and reason must assert and desire pursue the same things. This, then, is thought, and truth, of a practical sort.

Aristotle holds that practical wisdom does not consist simply in knowing and applying commandments and prohibitions, for he does not think it possible to formulate any set of general rules that can settle every particular choice that we meet in life: "the agents themselves have to consider the circumstances relating to the occasion" (1104a9). The wise person, the *phronemos*, learns from practical experience and will have to be trusted to make wise decisions in new cases.

Indeed, the whole of Aristotle's inquiry in the *Ethics* is undertaken not for the sake of theory, but to help people to become good (1103b27, 1179b1 ff.). His fundamental concern is not to display philosophical virtuosity and make an academic reputation, but to help promote virtue. It has to be admitted, though, that the demanding intellectual effort needed to understand Aristotle's intricately wrought philosophical prose is unlikely to make anyone virtuous who is not already well disposed. Aristotle is well aware that there is no substitute for a good upbringing, a training in virtuous habits from childhood. But the hope is that his laborious elucidation of the nature of human virtues may help social theorists and legislators ("political experts," as he calls them) in their thinking about how to organize society so as to promote human virtue and fulfilment (NE I.3).

The central books of the *Nicomachean Ethics* discuss particular practical excellences or virtues in considerable detail. As well as practical wisdom (often called "prudence"), there are the other three in the traditional list (deriving from Plato), namely moderation (or "temperance"), courage, and justice. But Aristotle extends this list considerably, and he offers a new analysis (which applies to many if not all of them) of virtue as a mean between two extremes. Courage is the right balance between cowardliness and rashness; temperance (with respect to bodily pleasures) is the mean between overindulgence and asceticism; "open-handedness" about money is the right balance between being spendthrift or miserly; "mildness" (in one's display of anger) is the mean between irascibility and meekness (NE III.6–V). To those who find Aristotle overly serious, it may be a relief to find him admitting that "life also includes relaxation, and relaxation includes amusement of a playful sort" (IV.8, 1127b35), though even here he does not relax his intellectual grip, but offers an analysis of wit as the appropriate mean between over-the-top buffoonery and humorless boorishness or stiffness!

Aristotle adds some virtues that seem more peculiar to the society of ancient Athens, such as "greatness of soul" (being worthy of great things and being conscious of it) and "munificence" (the appropriate and tasteful spending of money on public projects). The former, a suitable sense of one's own worth and honor, can be represented as a mean between conceitedness (thinking one is worthy when one is not) and "littleness of soul" (thinking one is less worthy than one is) (NE IV.3). But it is not universally agreed that greatness of soul is a virtue: the "beatitudes" in Jesus' sermon on the mount, "Blessed are the poor in spirit . . . " and "Blessed are the meek . . . " (*Matthew* 5:3–5), strongly suggest the contrary. Yet Nietzsche, in the late nineteenth century, fiercely rejected Christian humility and recommended something like Aristotelian greatsouledness instead.

The virtue of justice (in something more like the modern rather than the Platonic sense) does not seem to fit into the pattern of a mean between two extremes. There is the corresponding vice of injustice or unfairness, of course, but there does not seem to be such a thing as being *too* just or *too* fair (although people can be overly scrupulous about exact equality in things that do not matter). Justice crucially involves other people, not just particular others to whom one is related by ties of family or friendship or contractual obligations, but potentially everyone in one's society (however the bounds of that society are delimited—for Aristotle it would be the *polis*). He is aware of the importance of equality before the law for commercial transactions and the solidarity of society. He writes: "it is reciprocal action governed by proportion that keeps the city together" (NE 1131b35).

All this examination of virtues has been outlining positive ideals for human life. Things go wrong when human actions, characters, and lives do not measure up to these ideals. Aristotle does not offer any all-embracing diagnosis of why, for although there is (he takes it) just one basic ideal of human fulfilment, he is aware that there are *many* different ways of falling short of it (1106b31). As we have seen, for most of the virtues there are two corresponding vices, which fail either by deficiency or by excess. The various possibilities arise from our mixed nature, as animals with bodily instincts but also with strong social susceptibilities and rational capacities. We can be tempted away from temperance by pleasure and from courage by fear. We can be moved to rashness by social ambition and to injustice by selfishness.

There is a further twist to Aristotle's diagnosis when he distinguishes three kinds of undesirable states: badness, lack of self-control, and brutishness (NE 1145a16). The first is the opposite of virtue, namely a settled disposition to do the wrong thing—not innately there from birth, but formed through some combination of bad training and wrong choices. The third is some innate, incurable disposition to act in ways that are "inhuman," whether harmful to others or just weird (e.g., psychopaths or congenital idiots). The second is the most interesting to Aristotle, and he gives a subtle philosophical analysis of self-control and the lack of it in Book VII.

As we saw in Chapter 4, Socrates held that nobody does what he knows to be wrong. But this conflicts with the fact of human experience that St. Paul reports: "For the good that I would I do not: but the evil which I would not, that I do" (Romans 7:19). Plato distinguished conflicting parts of the soul and posed the practical problem of how one can achieve inner harmony. One of Aristotle's important contributions is to point out that the person who lacks self-control is significantly different from he or she who is simply bad or vicious, for the latter typically has no awareness of how bad he or she is, whereas the former is painfully conscious—like St. Paul—of the gap between his or her aspirations and deeds (NE 1150b36). There is more hope of "curing" or improving the former, but we should totally give up on the latter, for perhaps such people can be *made* aware of the wrongness of what they do.

On the positive side, there is a corresponding distinction between the person who does the right thing, but only after exercising self-control to master his or her inappropriate desires, and the person who is sufficiently advanced in virtue (inner harmony, enlightenment, or the spiritual life) as not to feel inappropriate desires (or at least, not so strongly as to experience inner conflict), so that they do the right thing easily and gracefully. Aristotle's discussion puts this latter ideal of *sophrosune* before us (though "moderation" and "temperance" are rather pale words to express it in English).

REALIZATION OR PRESCRIPTION: POLITICAL EXPERTISE AND INTELLECTUAL CONTEMPLATION

How can human fulfilment be achieved? How can inner harmony be attained? Aristotle holds that virtue and vice are formed by "habituation"; that is, one's character is a result of one's past actions, so it seems that we can be held responsible for what we have made of ourselves, at least to some extent. Exhortation, praise, and blame can have some effect in promoting appropriate action in particular situations, but Aristotle ruefully acknowledges that "most people are not of the sort to be guided by a sense of shame but by fear" (NE 1179b11) and he is well aware that "it is not possible, or not easy, for words to dislodge what has long since been absorbed into one's character-traits" (1179b18).

So, because appropriate upbringing is the crucial ingredient in character formation, and upbringing and education presuppose a preexisting human society, Aristotle is led, like Plato, to inquire into how society should best be organized. The *Nicomachean Ethics* is mostly concerned with setting forth an ideal of human happiness or fulfilment, but as early as the second page Aristotle points out that putting it into practice is a matter of "political expertise":

> For even if the good is the same for a single person and for a city, the good of the city is a greater and more complete thing both to achieve and to preserve; for while to do so for one person on his own is satisfactory enough, to do it for a nation or for cities is finer and more godlike. So our inquiry seeks these things, being a political inquiry in a way. (1094b8)

And the *Ethics* ends by setting out a program for another inquiry into constitutions, legislation, and good government (1181b13).

Most of the detail of Aristotle's prescription is set out in this other work, the *Politics*, which like Plato's *Republic* covers a much wider range than its title suggests. It deals with such matters as marriage, parenthood, slavery, and household management (Book I); population, territory, town planning, nursery education, and the training of youth (Books VII–VIII); as well as citizenship and constitutions, revolution and reform (Books II–VI). Aristotle is more realistic than Plato in allowing for family life and private property, so he recognizes some limits to state power. But in other ways his ideal *polis* is still somewhat totalitarian, for he regards the upbringing of children and youth as so crucial for their moral development, and thus for the moral health of society, that "their upbringing and patterns of behavior must be ordered by the state" (NE1179b35). It seems that, from a very young age, the state must take a controlling power over the lives of children. It has been remarked that for Aristotle the ideal *polis* is like Calvin's Geneva in the sixteenth century in its power over the morals of its citizens. It is common these days to try to make a distinction between questions of politics and legislation on the one hand and "private" morality on the other, but Aristotle's view challenges us to consider whether any community or society or nation can survive and flourish without some measure of agreement on the most fundamental questions about how human life should best be lived.

Before leaving Aristotle, we should return to his notion of ideal happiness and consider the prescription that he himself favors in the last book (NE X.6–9). Here he argues that of the three conceptions of fulfiled life mentioned in I.5 (namely, lives devoted to pleasure, to political success and honor, or to intellectual inquiry and reflection) the third is best.

He quickly dismisses the hedonistic life (X.6), he finds practical political activity second best (X.8, 1178a9 ff.), and awards the palm to the life of reflection (X.7–8). Aristotle's argument for this is that the best kind of happiness will be activity of the "highest" element within human nature, the ruling part, that which has "awareness of fine things and divine ones"—and that is, in his view, reflective activity (1177a13 ff.). This is the most self-sufficient kind of human activity, requiring only modest resources. Aristotle also claims, implausibly, that it is the only sort of activity that is done for its own sake (1177b1), thereby inviting the wrath of musicians, golfers, lovers, and anyone who enjoys a country walk!

At this point, comparison with "the gods" enters into Aristotle's argument (though one wonders how literally he takes them):

> If, then intelligence is something divine as compared to a human being, so too a life in accordance with this will be divine as compared to a human life. One should not follow the advice of those who say "Human you are, think human thoughts," and "Mortals you are, think mortal ones," but instead, so far as is possible, assimilate to the immortals and do everything with the aim of living in accordance with what is highest of the things in us; for even if it is small in bulk, the degree to which it surpasses everything in power and dignity is far greater. (1177b31 ff.)

Aristotle goes on to say that it is absurd to attribute practical doings to the gods, yet we believe they are blessed and happy in the highest degree and we conceive of them as alive and hence as active in *some* way—so that can only be the reflective way, which must be the highest kind of activity (1178b8 ff.). Moreover, if the gods care at all about humanity, he supposes they delight in what has the greatest affinity to themselves, namely our exercise of intelligence (1179a25).

All this argument is supposed to support Aristotle's rating of intellectual activity as the supreme kind of human happiness. But why need there be a first prize here, a picking out of one kind of fulfilment as the highest, all things considered? Obviously, Aristotle himself pursued the life of the mind, became a world leader in it, and must surely have derived immense satisfaction from it. But that need not commit him to rating other pursuits as inferior. Why can't they just be good in different ways? We might enlarge the scope of "intellectual activity" to include the creative arts. We can admire the successful politician—at least he or she who does not pursue power for its own sake, but uses it to promote peace, prosperity, and social justice. We can also admire less exalted ways of life (e.g., craftsmen, farmers, engineers, athletes, teachers, and housewives or househusbands who devote much of their lives to their families). Indeed, many lives are devoted to multiple ideals (e.g., career, family, church, political commitment, music, sports) and there is no compulsion for everyone to have a single or permanent highest priority.

If we subtract from Aristotle that final overvaluation of the purely intellectual and replace it with a multiple set of human ideals (things worth doing for their own sake, none of which is compulsory), we have a more attractive conception of human flourishing that conforms to his formula (in I.7) of activity using our rational capacities, conducted "well and finely" over a lifetime—where "rational" includes practical as well as theoretical rationality. We have here the basis of a human-centered or humanist ethics.

But is there something missing? We may have qualms when we reflect that people in a fortunate class or nation might live very fulfilled lives by this sort of criterion—enjoying careers, family and friends, the arts and sciences, sports and hobbies, and so on, in whatever mixtures suit each individual—while many other people have little or no opportunity for such fulfilments. In Aristotle's own society, slaves or barbarians had few rights, if any; and it seems that even among male Greeks, only high-born aristocrats could aspire to intellectual or political careers. In our own time, in our so-called liberal, freedom-loving (and prosperous) democracies, it is painfully obvious that not everyone in our own society has the same opportunities for human fulfilment, let alone everyone in the wider world on which we depend for our resources.

It may be salutary, then, to compare the modified Aristotelian humanist ethic just outlined with Jesus' summary of the commandments: "Love the Lord thy God with all thy heart and all thy mind and all thy soul . . . and love thy neighbor as thyself" (Mark 12:30–31). Let us factor out the question of the *existence* of the Judeo-Christian God or the Aristotelian gods, and just compare the ideals involved. The two conceptions of the divine, and the ideals thereby set up for human aspiration, are importantly different. Aristotle's gods are purely intellectual beings, and if they care at all about human affairs, he represents them as caring only that we (or the cleverest of us) should emulate their intellectual insight. But the Hebrew God was a God of love as well as knowledge, who is represented as caring about His people collectively and individually, and in particular as caring about social justice (e.g., about the fate of the poor and the orphaned) and as capable of forgiveness. All this carries over to the Christian conception of a God of Love (see Chapter 6).

Aristotle is far from ignorant of the importance of human love; indeed, he devotes two whole books (NE VIII and IX) to the topic of friendship. (These are some of the most readable sections and can be read almost independently of the rest.) And he notes that there is a sense in which one should love oneself, namely wishing for the very best for oneself (1168b30). But friendship (*philia*) is, on Aristotle's conception, only possible with a few people; moreover, it can only really exist between good people. In contrast, the New Testament conception of love (*agape*, formerly translated as "charity") is supposed to be universal and unconditional. It involves more, I take it, than Aristotle's "good will" (NE1166b30). The ideal it puts before us is first that we should be loving or compassionate to *all* our fellow human beings, regardless of sex, race, class, ethnicity, or nationality. And, second, that our love or compassion should not depend on good behavior or individual talents, so that a change of heart and forgiveness should always be seen as possible. This twin ideal is almost impossibly demanding on our frail human nature. But we may feel that there is something missing from an ethic that does not even set it before us.

FOR FURTHER READING

Basic text: Aristotle's *Nicomachean Ethics*. There are several English translations, of which the latest is *Aristotle, Nicomachean Ethics, Translation, Introduction, and Commentary* by Sarah Broadie and Christopher Rowe (Oxford University Press, 2002). Broadie provides an excellent introduction to the philosophical issues and presents a detailed argumentative commentary. J. O. Urmson gives a rather easier introduction in *Aristotle's Ethics* (Oxford: Blackwell, 1988).

Aristotle: Selections, edited by T. Irwin and G. Fine (Indianapolis: Hackett, 1995), is a good introductory selection from the whole of Aristotle's work.

There are several excellent introductions to the whole of Aristotle's philosophy: J. L. Ackrill, *Aristotle the Philosopher* (Oxford University Press, 1981), is good at relating Aristotle to contemporary philosophy; *The Philosophy of Aristotle*, 2nd ed., by D. J. Allan (Oxford University Press, 1970), goes into more detail about the texts and their historical background; Jonathan Barnes has a masterful "Very Short Introduction" in the Oxford University Press series.

There is a useful introduction to the *Politics* in *The Politics of Aristotle,* translated with an introduction, notes, and appendices, by Ernest Barker (Oxford University Press, 1946).

6

The Bible: Humanity in Relation to God

This chapter will examine ideas about human nature and destiny in the Bible. The Hebrew scriptures, known to Christians as the Old Testament, contain a variety of writings—creation stories, histories of the Jewish people, their ancestry and laws, the Psalms and wisdom literature, and the prophetic writings—dating from about the eleventh century to the second century B.C.E. It is recognized as the authoritative Word of God by both Jews and Christians. The much shorter New Testament, from the first century C.E., is distinctive of Christianity and not accepted by Judaism. I will therefore treat these separately. (Quotations will be from the Revised English Bible.) In both cases there was a complex historical process by which certain texts became recognized as religiously authoritative and worthy of inclusion in "the canon" of sacred scripture. There was some disagreement about *which* texts should count as canonical; even now the status of some of the Old Testament Apocrypha remains disputed.

Judaism as it exists today as a world religion has developed not only from the Hebrew Bible but from the Rabbinic tradition that compiled the Talmud from the second century C.E. onward, *after* the birth of Christianity and in reaction to it. I will not attempt to deal with post-Talmudic Judaism, but will confine my attention to the Old Testament.

Christianity has had a continuous and complex history of development, through the early Church Councils that formulated the Creeds, the emergence of the Papacy, the schism between Roman and Orthodox Christianity in the eleventh century, the Protestant Reformation in the sixteenth century, the Catholic Counter-Reformation, and many more developments and splits since. And we should not forget those early streams of Christianity that never came within the Western ambit and still survive in the Coptic churches of the Middle East, Africa, and India. I will not attempt to deal with all this, but will concentrate on the text of the New Testament.

The third great monotheistic world religion of Semitic origin is Islam, which originated in the Arabian peninsula with the visions of Muhammed in the seventh century C.E. Islam recognizes as forebears Abraham and the succession of Old Testament patriarchs and prophets leading up to Jesus, but asserts that Muhammed is the last and greatest of God's prophets, and that the Qur'an is the uniquely authoritative message of God ("Allah"), delivered word by word to Muhammed. I will not attempt to review Islam here—one reason being that it is not clear to me that Islam has much to add to Judaism and Christianity about *human* nature (though I stand open to correction).

There are obvious problems in interpreting and assessing ideas from the Bible. On the one hand, believers (of one tradition or another) treat it as sacred text, revealing the nature and will of God Himself; some treat every sentence as infallibly authoritative, and many appeal to it for ethical guidance. Judaism and Christianity are not mere theories, they are living religions that interpret and guide the lives of their adherents. Moreover, they are not attributable to a single thinker. Moses is not now believed to be the author of the Pentateuch (the first five books of the Hebrew scriptures). Jesus is central to Christianity of course, but even if he can be credited with many of the sayings attributed to him, he did not leave any writings—but St. Paul and others certainly did. And Judaism and Christianity have each split into notoriously rival versions.

On the other hand, there has grown up, especially over the last two centuries, a great body of expertise in the ancient languages of Hebrew, Aramaic, and Greek, and in the archaeology and history of the communities that produced the biblical texts, so that there is now a huge industry of academic study and interpretation. The texts are of different dates, written and edited by different hands, produced and used for different purposes. And they have been used by theologians down the centuries to support rather different theological positions. To say there is a Judeo-Christian belief in X, a Hebrew conception of Y, or a New Testament view of Z is to risk oversimplification.

It will be impossible to please everyone—the believers with their rival versions of faith and the scholars with their academic controversies. There is no such thing as an objective, neutral approach to the Bible, innocent of all preconceptions. So it is perfectly fair for the reader of this chapter to ask where I am "coming from," what my preconceptions are likely to be. All right then: I was brought up in an Anglican home, but soon started to question the fundamentals. Converted to an evangelical form of Christianity as a student, I then gradually diverged from it and came to think of myself as an atheist for a quarter century or so. Then I sampled the Quaker approach and was attracted by their spirituality and ethical/social commitment without dogma or creed, so I joined the Religious Society of Friends, which understands Christianity as "not a notion, but a way."

In this chapter I will first examine the background "theory of the universe" that is common to Judaism and Christianity (and Islam)—namely, the monotheist conception of God. I can hardly avoid this eternally debated topic here, but I can only offer a brief review, for the main agenda is the Hebrew and Christian conceptions of human nature. I will examine these in turn, under the headings of theory, diagnosis, and prescription.

METAPHYSICAL BACKGROUND: THE JUDAIC-CHRISTIAN CONCEPTION OF GOD

The opening three chapters of Genesis, the first book of the Hebrew Bible, tell of the divine creation of the whole world, including human beings. The story continues with the descendants of Adam (Chs. 4–5), the flood and Noah's ark (Chs. 6–9), Noah's descendants and the tower of Babel (Chs. 10–11). All this is told as *universal* human history. God's call of Abram to become the ancestor (renamed Abraham) of His chosen people, the Jews, begins at Chapter 12, and all the rest of the Hebrew Bible relates to the history of "the children of Israel."

Let us consider how God is represented in the opening universal chapters. In Genesis 1–2:3 the Hebrew word for God is *elohim*, which is a plural form, whereas in the second version of the creation story in 2:4 ff. God is also referred to as "JHWH," a singular form with consonants only, usually read as "Jahweh." It looks as if the book of Genesis has been put together from at least two sources. The text we have, whatever people believe about its ultimately divine inspiration, is surely a result of human editorial processes long ago. In these opening verses, it is not clear that the conception invoked is of a single superhuman person, they might be translated as "In the beginning the gods (or divine powers) created the heavens and the earth. . . ."

It sounds as if God does not need to physically do anything to create: He does not get His hands dirty (if He has hands at all!)—He just gives the command and the result follows. In the traditional interpretation, God creates *ex nihilo*, he does not work on preexisting material like Plato's demiurge in the *Timaeus*, but calls everything into existence in the first place. This Hebrew God is a language user: He has conceptions of things before they come into existence, and He gives names to things when they do ("God called the dry land earth," 1:10 etc.). God is the conceptual power (or powers?) behind everything. At each stage of creation, God "saw that it was good" (1:10, etc.). He is represented as making judgments of value, not arbitrarily choosing what is to be called "good" but recognizing, in what He has created, the application of a preexisting, objective standard of value. The point is reinforced at the end of the sixth "day" of creation, when God "saw all that he had made, and it was very good" (1:31). There is a fundamental point made here, about the intrinsic goodness of all that exists, including human beings (before the Fall).

However, things soon go wrong. In Genesis Chapter 3 we are told of the first human disobedience by Eve and Adam, in Chapter 4 Cain murders his brother, and in 6:5–7 God bitterly regrets His creation of human beings because of their great wickedness, and angrily resolves to wipe out not just humans, but all living things—until Noah finds favor in His eyes and is allowed to save his family and other animals (6:8–9:19). God is here represented as moodily changing his mind, first about the value of the whole business of creation, and then about his decision to extinguish the human race (6:7). This hardly fits with later theological conceptions of God as omnipotent, omniscient, and perfectly good!

In the preceding short fragment (Genesis 6:1–4), there is an intriguing reference to "the sons of the gods" having intercourse with human females, and to "the Nephelim" (apparently a race of giants) being on the earth in those days. This confirms that the text is a compilation of several ancient stories containing different conceptions of the divine.

In subsequent books, God is represented as *speaking* to individual people—to Adam and Eve (Genesis 2–3), to Noah (6:13), to Abraham (12:1 ff., 22:1 ff.), to Jacob (31:3), repeatedly to Moses, notably from the burning bush (Exodus 3:4 ff.) and when delivering the Ten Commandments on Mount Sinai (Exodus 31, 34), to Joshua (Joshua 1:1 ff.), to Samuel (1 Samuel 3:4 ff.), to Elijah (1 Kings 17:2 ff., 19:13), and to Job (Job 38:1). Typically, God instructs individuals what they should do. Moses is represented as having a particularly intimate relationship with God, talking with him face-to-face, as one man speaks to another (Exodus 33:11); yet Moses was afraid to look at God (3:6), and later he is not allowed to see God's face (33:20). Note the implication that God is visible and has a face! More usually, God is represented as having a voice, but not a body or a locatable spatial presence (although Job is said to *see* God with his own eyes—Job 42:5).

The Psalms are a collection of prayers, typically addressed to God. They are poetic in form, and some of what they say about God obviously has to be taken as metaphorical: for example, God as a shield (Psalm 3:3), the heavens as the work of His fingers (8:3), the Lord's throne in heaven (11:4), the Lord is my lofty crag (18:2), smoke went up from his nostrils . . . he flew on the back of a cherub . . . he loosed arrows, he sped them far and wide (18:8–14), the Lord is my shepherd . . . you have richly anointed my head with oil (23:1–5), and so on. But with other talk of God, it is not so clear whether we should take it metaphorically or literally: for example, the Lord's anger may flare up in a moment (Psalm 2:12), he answers from his holy mountain (3:4), he has heard my weeping (6:8), the Lord passes sentence on the nations (7:8), it is God who girds me with strength (18:32), you are he who brought me from the womb (22:9), he revives my spirit, for his name's sake he guides me in the right paths (23:3), and so on.

By the time of the prophets (the books of Isaiah, Jeremiah, and those that follow), God is usually represented as speaking through an intermediary—the prophet who has a vision (Isaiah 1:1) or receives the word of the Lord (Jeremiah 1:4 ff.), and then delivers the message to the people, using the phrase "Thus says the Lord. . . ." Typically, the prophets foretell what is about to happen and interpret the events of human history—past, present, and future—in terms of God's will. Predictions of invasion and destruction, of enslavement and exile, and of return, rebuilding, and restitution are expressed in terms of God's purposes, whether punishment for disobedience, disloyalty and sin, or merciful forgiveness.

In the so-called wisdom literature, such as Proverbs, Ecclesiastes, and (in the Apocrypha) the Wisdom of Solomon, there is noticeably less explicit talk of God. Scholars detect Egyptian or Greek influences in these writings, but the first two are generally accepted as part of the canon. "The fear of the Lord is the foundation of knowledge," we are told at the beginning of Proverbs (1:7), yet the rest of the book hardly mentions Him. In the Wisdom of Solomon, wisdom is personified, almost deified—and in female gender: "The spirit of wisdom is kindly towards mortals. . . ." (1:6) ". . . Like a fine mist she rises from the power of God . . . She is but one, yet can do all things . . . age after age, she enters into holy souls" (7:25–27). Such talk of wisdom is personification, like Aphrodite as the goddess of love in Greek thought, or Virtue as a female person in poetry and paintings. But what about the talk of *God*—is it also personification, mere figures of speech? (Put the other way around, however, is wisdom any less real than God? Wisdom is often noticeable by its absence, but in some people its presence can be recognized.)

In the third edition of this book, I wrote that God can hardly be treated as a mere symbol in the Bible; much else may be poetry, parable, symbol, allegory, or myth, but not God Himself, who is obviously conceived of as the supreme Reality. Now I am not so sure. Where should we draw the line between symbolic or metaphorical talk of God and realistic, literal talk of Him? When God is described as having a face, nostrils, breath, arms, hands, and fingers, contemporary theologians take all that as metaphor, poetry, or picture-thinking. They tell us that God does not have a body. Artists like Michelangelo or William Blake painted God as a bearded European man of a certain age (and thereby exerted a stranglehold over our visual imagination that still persists), but theologians will now say those are mere pictorial images and that anyone who thinks *that* is the sort of God that the Judeo-Christian tradition believes in is missing the point. (We may feel some sympathy with the forbidding of graven images at Exodus 20:4 and with the Islamic ban on representational art.)

We are typically told that the biblical God is not supposed to be, or to have, a material body. He is not one object among others in the universe, He does not occupy a position in space, or last for a certain length of time. Nor is He to be identified with the whole universe, the sum total of everything that exists—that is pantheism, not theism. God is said to be transcendent as well as immanent: although in some sense present everywhere and all the time, He is also thought of as beyond the world of things in space and time (Psalm 90:2, Romans 1:20). God is not supposed to be like the unobservable entities (atoms, electrons, magnetism, quarks, superstrings, etc.) that scientific theory invokes to explain what we observe through our senses: He is not a scientific postulate. The existence and nature of God are surely not empirical hypotheses to be tested by observation and experiment.

Yet God is not a mere abstraction like numbers and shapes and the other objects of mathematics. He is supposed to be a personal Being who creates us, loves us, gives us guidance, enters into agreements or covenants with individuals or nations, judges us, and may redeem or save us. So although lacking a body, He is still thought of as *a person*, a superhuman mind endowed with intelligence, knowledge, desires, and purposes; and capable of anger, love, and forgiveness, of intentions, actions, and some kinds of intervention in the world, whether by "speaking" to people in their minds or perhaps more directly by miraculous exertion of His omnipotent power to change the course of physical events. But His significance is at least as much moral as cosmological: belief in Him is supposed to affect how we conceive of ourselves and how we ought to live.

Much thought and debate, both at the popular level and at more intellectual levels, has assumed that the traditional biblical talk of God has to be interpreted realistically, at face value, as implying the existence of a superhuman person. If He is not an embodied person—that, we agree, is too crude and makes the mistake of taking metaphors literally—then, it is usually said, we have to think of Him as a *dis*embodied person with superhuman properties of omniscience, omnipotence, and total benevolence—a conception of someone who is greater and better than anything or anyone else we can conceive of (as Anselm put it).

But this runs the risk of avoiding empirical falsification at the cost of metaphysical obscurity. Can we really make sense of the notion of a disembodied person—especially one with those idealized superlative properties? Of course, we can utter the relevant *words* and seem to understand something by them. But what is meant by the claim that there *exists* such a supernormal person? It is not, we agreed, an empirical hypothesis that might even yet be confirmed or disconfirmed by some new, esoteric bits of scientific evidence (though there are still some who take it that way). What, then, is the point of the speech-act of asserting this metaphysical claim?

This is not a book about the philosophy of religion, and the main business of this chapter is the biblical account of human nature. I can only leave the reader with the suggestion that there is a nonliteral, less naively realist way of interpreting the biblical talk of God, taking it as an overarching picture or metaphor—or perhaps a recipe for generating many metaphors. It provides a scheme of interpretation that many people from biblical times down to the present day have found helpful, useful, or illuminating in the effort to understand and express their experience of life—its ups and downs, its delights and disasters, its loves and hates, its moral failures, its illuminations, and its new possibilities. Others, however, have discarded such language or have never used it. Perhaps the difference between theism and atheism is not so much a question of metaphysical fact concerning the existence of a supernormal incorporeal person, but rather a question of how helpful, useful, and illuminating a person finds theistic figures of speech in talking about life. The answer to that can be a matter of degree.

THE HEBREW THEORY OF HUMAN NATURE

The Hebrew conception of humanity sees us as existing primarily in relation to God, who has created us to occupy a special position in the universe when He said "Let us make human beings in our image, after our likeness, to have dominion over . . . all wild animals . . ." (Genesis 1:26). The question immediately arises whether we should read this story literally as narrating historical events that occurred at some specific time in the distant past, or as mythology—which may poetically express important truths about the human condition, but not as history or science. Probably the original writers, editors, readers, and listeners did not make any such distinction, but it is a question we cannot avoid now.

Two large difficulties face any attempt to see literal truth here. The first is that the text displays inconsistencies, for there are *two* stories of the creation of human beings in Genesis, which give different accounts at several points, notably on the creation of woman. The first story has God creating men and women in the plural at 1:27, whereas the second has God creating a single man at 2:7, then fashioning a woman out of his rib at 2:22. The other difficulty is the inconsistency of the literal text with the results of cosmology, geology, and evolutionary biology. Science has given us entirely different accounts of the origin of the material universe in the Big Bang, the formation of galaxies, stars, and the solar system, the origin of seas and continents, and the evolution of humans from lower forms of life. There is even a contradiction with common sense, for how did the sons of Adam and Eve find wives (4:17), if *all* humans are descended from that first couple? I propose that only symbolic readings of the creation stories can be taken seriously. It is now widely—though not universally—accepted that they are myths (symbolic of deep religious truths), so there need be no incompatibility with science. To assert the historical existence of Adam and Eve as the ancestors of all humanity is in my view to insist on an overliteral interpretation of scripture.

What can it mean to say that we are made in the image of God? The believer will say that human beings are unique in that we have something of the rationality and personhood of God. But that statement can be turned around to say that our conception of the perfect rationality and moral personhood of God is an idealization from our own imperfect rationality and morality (see the mention of Feuerbach in Chapter 8). We can agree that we are (imperfectly) rational beings and that we are also persons, with self-consciousness, freedom of choice, and the capacity for loving personal relationships, as well as the capacity for hatred and vice. What can it mean to say that human beings are made to have dominion over the rest of creation? We have (for better or for worse) a certain degree of power over nature: at the time of Genesis, people in the Middle East had already domesticated animals and were growing food by agriculture; they had passed beyond the hunter-gatherer stage.

But although human beings are thus seen as having a special role compared with the rest of creation, we are also seen as continuous with nature.

The first human was made of "dust from the ground" (Genesis 2:7), that is, of the same matter that composes the rest of the world. "God breathed into his nostrils the breath of life" (are we to take *that* literally—does God breathe?). It is a recurring misinterpretation of the Bible that it implies a distinction between material body and immaterial soul or spirit. The Hebrew word translated as spirit, *ruach*, also means wind or breath and need not be interpreted as referring to a separable Platonic soul, but rather the essence of life or the function of being alive, perhaps more like Aristotle's nonsubstantial conception of soul (see Chapter 5). Dualism of body and soul is a Platonic idea that is *not* to be found in the Old Testament (or in the New—see the discussion that follows). Nowadays we are so influenced by the distinction between body and soul that we have inherited from Plato and Descartes that we tend to read it into the Bible, although it is not really to be found there.

According to the biblical conception, we are *persons*, importantly different both from inanimate matter and from other animals, but our personhood does not consist in the possession of an immaterial entity that is detachable from the body. There is no firm expectation of life after death expressed in the Hebrew Bible. The Jews did not develop any belief in an afterlife until shortly before the time of Jesus, and they did not agree about it: the gospels mention the Sadducees, who denied the Resurrection.

The relation of women to men in the Hebrew scheme of things is somewhat ambiguous from the start. As we have seen, one creation story suggests equality of the sexes, but the other implies that the male is the primary form of humanity. Moreover, in the story of human disobedience, "the Fall," the woman is represented as giving in to temptation and then persuading her husband to follow her (Genesis 3:6). There has been a tendency to see women as somehow more subject to sin and as tempting men to sin. And there was an early association of sexuality with sin, because as soon as Adam and Eve disobey God's prohibition, "the eyes of both of them were opened, and they knew that they were naked; so they stitched fig-leaves together and made themselves loincloths" (3:7). As punishment for disobedience, God decrees that the wife will desire her husband, but he will be "master" of her (3:16). In the stories of Abraham and his descendants, there is a tremendous emphasis on the importance of producing *male* heirs (typical of many cultures down to the present day). And, of course, God Himself is almost always described in masculine terms. For several religions and cultures, there is unfinished business to do with the equality of the sexes.

Probably the most crucial point in the biblical understanding of human nature is the notion of freedom, conceived of as the choice between obedience to God's will, faith in Him, love for Him—or disobedience, faithlessness, and pride. The necessity for choice between obedience or disobedience, good and evil, is presented in Genesis 2:16–17, where God forbids Adam to eat from the tree of knowledge of good and evil. But why should knowledge of good and evil be a bad thing, one wonders? Isn't that what one would expect of human *maturity*? Perhaps the thought is that there is a primeval stage of innocence, before moral distinctions are understood, in early childhood—and maybe also in early human evolution.

Greek thought puts great store on the intellect, on our ability to attain knowledge of truth (including moral truth); the highest fulfilment of human life was thought by Plato and Aristotle to be attainable only by those who are able to gain such rational knowledge. The Judeo-Christian tradition, in contrast, puts the emphasis on human goodness, a matter of basic attitude—of "heart" or will rather than mind or intellect—which is something open to all, independently of intellectual ability.

There is thus a democratic impetus, an ideal of the equality of all finite human beings before God, implicit in the Bible. (Though it can, of course, be questioned how well Jewish and Christian practice has lived up to this ideal.) The concern with human goodness is not just with right action: it is at least as much with the foundation in human character and personality from which such actions will flow. And it goes beyond the conceptions of human virtue offered by Plato and Aristotle, for the biblical writers see the only firm foundation for human goodness as faith in the transcendent yet personal God. The idea is that God created us for fellowship with Himself, so we fulfil the purpose of our life only when we love and serve our Creator.

There are various dramatic exemplifications in the Old Testament of this ultimate requirement of obedient submission to God rather than use of the intellect to reason things out and make one's own judgments about truth and morality. One is in the story of Abraham being commanded by God to sacrifice his only son, Isaac (Genesis 22). God rewards Abraham for being a "god-fearing" man, ready to give up even his own child in response to divine requirement; so God promises that he will be the patriarch of innumerable descendants. (A different response to the situation would be to reject any such killing of an innocent child as immoral and to conclude that any such "command" could not really come from a good, loving God. Even if it was only given as "a test of faith," what sort of God would play such a trick?) An anthropological interpretation is that this story shows the early Jewish tradition rejecting the practice of child sacrifice, which was found in some neighboring religious cultures.

Another famous case of faith being preferred to reason is in the book of Job, where Job and his interlocutors struggle with the problem of undeserved suffering. Job is a blameless and god-fearing man, but Satan persuades God to test him by letting him be subjected to catastrophic losses and afflictions (Job, Chs. 1–2). Despite all the efforts of Job's would-be comforters, no reasoned explanation of his suffering is offered (Chs. 3–37). In the end, God Himself simply appears and asserts His power and authority, and Job submits (Chs. 38–42). The answer, such as it is, seems to lie in adopting the appropriate attitude of humility before God (or fate, or the laws and accidents of nature) rather than in attaining some kind of intellectual insight.

DIAGNOSIS: HUMAN DISOBEDIENCE

Given this picture of humanity as made by God, the diagnosis of what is basically wrong with humankind follows. We misuse our God-given free will, we choose evil rather than good, we are infected with sin, and we therefore disrupt our relationship to God (Isaiah 59:2). But as argued before, the Fall need not be thought of as a particular historical event: the story of Adam and Eve eating the forbidden fruit can be read as a symbol of the fact that although we are free, there is a fatal flaw in our nature: we are all liable to sinful misuse of our freedom, and we suffer from the consequences.

Genesis 3:14–19 represents certain familiar features of human life as results of the Fall—punishments imposed by God for disobedience—such as the necessity to work to get food, the pain of childbirth, and even death itself. We can all wish for a life in which these things were not necessary, we may fantasize about a primeval Eden (or a heavenly paradise after death) in which there is no tension between inclination and necessity, desire and duty. It seems odd, however, to conceive of these fundamental biological features of life as the result of human moral failings.

Identifications and condemnations of human sinfulness recur throughout the Old Testament. Cain and Abel, the two sons of Adam and Eve, begin the fratricidal history of humanity when Cain murders his brother. In Genesis 6:5–7, God regrets His creation of humankind—until Noah finds favor. In Genesis 11:1–9, God is depicted as confusing the original single language because humankind was growing too proud and had tried to build the tower of Babel up to the heavens. Throughout the subsequent history of the children of Israel, there are repeated prophetic denunciations of their disloyalty and unfaithfulness to God, pride, sinfulness, selfishness, and injustice (see Exodus 32, Numbers 25, 1 Samuel 19, 2 Samuel 11, Isaiah, Jeremiah, Amos, etc.).

GOD'S COVENANTS AND REGENERATION

The Hebrew prescription is based on God, just as much as the theory and diagnosis. If God has made us for fellowship with Himself, and if we have turned away and broken our relationship to Him, then we need God to forgive us and restore the relationship. Hence the idea of salvation, of a regeneration of humanity made possible by the mercy, forgiveness, and love of God. In the Old Testament we find the recurring theme of a "covenant," a quasi-legal agreement like that between a powerful conqueror and a subject state, made between God and His chosen people. One covenant was with Noah (Genesis 9:1–17), another with Abraham (Genesis 17), and the third, most important one is with the "children of Israel" led by Moses, by which God redeems them from their bondage in Egypt and promises that they will be His people if they keep His commandments (Exodus 19).

But none of these covenants seems to be totally effective: sin does not disappear from the face of the earth (nor has it still, we may want to add!). There is even a danger of spiritual pride if members of a group conceive of themselves as "God's chosen people" and feel justified in conquering and oppressing their neighbors. The Hebrew Bible records genocide by the children of Israel as they took over "the Promised Land," and God is even represented as ordering it (Joshua Chs. 8–11). There is a tension between the exclusive tribalism—worshipping Jahweh as the God of Israel, as opposed to the gods of other peoples—that characterizes the early stories of the deliverance from Egypt and the conquest of Canaan, and the later, universal tendency—worshipping the God of *all* humankind—that appears in the prophets, such as in Isaiah 49:8: "I have formed you, and destined you to be a light for peoples."

When the people failed to obey God's commandments and laws, there arose the prophetic idea of God using the events of history, especially defeat by neighboring nations, to punish the people for their sin. But there is also a promise of God's merciful forgiveness, and His regeneration of not just the people of Israel, but the whole of creation. In particular, the author of the second section of the book of Isaiah uses ecstatic language (unforgettably set to music in Handel's *Messiah*) to express this vision of God's forgiveness, redemption, and new creation: "Then will the glory of the Lord be revealed, and all mankind will see it" (40:5); "You will go out with joy and be led forth in peace, before you mountains and hills will break into cries of joy. . . ." (55:12); "See, I am creating new heavens and a new earth!" (65:17). Thus the hope arose among Judaism for the coming of a God-appointed savior, "the Messiah," which Christians identify in Jesus.

THE NEW TESTAMENT

The Jewish rabbi, or religious teacher, Jesus of Nazareth did not leave any writings (none that we know of, anyway). But he exerted a magnetic personal influence on his disciples and those who met him, and an indirect influence down the centuries through the writings of his followers. (In this respect, there is a parallel with Socrates—see Chapter 4). The new world religion of Christianity quickly developed out of the early reactions to Jesus' life, teachings, Crucifixion, and reported Resurrection. The first Christian documents were letters ("epistles") of St. Paul (and others) to the early Christian communities. Most of these epistles are reckoned to predate the compilation, between about 70 and 100 C.E., of the four gospel narratives of Jesus' life and death.

For Christians, the coming of Jesus changed their conceptions both of God and of human nature. The God of the Old Testament became for them God the Father, and Jesus was identified as embodying or instantiating the divine, or being one with God (John 10:38), so that he was described as "God the Son." The distinctively threefold Christian conception of God was completed with the recognition of God the Holy Spirit acting inspirationally within Christian believers. The Spirit was powerfully experienced by the apostles on the day of Pentecost, according to Acts 2:1–5, and—in retrospect—could be identified as far back as Genesis 1:2. All this was later summed up in the paradoxical formulation of the doctrine of the Trinity: "three persons in one God."

Because of the enormous influence of Christianity in Western civilization down to our own time, the word "Christian" is often used in honorific ways. Until quite recently, it was shocking, even foolhardy, to declare oneself *not* a Christian (in some circles, it still is). But what *are* we to mean by the word now? What criteria does someone have to satisfy to count as a Christian? And why is this question regarded as so important? It is surely because of a cultural inheritance that has for so long been fundamental in the West: an assumption that "we" are Christian and that we need to define what Christianity is to distinguish ourselves from others—from pagans, atheists, Muslims, and so on. (Notoriously, further divisions are made when various brands of Christianity differentiate themselves from rivals. Those labeled "heretics" have sometimes been burned or massacred.)

Whatever extra connotations the term "Christian" has come to have, it at least involves some theological claim about Jesus. To be a Christian, it is hardly enough to say that Jesus was a very good man or a person of great spiritual insight—for atheists and members of other faiths may say such things. The most central Christian claim has been that there was a special revelation of God in this particular historical figure who lived, preached, and was crucified in Roman-occupied Palestine in the first century. This has been traditionally expressed in the doctrine of *incarnation*: that Jesus is both human and divine, the eternal Word of God made flesh (John 1:1–18). The later creedal formulations of this doctrine in Greek philosophical terms ("two natures in one substance") are perhaps optional, but the basic idea of incarnation, that God was *uniquely* present in Jesus, seems basic to Christianity, if anything is.

Yet even here, there is some room for shading at the edges. If we are pressed to say in what respect Jesus is different in kind from other great spiritual figures of history, such as the Buddha or Socrates or Muhammed (or more recent inspirational figures), the orthodox thing to say is, of course, that he was the Son of God, the divine Word incarnate in human form. However, he is said to have to have given, to those who received him, the power to become sons of God themselves (John 1:12). So what does the crucial phrase "Son of God" mean? For Christians, it does not mean that God the Father literally impregnated a woman and thus produced human progeny, as some of the Greek gods were said to do. (The Qu'ran dismissed such a thing as far beneath God's dignity.) The phrase "Son of God" thus launches us into controversial theology. But surely one can be impressed and inspired by the life and teaching of the Jesus represented in the gospels—perhaps more than by any other figure— without having to take a stand on a metaphysical claim about incarnation.

THE NEW TESTAMENT THEORY
OF HUMAN NATURE

The coming Jesus also expanded the conception of human nature for Christians by showing that in some sense human nature can become divine (see John 1:12 again). But what can that mean? In Romans 8:1–12, Paul makes a crucial contrast between "the spirit" and "the flesh." The latter term was the traditional translation in the Authorized Version, but the Revised English Bible has "our old nature," and the Jerusalem Bible has "human nature." A similar distinction is attributed to Jesus in John 3:5–7 (also 6:63):

> In very truth I tell you, no one can enter the kingdom of God without being born from water and spirit. Flesh can give birth only to flesh, it is spirit that give birth to spirit. You ought not to be astonished when I say "You must all be born again."

There is a tendency for us to interpret this in metaphysically dualist terms, involving a contrast of incorporeal soul with physical body (as in Plato and Descartes). But Paul's distinction seems to be not so much between mind and matter, nor between our spiritual nature and our human nature—which would suggest that our human nature is intrinsically bad, contrary to the idea of humanity being made in the image of God—but rather between regenerate and unregenerate humanity, redeemed and unredeemed human nature. The fundamental contrast is between two ways of living:

> Those who live on the level of the old nature have their outlook formed by it, and that spells death; but those who live on the level of the spirit have the spiritual outlook, and that is life and peace. (Romans 8:5–6)

Of course, it is tempting to identify "the flesh" with our biological nature—our bodily desires, especially our sexuality (compare Plato's conflict between Appetite and the higher parts of the soul, in Chapter 4). But it is a misinterpretation of the Christian conception of human nature to identify the distinction between good and evil with that between our mental and physical nature. Desires for wealth or fame or power are more mental than physical, but Jesus' teaching condemns these desires as worldly, not spiritual (see the Sermon on the Mount in Matthew Chs. 5–7), and for Paul too they are surely part of "living on the level of the old nature."

It has to be admitted, however, that the ascetic view that our sexual desires are intrinsically evil has had a strong influence in the history of Christianity. We can find this tendency in Paul (see 1 Corinthians Ch. 7, where he describes marriage as second best to celibacy), and it was more influential in the writings of St. Augustine. Paul was especially scathing about homosexuality (Romans 1:27)—as were Jews in general—but it is not obvious that this view is essential to Christianity rather than a cultural attitude of the time. Christians (and Jews and Muslims, too) have to ask themselves which bits of scripture reflect elements of ancient culture that are not compulsory for them now, and which bits express eternal spiritual insight. It is notable, for instance, that Paul does not condemn the institution of slavery (1 Corinthians 7:20–24).

On the question of equality between the sexes, we should note that in the Gospel stories, Jesus treats women with great respect. However, he did not choose any women to be his disciples: in that respect, he was presumably a man of his time, a Jewish rabbi. Paul said that in Christ there is so such thing as Jew and Greek, slave and freeman, male and female (Galatians 3:28), and yet he seems to support patriarchy when he wrote that wives must be subject to their husbands (Ephesians 5:22; see also 1 Corinthians 11:8–9, which refers to the second Creation story in Genesis). Paul also required the covering of women's hair in church. Much Christian thought has found females theologically problematic ever since—witness the continuing controversies about the ordination of women.

Is the distinction between living on the level of the old nature and living on the level of the spirit to be made purely in this life, or does it also

involve life after death? Here there is a divergence between a purely spiritual interpretation of Christianity and a supernatural or eschatological
version (the word "eschatological" means to do with the end of the world,
"the last things"). Jesus is said to have proclaimed the coming of "the
Kingdom of Heaven" or "the Kingdom of God" (Matthew 4:17, Ch. 23,
Mark 1:15). But it is not clear whether this means a psychological or a
political or a metaphysical change (apparently it was not clear to Jesus'
followers either). The phrase "eternal life" (or "everlasting life") is used
in the Gospel of John, where Jesus is represented as offering eternal life
to whoever will believe in him (John 3:16), to those who are "born again."
But we need not jump to the conclusion that these phrases mean the continuation of human life after death. Could they mean a new and better
way of living in *this* life—a way that relates properly to eternal truths and
values?

Some of Paul's writings can be taken in this way. Consider this vivid
passage in Galatians 5:16–25:

> What I mean is this: be guided by the Spirit and you will not gratify the
> desires of your unspiritual nature. . . .
>
> Anyone can see the behavior that belongs to the unspiritual nature: for-
> nication, indecency, and debauchery; idolatry and sorcery; quarrels, a con-
> tentious temper, envy, fits of rage, selfish ambitions, dissensions, party
> intrigues, and jealousies; drinking bouts, orgies, and the like. . . .
>
> But the harvest of the Spirit is love, joy, peace, patience, kindness, good-
> ness, fidelity, gentleness, and self-control, against such things there is no
> law. Those who belong to Christ Jesus have crucified the old nature with
> its passions and desires. If the Spirit is the source of our life, let the Spirit
> also direct its course.

This passage confirms that the old, unspiritual nature is the source of
worldly passions as least as much as bodily debaucheries. It is in some
ways more specific than Paul's oft-quoted hymn to "love" (*agape*, traditionally translated as "charity") in 1 Corinthians Chapter 13—which is
easily sentimentalized. And it is clear that we are not merely being re-
minded here of what is right and wrong; we are being promised a fundamental transformation of mind, from which ethical behavior will flow.

In the New Testament, love of God, and life according to His will, is
open to all regardless of intellectual ability (1 Corinthians 1:20). Jesus famously summed up the Old Testament law in two injunctions: "Love the
Lord your God with all your heart, and with all your soul, and with all
your strength, and with all your mind; and your neighbor as yourself"
(see Matthew 22:34–40, Mark 12:28–31, Luke 10:25–28, and the antici-
pations in Deuteronomy 6:5 and Leviticus 19:18). The "love of neigh-

bor" that is meant here is different from mere human affection; it must be divine in nature, as the First Epistle of John 4:7–8 makes clear:

> Let us love one another, because the source of love is God. Everyone who loves is a child of God and knows God, but the unloving know nothing of God, for God is love'.

"Eternal life" implies *at least* a Spirit-inspired, divinely loving life in this world, but it is impossible to ignore that the New Testament also lays great stress on resurrection, a last judgment, eternal punishment for the wicked, and everlasting life for all believers (Matthew 7:21–23, 13:36–43, and Chs. 24–25). Traditionally, the resurrection of Jesus after his death on the cross has been proclaimed as God's guarantee that there is a life after death for everyone—or at least for "the saved". We are offered hope of a regenerate, spiritual life: "For anyone united to Christ, there is a new creation" (2 Corinthians 5:17). This is seen as a lifelong process, which looks beyond to life after death for its completion (Phillipians 3:12–14). The Christian expectation of resurrection for all, or at least for all believers, is made quite explicit in 1 Corinthians Chapter 15.

THE NEW TESTAMENT DIAGNOSIS OF SIN

The doctrine of original sin does not imply that we are totally and utterly depraved. But it does mean that nothing we can do can be *perfect* by God's standards: "All alike have sinned, and are deprived of the divine glory" (Romans 3:23). We find ourselves in inner conflict. We often recognize what we ought to do, but somehow we fail to do it. St. Paul expresses this vividly in Romans 7:14 ff.; he even personifies sin (rather like the Freudian unconscious, or id), saying, "It is no longer I who perform the action, but sin that dwells in me" (7:17). This threatens to excuse the sinner from responsibility, which was surely not his intention. John also contrasts slavery to sin with being set free by knowing the truth in Jesus (John 8:31–36).

As we have seen, sin is not intrinsically bodily in nature: sexuality has its rightful place in marriage. The true nature of sin is mental or spiritual; it consists in pride, in the preference for our own selfish will against God's will, and our consequent alienation from Him. But this surely does not mean that all self-assertion is sinful. Nietzsche characterized Christianity as recommending "slave morality" in praising meekness and self-abasement, and discouraging vigorous human self-assertion and living life to the fullest. A superficial reading of the beatitudes (Matthew Ch. 5) may suggest this. "Blessed are the poor in spirit," Jesus said, but it is not obvious how we are to understand those mysterious words. Some of the stories of Jesus (such as his expulsion of the money-changers from the temple) and of Paul's preaching suggest no inhibition on clear moral judgment, righteous anger, and resolute action.

The Fall of humanity is seen as involving the whole creation (Romans 8:22): everything falls short of the glory of God. But one wonders if it is necessary to personify evil in the concept of Satan or other demonic powers—though those notions certainly appear in the New Testament (Matthew 4:1–11, Mark 5:1–13, Acts 5:3, 2 Thessalonians 2:3–9, Revelation 12:9). And it is Manichean, not biblical, to believe in twin and equal powers of good and evil: for Jew and Christian alike, God is ultimately in control of all that happens, despite the manifold appearances of evil in the world.

GOD'S SALVATION IN CHRIST

Scholars and theologians have long debated what Jesus' conception of himself was. In the Gospels he is represented as making dramatic theological claims about himself, especially in the Fourth Gospel, where he claims to be the Messiah (John 4:25–26), the Son of God (5:16–47), the bread that comes down from heaven (6:30-58), and to have existed before Abraham was born (8:58). But the gospels were compiled after Jesus' death, by writers who were already believers in his divine status. We cannot be at all sure that Jesus himself made such claims. It is in the writings of Paul that we find the earliest written formulations of the Christian theory of incarnation and salvation. The central claim is that God was uniquely present in Jesus of Nazareth, and that God uses Jesus' life, death, and resurrection to restore us to a right relationship with Himself:

> . . . as the result of one misdeed [Paul is thinking of Adam's Fall] was condemnation for all people, so the result of one righteous act [i.e. Jesus' death on the cross] is acquittal and life for all. For as through the disobedience of one man many were made sinners, so through the obedience of one man many will be made righteous. (Romans 5:18–19)

Paul writes with great eloquence and conviction, and his language has acquired great authority for many, but if we stop to think about what he is saying here, it seems to run counter to our ordinary convictions about responsibility and blame. How can it be just to blame all humanity for a misdeed of one man long ago (supposedly, Adam)? How can it be right to acquit or "make righteous" the whole of sinful humanity because of the obedience of another individual man (Jesus)? There is a controversial theological theory of *atonement* here, that the particular historical events of the life and death of Jesus are the means by which God reconciles the whole of creation to Himself (Romans 5:6–10, 2 Corinthians 5:18–21).

For many Christians, it is not enough to say that Jesus provides an example of someone being prepared to suffer death rather than go against his most fundamental values. Socrates and other historical figures including the Christian martyrs also provide such examples, but they are not divinized in the same way. Paul and other Christian writers (Hebrews Ch. 10) are obviously thinking in terms of Old Testament ideas of sacrifice, but not many theologians are now prepared to interpret Christ's "saving work" as a propitiatory sacrifice—as if God requires blood to be shed (any blood, even that of the innocent?) before he will be prepared to forgive sins. But how, then, is the crucifixion of a Jewish religious teacher under the Roman governor Pontius Pilate in Jerusalem about the year 30 supposed to effect a redemption of the whole world from sin?

The Christian prescription is not complete with this mysterious "saving work" of Jesus Christ. It needs to be accepted by each individual person and to be spread throughout the world by the Church. But there is some obscurity about just what is required from individuals to be "saved." Baptism became the traditional ritual for becoming a Christian, but that is only an outward and visible sign of an inward and spiritual change. There are familiar, constantly invoked phrases for the latter: being "born again," "believing in Christ," having "faith in Christ," "being justified by faith alone," and many variations on these. But what do these pious phrases really mean? Do they require a propositional belief in a theological claim that Jesus is the Son of God? And that his death atones for the sins of the world? Or do they mean rather a personal relationship of trust in Jesus as a religious authority, a "guru," a revealer of God, a guide to life, a source of spiritual life? But how can people who have never met him in the flesh have a personal relationship with him? What can that mean other than treating him—or rather the written representations of him that we are left with—as a supremely inspiring example of selfless living, life "in the spirit?"

A traditional problem arises over the parts played by human beings and God in the drama of salvation. The fundamental conception is that redemption can only come from God, through His offering of Himself in Christ. We are "justified" in the sight of God not by our own good works, but by faith (Romans 3:1–28), by our mere acceptance of what God does for us. We are saved by this free grace of God, not by anything that we can do ourselves (Ephesians 2:8). Yet, just as clearly, there is an assumption that our will remains free, for it must be by our own choice that we accept God's salvation and allow His regeneration to transform our lives. The New Testament is full of exhortations to repent and believe (e.g., Acts 3:19) and to live the life of the Spirit. There is thus a tension between the view that salvation is entirely due to God's grace and the insistence that it depends on our freely chosen response (see the mention of Augustine and Pelagius in the Historical Interlude).

SPIRITUAL OR SUPERNATURAL VERSIONS OF CHRISTIANITY?

The doctrines of incarnation, atonement, resurrection, and the end of this world present problems to secular human rationality, and their formulation has provoked much internal debate in the Christian tradition. How can one particular human being be a member of the transcendent, eternal Godhead? The doctrine of the Trinity—that there are three persons in one God—multiplies the conceptual problems. The standard response is that these are mysteries rather than contradictions, that human reason cannot be expected to understand the infinite mysteries of God, and that we have to accept in faith what God has revealed to us. But this sort of statement from within the perspective of faith does nothing to answer the difficulties of the unbeliever or the puzzled.

Unlike early Judaism, Christianity developed a clear expectation of life after death. But this is different from the Greek idea of the survival of an incorporeal soul. The Christian Creeds express belief in the resurrection of the *body*, and the main scriptural warrant for this is in 1 Corinthians 15:35 ff., where Paul wrote that we die as physical bodies but are raised as "spiritual bodies." It is not clear what a spiritual body is supposed to be, but Paul did use the Greek word *soma*, which means "body." Christians claim that the resurrection of Jesus was both a real, observable event in history and a unique act of God. (The idea of the Virgin Birth is almost as miraculous, but is perhaps less crucial to Christianity.) And Jesus' resurrection is supposed to show the possibility of a similar resurrection for everybody.

Is it meant that there will be a time in the future of this world at which the general resurrection will take place? Paul says "we shall all be changed, in a flash, in the twinkling of an eye, at the last trumpet-call" (1 Corinthians 15:51–52), and Peter predicts that on "the day of the Lord . . . the heavens will disappear with a great rushing sound" (2 Peter 3:10). Jesus himself is reported as predicting the imminent end of the world (Matthew Ch. 24). Paul keeps reminding his readers that the time is short, and in 1 Thessalonians 4:16-17 he writes his most vivid description of what he expected:

> . . . when God's trumpet sounds, then the Lord himself will descend from heaven; first the Christian dead will rise, then we who are still alive shall join them, caught up in the clouds to meet the Lord in the air. Thus we shall always be with the Lord.

Paul thus envisages a cataclysmic divine event that will dramatically and visibly intrude into our time and space. The book of Revelation is full of vivid descriptions of such eschatological events, including strange beasts, battles, and tortures—and displaying a certain obsession with numbers. (To my mind, it is like the script for a science-fiction movie, with lots of special effects in rather questionable taste: even the description of the new Jerusalem in Chapter 21 seems more interested in its jewelry and its dimensions than its spiritual qualities.) It is clear that the early Christians had a definite expectation of an end to human history, a taking up of humanity into a metaphysically different kind of existence. It would be nice to think that all will then be "saved," but many passages foresee a last judgment and a final division between the saved and the damned (Revelation destines some for "the second death" at 21:8).

How are we to understand this eschatological prediction or vision? (Are we meant to *understand* it at all? But unless we understand it, how can we believe it?) If bodies are resurrected, then presumably, as *bodies* of some kind, they have to occupy space and endure through time. It is surely not meant that they exist somewhere in our physical universe, so that somewhere, presumably at some large distance from the earth, there exist the resurrected bodies of St. Paul, Napoleon and Great-Aunt Agatha. That would make the belief into a scientific hypothesis, to be tested empirically. Rather, it seems that what we have to try to make sense of is the idea that there is a space in which resurrected bodies exist, but which has no spatial relations with the space in which we live.

The question of time is at least as difficult. Is it meant that there exists a system of events that bear no temporal relation to the events of this world (neither before nor after nor simultaneous)? Or is the resurrection world supposed to be timeless, in which case what sense can be made of the idea of resurrected *life*, for life as we understand it is a process in time in which people act and change, interact and communicate. If we think rather of a resurrected life that literally goes on forever, is that even an *attractive* prospect? The answer is, I suggest, not obvious. Could life remain meaningful if we knew there could be no end to it?

Many thinking Christians may acknowledge such intellectual problems. But they remain practicing members of a Christian community, and in some sense "accept" or "go along with" the orthodox doctrines because of what they find in the life and worship of the Church and in reading the Bible—a certain growth in the spiritual life. They may well say that Christianity is not just a theory, it is a way of life. Perhaps we can reach some degree of agreement on what counts as "spiritual growth," in terms of the sort of "fruits of the spirit" mentioned in Galatians 5, James, and 1 John. But any claim that it can be achieved only by accepting the metaphysical, supernatural, and eschatological claims of New Testament Christianity is highly disputable.

FOR FURTHER READING

There are many different English translations of the Bible. One excellent version for present purposes is the *Oxford Study Bible: Revised English Bible with the Apocrypha*, edited by M. J.Suggs et al. (Oxford: Oxford University Press, 1992). This volume contains explanatory footnotes as well as helpful essays on the historical, sociological, literary, and religious background of the biblical texts.

In the Very Short Introduction series published by Oxford University Press, see the titles on the Bible by J. Riches, on Judaism by N. Solomon, on theology by D. F. Ford, on Paul by E. P.Sanders, and on atheism by J. Baggini. There is also a title on Jesus, by H. Carpenter, formerly in Oxford University Press's Past Masters series.

For more on Christian understandings of human nature, see Reinhold Niebuhr, *The Nature and Destiny of Man* (New York: Charles Scribner's & Sons, 1964); E. L. Mascall, *The Importance of Being Human* (New York: Columbia University Press, 1958), which presents a neo-Thomist view; *Man: Fallen and Free*, edited by E. W. Kemp (London: Hodder & Stoughton, 1969), which contains an interesting variety of essays, including a notable summary by J. A. Baker of the Old Testament view; and J. Macquarrie, *In Search of Humanity* (London: SCM Press, 1982; New York: Crossroad, 1983), which offers a more existentialist view.

For a feminist critique of Christianity, while retaining theism, see Daphne Hampson, *After Christianity* (London: SCM Press, 1996).

Books on philosophy of religion are countless. One comprehensive set of readings is *Philosophy of Religion: Selected Readings*, edited by M. Peterson et al. (Oxford: Oxford University Press, 1996).

Historical Interlude

In our selection of ten theories of human nature, we are jumping over a long historical gap from the ancient worlds of China and India, Greece and Rome, to eighteenth-century Europe. In an introductory textbook we cannot offer comprehensive coverage of intellectual history. But it should aid readers' understanding of Kant and subsequent theories if we provide some thumbnail sketches of major intellectual developments in the intervening centuries.

THREE RELIGIONS WITH A COMMON ROOT: JUDAISM, CHRISTIANITY AND ISLAM

Judaism as it exists today is very different from what it was in Jesus' time. In 70 C.E., the ancient state of Israel was wiped off the face of the map and the temple destroyed by the Romans, after an armed Jewish uprising. The Jews were then dispersed into many countries, where they became immigrant minorities, often persecuted. But the Jewish religion was maintained and developed by the rabbis, and Judaism underwent considerable changes over the next two thousand years, in reaction to exile, the growth of Christianity, and the later rise of science. Over the years

Judaism has split; these days there are differences between various Orthodox and Reformed groups, in the modern state of Israel and elsewhere. There are disagreements, for example, over the separation of religion and state.

The third great monotheistic world religion of Semitic origin is Islam, which arose in the Arabian peninsula in the seventh century C.E., when the prophet Muhammed had a series of visions in which, Muslims believe, he was given a series of direct revelations from Allah: when written down, these became the text of the Qur'an. Muhammed converted the Arabs of Medina and Mecca from paganism, convincing them that they had been given a divine revelation of their own that superseded those of the Jews and the Christians. Ever since then, Mecca has been the center of worldwide Muslim pilgrimage.

After the death of Muhammed, differences about religious authority and interpretation arose. There was a schism between Sunnis and Shi'ites, which remains the main division between Muslims today. Iranians and a majority of Iraqis follow the Shi'ite tradition, but most of the Muslims in the world are Sunni, including those in Saudi Arabia who control the sacred site of Mecca. The armies of early Islam spread rapidly from its Arabian home, conquering eastward as far as India and westward across the whole of North Africa and half of Spain. There followed a golden age in which Islamic civilization led the world in science, medicine, philosophy, and scholarship. Some Muslim thinkers tried to interpret the theology of the Qur'an in terms of classical Greek philosophy, as we will see later on. However from the eleventh century onward, conflict arose with the rising powers of Europe. The Crusades were a series of invasions by European armies, instigated by the pope, with the aim of expelling Muslims from the Holy Land of Palestine. They were ultimately unsuccessful, but from the fifteenth century onward, European exploration, military, and economic development began to dominate the whole world.

Since then, Muslims have debated about how to react to Western science, technology, empire building, and culture. Some have favored a degree of assimilation, but others have reacted by strongly affirming separate Muslim religious and cultural identity (though they have usually been ready to use the latest technology). Many Muslims have had a sense of frustration and resentment against the conquering West which has led to extreme violence; for instance, the British Empire fought Muslim rebellions in the Indian Mutiny of 1857 and by the Mahdi and his followers in the Sudan at the end of the century. For better or for worse, Islam has not developed much conception of the separation of religion and state. Their social ideal has tended to be a society whose every aspect is formed by the teachings and traditional culture of Islam—hence the demands for "Sharia law." It seems that Islam's relationship to modernity has still to be worked out. (An extended argument for selective assimilation can be found in *Western Muslims and the Future of Islam*, by Tariq Ramadan, Oxford University Press, 2004.)

THE MIDDLE AGES: WHAT PART DOES REASON PLAY IN FAITH?

Augustine (354–430)

In the early fourth century C.E., the Roman emperor Constantine adopted Christianity as the official religion of the empire, and Christians made the transition from a persecuted minority to membership in the power structure.

St. Augustine was the most crucial connecting link between the thought of the ancient world and the Christian medieval worldview that was to dominate the next millennium in Europe. He came from North Africa, then part of the Roman Empire; although he had a Christian mother, he did not start out as a Christian himself. He was trained in the Roman tradition of rhetoric (public speaking), and he avidly studied the writings of the Manicheans, who held that there are twin Powers of Good and Evil, and the neo-Platonists, who revived and extended Plato's ideas. After contact with influential Christians and studying the Bible, Augustine converted to Christianity following a prolonged intellectual and moral struggle that he famously describes in his *Confessions*. He was ordained as a priest and was soon pressed into service as a bishop.

Augustine's deep and extensive writings effected a synthesis of Christianity and Platonic ideas (he had little knowledge of Aristotle). He was strongly influenced by the thought of the neo-Platonist philosopher Plotinus, who saw a Platonic God as the Source of everything that exists, and human beings as capable of inner illumination. These conceptions could be readily integrated with belief in God as Creator and the Christian gospel of salvation. Despite the intellectual power of his mind, Augustine, once converted, saw the intellect as subservient to faith. In a famous phrase, he said, "I believe in order to understand," by which he meant that reason alone cannot reach the most important truths; he·saw an act of will, the disposition of the whole person, as crucial.

Augustine had a strong belief in human free will, but an even stronger sense of human sinfulness. He held that nothing we can do by ourselves can reconcile us to God. Mired in original sin, we cannot free ourselves from it. Only God's free action, His "grace," can save us; and if some are saved (and "predestined" for it by God's "election") while others are not, this is not because of any individual merit. Augustine defended these views in a famous controversy with Pelagius (the first thinker from the British Isles to appear in history), who maintained that ultimately we save ourselves by our free choice. Augustine persuaded a Church Council to condemn Pelagius' view as heretical, but the relation between human freedom and divine grace remains a crucial problem for theology.

Augustine's sense of human sin as manifest in our bodily desires had a baneful influence on much subsequent Christian thought, which tended to identify sin with sexuality—or at least to concentrate attention on sex as the primary exemplification of sin. This was connected with a tendency to devalue women as supposedly more involved with unspiritual bodily matters than men, and to regard marriage as second best to celibacy.

Augustine had a strong sense of history and divine providence. He made a famous distinction between the City of Man—the temporal order of human politics and power (represented in his own time by Rome)—and the City of God—the ideal human destiny in which God's will is eventually fulfilled. But the Romanized Christian Church occupied an ambiguous position between the two—an imperfect human institution, changing and developing in time along with secular history and culture, yet believed to embody and fulfil God's will. Augustine had a very strong belief in the authority of the Church and in the importance of its unity. When a division emerged between orthodox Catholicism and the "Donatist" Christians of North Africa, he was quite prepared to use the civil powers to enforce conformity.

The Islamic Philosophers

From the ninth to the thirteenth centuries, a great flowering of Islamic civilization took place all around the Mediterranean. In this period, Islamic theology, philosophy, science, and medicine were more advanced than in medieval Europe. Islamic philosophers developed various intellectual systems that tried to combine Greek philosophy with religious faith (as did their Christian contemporaries). An influential tradition of Islamic mystical spirituality could also be found in the Sufi movement (which still survives). For a while some fruitful contact occurred between the rival civilizations; crucially, much of the thought of Aristotle that had been lost to the West was rediscovered from the Muslim scholars via the school of translators at Toledo in central Spain, then on the border line between the Christian and Muslim worlds.

Islamic thought resembles medieval Christianity in assuming as an unquestionable premise the authority of a religious tradition based on a claimed divine revelation. But there emerged some hotly debated differences (comparable to those in the Christian world) about the relation of reason to faith, and of individual religious experience to religious authority. One such dispute resulted in the execution of al-Hallaj in the tenth century for proclaiming his Sufi belief in his attainment of mystical union with God—which was seen as heretical. Ibn Sina (Latin name: Avicenna, 980–1037) used Aristotle's subtle distinction between active and passive elements within the human mind to give a theory of "prophecy" or revelation: God was said to speak through the divine, active intellect working in the mind of Muhammed, whereas the more passive, imaginative side of the prophet's mind expresses religious truths in terms of vivid images. According to ibn Sina, imagery is needed to persuade most human beings of religious truth and to impel them to action, but philosophers can interpret the images in terms of higher spiritual truths. He voiced doubts about the literal truth of bodily resurrection, and his orthodoxy was questioned.

Al-Ghazali (1058–1111) was a brilliant scholar who gave up his professorship in Baghdad for the life of a wandering ascetic and Sufi. In a book aggressively entitled *The Incoherence of the Philosophers*, he criticized previous Islamic philosophers for being overinfluenced by Greek ideas and departing from Qur'anic orthodoxy. He also made a striking anticipation of Hume's denial of the necessity of the cause-effect relation and used this to question metaphysical theories of God. He defended the Sufi appeal to religious experience rather than philosophical argument.

In Spain there was a redefense of philosophy by ibn Rushd (Latin name: Averroes, 1126–1198). He argued that Muslims cannot avoid the use of reason, since the text of the Qur'an sometimes stands in need of rational interpretation, and jurists tend to disagree on questions of law and ethics. He wrote a reply to al-Ghazali entitled *The Incoherence of "The Incoherence,"* arguing that it was inconsistent to use reason to subvert reliance on reason. He thus tended to subordinate theology to philosophy once again.

Avicenna and Averroes had considerable influence on medieval Western thought. In the twelfth and thirteenth centuries, there developed a fascinating three-way debate, also involving Jewish philosophers such as Maimonides (1135–1204), who wrote a famous work entitled *Guide for the Perplexed*. But this medieval episode of multiculturalism was not to last: intolerance and conflict took over, and after the Reconquista of Spain by the Spanish Catholic monarchy, Jews and Muslims were forcibly expelled.

Aquinas (1224–1274)

As we have just seen, most of the works of Aristotle did not become available to the West until the twelfth century. This produced a revolution within late medieval thought, even though some conservative Church authorities tried to ban the study of Aristotle. St. Thomas Aquinas's magnificent Christian systematization—expounded in his *Summa Theologica*—was based on Aristotle's philosophy, plus, of course, the Bible and the Church Fathers. The *Summa* is like a medieval cathedral—an enormous, impressive structure of high religious aspiration, full of intricate detail that makes one marvel at the faith and the workmanship that produced it. Though controversial in its time, it has since become Roman Catholic orthodoxy, backed by papal authority.

Aquinas allowed that the natural powers of human reason have a legitimate, if limited, place in the defense of Christian faith (something that Augustine and his late medieval followers like St. Bonaventure tended to deny). Aquinas held the Aristotelian (and empiricist) view that all human knowledge starts with sense perception, but he acknowledged that we have to use our intellect to recognize types or "forms" of things and to attain systematic scientific knowledge of the world. Crucially, he distinguished between rational theology and revealed theology: in the former, we can use unaided human reason to prove the existence of God (by the famous "Five Ways"); in the latter, we receive in faith the revelation of God through the Bible and the Church. Faith, it emerges, is not something under the control of our will; rather, it is infused by the grace of God (*Summa Theologica*, II–II, Q.6, art. 1).

On human nature, Aquinas follows a basically Aristotelian analysis of our "rational soul" as consisting in our capacities for perception, intellectual conception, theoretical reasoning, and practical deliberation resulting in exercise of our free will in action. He Christianizes Aristotle's conception of *eudaimonia* by identifying our ultimate fulfilment as consisting in the knowledge and love of God. And he supplements the four classical Greek virtues of courage, temperance, prudence, and justice with the three "theological virtues" of faith, hope, and divine love (or "charity"), for which we need to receive divine illumination or grace.

On the question of immortality, Aquinas retained (with dubious consistency) an element of Platonism, saying that although the resurrection involves the re-creation of the human being as a living body, a union of body and soul, nevertheless the soul has a separate existence between death and resurrection. This formulation tries to solve the problem of maintaining personal identity over the interim period, but it invites the question of how such a temporarily disembodied soul can be a perceiving and acting person.

Aquinas's appeal to reason was real, but limited. The authority of the Catholic Church remained paramount for him in all matters of faith; and like Augustine, he was prepared to sanction the use of force against dissent. He wrote that those heretics who use their reason to produce perversions of the Christian faith may be "banished from the world by death" (*Summa Theologica*, II–II, Q.11, art. 3). His intellectual cathedral was built for the glory of God, but also to buttress the authority of the Church, and in some of its darker corners a whiff of burning can still be detected. He did not quite finish his great construction, for in the last year of his life he experienced a mystical vision, and said that all he had written now "seemed to him as straw."

THE REFORMATION: WHERE LIES
THE AUTHORITY FOR FAITH?

Christianity was the dominant system of belief in Europe for some fifteen hundred years, from the fall of Rome through the Dark Ages and the high medieval period and into the modern age. And, despite secular trends, it is still embedded in twenty-first-century Europe and America. The popes of the Western Catholic Church inherited from the Roman Empire their center of power in Rome and retain it to this day. But after the schism of 1054, the Eastern Orthodox version of Christianity became independent, centered in the Byzantine Empire in Constantinople until the fall of that city to the Muslim Turks in 1453, when it was renamed Istanbul. Orthodox Christianity continues to this day in Greece and Eastern Europe, and is resurgent in post-communist Russia. Other extant Christian churches date back to the early centuries of Christianity, such as the Coptic Church in Egypt and Ethiopia.

Four successive cultural movements of enormous world historical importance developed in early modern Europe: the Renaissance, the Reformation, the Rise of Science, and the Enlightenment. In the Renaissance of the fifteenth and sixteenth centuries, new attention was devoted to the literature, arts, and philosophy of the ancient world, and these exerted a new, invigorating influence on Western thought. The wisdom of the ancients was now seen more directly, rather than through the distorting prism of medieval Christianity. As a result, there arose a humanist style of philosophy concentrating more on human nature than on metaphysics or theology (e.g., Pico della Mirandola in Italy and Erasmus of Rotterdam).

The religious Reformation is commonly said to have started when Martin Luther (1483–1546) nailed his ninety-five theological propositions on the church door in Wittenberg in Germany on November 1, 1517. But there had already been reforming voices within the Catholic Church, such as John Wycliffe in fourteenth-century England. Sometimes dissent was violently suppressed; for example, Wycliffe's follower John Huss was burned at the stake in Bohemia. Luther himself was a highly educated theologian in the Catholic tradition, but he soon began to question some of the ideas and practices of the Italian popes. He vehemently opposed the Church's sale of "indulgences," by which people were led to think that they could buy forgiveness and a place in heaven. The main theme of Luther's theology was the doctrine of justification before God by individual faith, by God's freely given grace, without the mediation of Church authority—and without appeal to reason, either: Luther notoriously condemned reason as a "whore."

Luther was also something of a German nationalist, in reaction against the power of Rome. He translated the Bible into German and wrote his controversial works in a witty and pithy language that the people could readily understand. The new movement of religious reform spread rapidly across Northern Europe, and the unity of the Western Church was shattered. A large number of different Protestant churches and sects developed, appealing to the Bible and to individual religious experience rather than the tradition of the Church. Translations of the Bible into the languages of the people became a crucial element in this new kind of spirituality. Until the Reformation, the Bible had been available only to priests and theologians who could read Latin or Greek. Some of the early translators such as William Tyndale were even burned by church authorities, who felt the threat to their own ecclesiastical power if everyone could read and interpret the sacred texts for themselves.

Appeal to scripture became the fundamental source of authority for protestants, especially the Calvinist or Reformed churches led by John Calvin (1509–1564), who systematized his thought in his *Institutes of the Christian Religion*. A theocratic Calvinist state (a society ruled by religious leaders) was established in Geneva in Switzerland. Calvinism spread to Scotland, to the Puritan movement in England, and then to America with the first settlers. There developed a doctrine of the infallibility of the Bible as the revealed word of God—a view that is still very much around. But the question of who has the correct *interpretation* always tends to arise whenever believers disagree. Some of the more radical protestant sects, such as the Anabaptists (or Radical reformation) on the Continent and the Quakers led by George Fox in England, though still strongly influenced by the New Testament, appealed to "the inner Light" of God's revelation in the individual mind or heart. They thus tended to place more emphasis on individual religious experience.

Religious disagreements often spilled over into violent conflict. There were "wars of religion" in early modern Europe, not only between Catholics and Protestants, but also between rival protestant sects. Luther appealed to the German rulers to suppress the Anabaptists by force. The Huguenots (French Protestants) were seen as traitors to the French Catholic state and were massacred or expelled. After the English civil war of the mid-seventeenth century, the monarchy and the Anglican Church were restored, and religious "nonconformists" were persecuted. Only gradually, after such painful experiences, did the European peoples begin to accept that different religions could be tolerated in the same country. A separation between church and state was enshrined in the American Constitution.

THE RISE OF SCIENCE: HOW DOES SCIENTIFIC METHOD APPLY TO HUMAN BEINGS?

Modern physical science arose in the seventeenth century. The combination of experimental method with systematic mathematical theory was triumphantly demonstrated in the work of Galileo and Newton. The explanatory success of the Newtonian system of mechanics showed how new knowledge about the universe—both in the heavens and on earth—could be firmly established on the basis of carefully measured observation. Appeal could no longer be made to the traditional medieval authorities of Aristotle, Bible, and Church on matters of fact about the workings of the physical world. The Catholic Church's attempt to retain a pre-Copernican, earth-centered cosmology in the face of the new discoveries of Galileo was a last-ditch defense of the indefensible.

The more difficult problem (which still faces us today) was how far can scientific method be applied to human beings? To this question, there often seem to be two starkly opposed answers, associated with the rival metaphysics of materialism or dualism. Are human beings entirely composed of the same kind of matter that makes up the rest of the universe, and subject to the same laws of nature? (The laws were assumed to be deterministic, until the advent of quantum mechanics in the twentieth century.) Or are we combinations of body and soul, where the latter is thought of as something nonmaterial, not subject to the laws of physical science, and thus leaving room for rationality and free will? These two metaphysical views were defended by Hobbes and Descartes, respectively. They still tend to dominate our own intellectual landscape, but as we will see, Spinoza suggested a third way.

Hobbes (1588–1679)

The Englishman Thomas Hobbes published his most famous work, *Leviathan*, in 1651, in the period of the English civil war. It is one of the great classics of political philosophy, but his social conclusions are derived from premises about individual human nature. Hobbes vehemently rejected dualism and medieval Aristotelianism, and argued that the very notion of soul as incorporeal substance is self-contradictory. He espoused instead an uncompromising metaphysical materialism about human nature, treating life as a motion of the limbs, sensation as motion within the bodily organs, and desire as the states of the body and brain that cause bodily movement. Hobbes's philosophy is one of the first to be systematically "naturalist," proposing to use the methods of the physical sciences to explain human nature and human society.

Hobbes had a bleak view of individual human nature as intrinsically selfish—each person's desires being for his or her own survival and reproduction. We look after our immediate family—which is, after all, part of human reproduction—but we have little or no concern for others. (This is a crude anticipation of Darwinian approaches that we will consider in Chapter 10.) Humans are inevitably in competition with each other—for food, for land, and all other resources. So if there is no common power to keep order, people tend to resort to robbery and violence, so there is no security of property or life. In Hobbes's most-quoted phrase, human life becomes "solitary, poor, nasty, brutish, and short." He therefore argued that there is a fundamental need for an authority with effective monopoly of the use of force, to save people from the evils of "the state of nature." Thus it is in each person's self-interest to give up some individual freedom for the sake of security, and to acknowledge the authority of whatever power is strong enough to enforce the rule of law.

Hobbes's account of human nature is implicitly atheist. He could not openly say so in the seventeenth century, so we still find talk of God in his writings. But it seems inessential to his main argument, in which there is no appeal to divine creation, purpose, redemption, or judgment. And in terms of actual power, he wanted to subordinate all churches to the authority of the state.

This is a good point at which to note that the phrases "state of nature" and "human nature" are extremely ambiguous. Some early modern thinkers such as Thomas Hobbes, John Locke, and Jean-Jacques Rousseau tended to mean by them the supposed nature of human beings before the advent of organized human society. But there is every reason to believe that human beings have always been highly social creatures, and that the idea of individuals coming together to form society is a myth.

Descartes (1596–1650)

The Frenchman Rene Descartes was a central figure in the scientific revolution of the seventeenth century. He contributed to the development of mathematics, physics, physiology, and philosophy. His scientific work has long been superseded, but his philosophical writings remain firmly on the syllabus, for they express fundamental conceptions and arguments that any philosopher must address.

What most concerns us here is Descartes' dualist account of human nature as consisting of body and soul—two distinct but interacting substances, each of which can exist without the other. In this he followed a long tradition (including Plato), but he put a new gloss on the distinction and gave new arguments for it. According to Descartes, the body occupies space and is subject to the laws of nature that science studies, but it has no mental properties. It is the mind or soul that thinks, feels, perceives, and decides (thereby exercising free will). The soul is incorporeal—i.e., it is not made of matter, it does not occupy space (although it undergoes changes in time), it cannot be studied by the methods of physical science. Moreover, the soul can survive the death of the body, carrying the identity of a person into the afterlife. Descartes was thus led to make a sharp distinction between humans as possessing immaterial souls and animals lacking all consciousness.

In his *Discourse on Method*, Descartes wrote a preliminary exposition of his ideas in semiautobiographical form. Expressed more carefully in the *Meditations*, his main argument for dualism starts from the reflection that whatever else one can doubt, one cannot doubt one's own existence as a conscious being—although one can (he claimed) doubt whether one has a body. Descartes thus used pure reason in a reflective, introspective way to try to prove fundamental metaphysical truths about the soul, and he then proposed to argue from the nature of our mental ideas to the existence of God.

In Part V of the *Discourse*, however, he offered a different empirical argument for dualism, as the hypothesis that best explains the observed behavior of people and animals. He argued that there is a distinction of kind rather than degree between the innate mental faculties of humans and animals, picking out language as a distinctive component of human rationality. It is this empirically based sort of rationalism (namely, the assertion of certain innate mental capacities as peculiar to the human species) that Noam Chomsky and others have renewed in the twentieth century (see Chapter 10).

Having thus bifurcated human nature into two different metaphysical realms—the physical and the mental—Descartes (like many others) thought he could apply scientific method to the physical part, studying our bodies in anatomy and physiology while remaining an orthodox Catholic believer in an infinite, immaterial God and a finite, immaterial, immortal soul with free will.

Spinoza (1632–1677)

The Dutch philosopher Benedict de Spinoza (who was descended from the Jews expelled from Spain in the Reconquista) offered a compromise between the stark alternatives of dualism and materialism. In his main work, the *Ethics* (which actually contains a lot more metaphysics than ethics), he identifies God with the whole of nature. He thus retains some reverential talk of "God or Nature," but not the biblical conception of God as transcendent personal Creator of the whole universe. Spinoza's view is pantheism, not orthodox theism.

On the question of human nature, Spinoza developed an interesting theory that matter and mind are not two separate substances, but two attributes of one complex underlying reality. This is called "dualism of attribute," or "double-aspect theory." His technical metaphysics of substances, attributes, essences, and so on is difficult to interpret, but it has an intellectual descendant in the twentieth-century identity theory of mind. This says that mental events are identical with brain events: there are two different sets of descriptions (mental and physical), but they apply to the one and the same events. This might also be expressed, using what we learned from Aristotle in Chapter 5, by saying that the mind is what the functioning brain *does*.

THE ENLIGHTENMENT: CAN SCIENCE BE OUR GUIDE TO LIFE?

From the mid-seventeenth century onward, as science became widely accepted as the only way to gain knowledge of the material world, the proposal was repeatedly raised to apply the methods of science to human beings. In the European movement of ideas called the "Enlightenment," centered in the eighteenth century, the hope emerged that this not only would give us knowledge of human nature, but also would enable us to solve the problems of humanity. The Enlightenment can be briefly summed up as belief (or faith!) in the power of human reason to improve the human condition. It was widely thought that rationality, applied to the benefit of human individuals in medicine and education, and to the reform of human society in economics and politics, could lead to hitherto undreamed-of human progress. In its more extreme versions, this became the claim that science can replace *all* other guides to life, such as religion, morality, the authority of monarchs and aristocrats, and social tradition.

The Enlightenment took somewhat different forms in the rival nation-states of Europe. In Britain, which had been through the searing experience of civil war in the seventeenth century, there was a gradual evolution and piecemeal reform of society, and democracy was introduced in stages. John Locke gave an empiricist account of the origin of all our ideas in experience in his *Essay Concerning Human Understanding* (1690). Though retaining dualism and theism, Locke appealed to reason and experience rather than to revealed religion. His political philosophy derived the need for government (and for limitations on its power) from individual human needs and rights, especially property rights. Locke's thought strongly influenced the drafting of the new American Constitution in 1776.

Hume (1711–1776)

One of the seminal figures of the Enlightenment was the Scotsman David Hume. His magnum opus is the three-volume *Treatise of Human Nature* (1739–40), written in his twenties; later he wrote more popular expositions of his main ideas in the two *Enquiries* (concerning the human understanding, and morals). He went on to treat many other topics, including religion, politics, and history.

Hume applied empiricism more rigorously than ever before: he held that all concepts are derived from experience, and that all knowledge about the world must be based on experience. Pure reason can prove results only about "relations of ideas" in logic and mathematics; it cannot yield any sort of substantive truth about the world. His *Treatise* is significantly subtitled "An Attempt to introduce the experimental Method of Reasoning into Moral Subjects" (here "experimental" meant experiential, and "moral" meant human). It was one of the first serious attempts at a scientific theory of human nature—yet it remains more a work of philosophy than psychology.

Hume's version of empiricism asserted that all ideas are derived from impressions, either of the senses or of "reflection" (i.e., introspective awareness of one's own states of mind). He argued that we have no idea of matter except as a bundle of perceptible qualities (following the lead of the Irish philosopher Berkeley). Hume went dramatically further than Berkeley, however, when he argued that we have no coherent notion of soul, or mental substance—we are aware of nothing but a succession of mental states in ourselves and therefore have no idea of a continuing "self." He also famously argued that we have no idea of causation or "necessary connection" except as a regular temporal succession of types of event. There is, in Hume's view, no rational reason to expect correlations already experienced to be continued in new cases; it is only our nonrational, instinctive human nature (which in this respect resembles animal natures) to expect the future to resemble the past.

There is thus a skeptical and subversive tendency at the foundation of Hume's theoretical philosophy, for he thought that our most fundamental beliefs cannot be proved by reason. But on practical matters he was more humane, cautious, and even conservative, appealing to (what he took to be) the well-known empirical facts about human beings, as evidenced by common sense, history, and anthropology. He gave an essentially humanist account of ethics and politics, in terms of our tendencies to benevolence as well as selfishness, our liability to emotions and our ability to moderate them by thought. He supported a gradual, progressive reform and development of human society.

In all this, Hume made no use of theological concepts. He was one of the first thinkers to attempt a social scientific account of religious belief and practice in his *Natural History of Religion*. He critically examined traditional arguments for the existence of God, especially the argument from apparent design, in his *Dialogues Concerning Natural Religion*—but such thoughts were far too controversial to be published in his own lifetime. In maturity Hume enjoyed fame as a central figure of the Scottish Enlightenment, along with Adam Smith and Thomas Reid. Yet his reputation as an atheist excluded him from appointment to a Chair of Philosophy in Edinburgh University, which he so richly deserved. He died in philosophic calm, with no expectation of an afterlife.

Rousseau (1712–1778)

In eighteenth-century France there emerged a group of radical thinkers who put their faith in the application of reason to human affairs. These so-called *philosophes* included Voltaire, Diderot, d'Alembert, Rousseau, and Condorcet. Under the prevailing French regime of absolute monarchy, aristocratic privilege, and the Catholic Church, such thinking was highly subversive. Voltaire was a deist (i.e., he believed in a God who created the universe, but does not intervene thereafter), but others were outright atheists, which was a new thing in European thought. Some were explicit materialists, notably Baron D'Holbach and de la Mettrie, who argued in *L'Homme Machine* that human beings are biological machines, made of nothing but matter. The *philosophes* had what we can in retrospect call a naive faith in the power of human reason to reform human affairs, which was severely tested by the violent aftermath of the French Revolution.

Jean-Jacques Rousseau, born in the city-state of Geneva, was one of the most influential thinkers of the Enlightenment, but he was an eccentric and atypical figure in many ways, especially in his appeal to instinctual feeling more than pure reason. In his *Discourse on Inequality* (1755), he argued for the basic goodness of human nature, offering a speculative history of the emergence of human society from primitive origins. He claimed to show how the growth of what is called "civilization" has corrupted people's natural happiness, freedom, and morality, and allowed unnatural, unjust inequalities to develop.

In his treatise on education entitled *Emile* (1762), Rousseau presented his idealistic vision of the essential goodness of human nature in the form of a detailed plan for how a boy could be brought up by a super-wise, all-controlling tutor (from infancy up to marriage). For all the impracticality of this scheme (coming from a man who consigned his own illegitimate children to orphanages!), Rousseau displayed insights into child development that have been very influential. He insisted that children are not miniature adults and should not be treated as such: their upbringing and education should be tailored to their particular mental stage. His prescription is basically that each individual should be allowed to develop his own innate nature, uncorrupted by society—especially by the wealthy, urban, fashionable society, which Rousseau so strongly felt was thoroughly corrupt. In one of his typically exaggerated sentences, he wrote that "human institutions are one mass of folly and contradiction."

Rousseau's writing has a kind of eloquence that many have found persuasive, and his influence is still with us in the widespread—but questionable—assumption that whatever is "natural" must therefore be good. "Oh man!" he wrote, "live your own life and you will no longer be wretched. Keep to your appointed place in the order of nature and nothing can tear you from it." This may sound great, but what counts as "one's own life," and what is "man's appointed place in the order of nature"? Rousseau does not seem to reckon with the thought that selfishness, rivalry, bitchiness, aggression, and bullying also seem to be very natural to human beings, perhaps even innate to them. And for all his progressiveness, he still treats girls and women as subordinate to the male sex (see the end of *Emile*).

In the section of *Emile* entitled "Profession of Faith of a Savoyard Priest," Rousseau expressed his attitude to religion. He defended belief in a deist conception of God and in an immaterial soul endowed with free will. But he was skeptical about the claims of revealed religion put forward by religious authorities and preferred instead a (rather naive) faith in the infallibility of each person's conscience as a guide to good and evil. For this he was condemned by both French Catholicism and Genevan Calvinism; he narrowly escaped arrest and had to live in exile for much of the rest of his life. Though he may have hoped to find a middle way between the irreligious French *philosophes* and authoritarian Christianity, Rousseau did not satisfy either. But his insistence on the natural equality of all human beings, and that "true worship is of the heart," was to influence many, including Kant. And his emphasis on the importance of human feeling was a precursor to the Romantic movement of thought that took over from the Enlightenment in the nineteenth century.

7

Kant: Reasons and Causes, Morality and Religion

LIFE AND WORK

Immanuel Kant (1724–1804) is generally recognized, along with Plato and Aristotle, as one of the three greatest philosophers of all time. He spent all his life in the small Prussian city of Königsberg, on the eastern edge of European culture. (Since 1945 it has been called Kaliningrad, in a sector of Russia on the Baltic Sea.) Kant is typical of much Western thought in inheriting the twin influences of Christianity and science, and in seeing a fundamental philosophical problem in how to combine the two.

The Christian inheritance includes the conceptions of God as omniscient, omnipotent, and benevolent, and of an immortal human soul endowed with free will and a strong sense of morality. A more specific influence on Kant came from the Pietism of his parents. Pietism was a radical spiritual movement within Lutheranism that emphasized personal devotion and right living above dogmas, creeds, and ritual. Although he soon rejected the exclusiveness of the Pietist movement, something of its ethos is expressed in Kant's late philosophy of religion.

On the scientific side, Kant soon acquired a thorough knowledge of the theories of his day. He understood the fundamentals of Newton's mathematical physics and regarded it as the paradigm of natural science. He himself contributed to science as a young man when he developed the nebular hypothesis, the first account of the origin of the solar system by accretion of the planets from clouds of dust. In the late eighteenth century, the chemical revolution—the second main stage of modern scientific development—was under way, and Kant used some examples from chemistry in his own philosophy. He predated the Darwinian revolution in biology, of course, so what he says about "teleology" (purposiveness in nature) needs rethinking in light of the theory of evolution by natural selection.

Kant also had a well-grounded humanistic education, embracing Greek and Latin philosophy and literature, European philosophy, theology, and political theory. At university, he was educated in the German rationalist tradition stemming mainly from Leibniz (1646–1716), who believed that pure reason could prove certain striking metaphysical claims, e.g., that God exists and orders the world for the best, and—less conventionally— that everything is made up of elementary minds called "monads." Kant's early ("precritical") writings waver between the competing influences of metaphysical rationalism and empirical science, but in his mature work he achieved a remarkable synthesis.

Kant was surely the deepest thinker of the European Enlightenment. He believed in the potential for human reason to improve the human condition (using "reason" in a wider sense than philosophical rationalism, to mean science and its social applications). One philosopher who made a special impression on the development of Kant's thought was Rousseau, the maverick of the French Enlightenment. Rousseau's ideas (see the preceding Historical Interlude) on human nature, culture, education and history, the importance of moral feeling, and the unimportance of metaphysical theology were absorbed by Kant into his own thinking.

The works of Kant's mature "critical" philosophy were published in the closing decades of the eighteenth century. His major writings are the *Critique of Pure Reason* (1781); *Groundwork* (or *Foundations) of the Metaphysics of Morals* (1785); *Critique of Practical Reason* (1788); *Critique of Judgment* (1790); *Religion within the Boundaries of Mere Reason* (1793); and *The Metaphysics of Morals* (1797). (References to the first *Critique* use the A and B page numbering of its first and second editions; references to the rest are to the volume and page number of the Prussian Academy edition.) None of these is easy reading, for Kant's thought and writing are formidably abstract and bristle with technical terms.

He also wrote some brief, stylish essays for the educated public on such topics as "What Is Enlightenment?" "Idea for a Universal History with

Cosmopolitan Intent," and "Perpetual Peace." He wanted to be not just an academic philosopher, but an influential progressive thinker as well. In some of his more popular essays, Kant expressed regrettably racist views that were characteristic of his time, but there is some evidence that he modified these views as his thought developed.

Kant repeatedly expressed his belief in the free, democratic use of reason to examine everything, however traditional, authoritative, or sacred: such reasoning should appeal only to the uncompelled assent of anyone capable of rational judgment. He argued that the only limits on human reason are those that we discover when we scrutinize the pretensions and limitations of reason itself: thus, human reason can provide its own self-discipline by philosophical reflection. The word "critique," which Kant made so much his own, means for him this self-conscious inquiry into the powers and limitations of the human mind. He thus made epistemology, the study of what we can and cannot know, the heart of philosophy. He applied his critical method, in turn, to science and metaphysics, to ethics, to judgments of beauty and of purpose, and to religion.

In old age, when his international reputation was well assured, Kant got into trouble with his government. For most of his life he had benefited from the comparatively liberal rule of Frederick the Great, king of Prussia, but after that monarch's death a more reactionary regime took over. Its censors detected an unorthodox tendency in Kant's *Religion* and forbade him to publish any more on the subject. There was no question of drinking hemlock, like Socrates—yet it was their alleged subversion of state-approved religion that got both philosophers into conflict with those in power. (There are still places where such things can happen.) Kant's response was wily, if not conspicuously courageous: he gave a promise to obey, but worded it so that he felt bound only for the lifetime of Frederick William II, whom he managed to outlive.

METAPHYSICS AND THE LIMITS OF KNOWLEDGE

The impact of science on Kant is obvious and deep. One fundamental theme of his philosophy was to explain how scientific knowledge is possible. He developed a theory of human cognitive faculties, which showed how science depends on certain fundamental presuppositions, e.g., that every event has a cause and that something (substance) is conserved through every change. He argued that these principles cannot be proved by mere observation (they are a priori rather than a posteriori), but nor are they mere tautologies (they are synthetic rather than analytic). Kant argued that they can be shown to be necessary conditions of any self-conscious, conceptualized perceptual experience of an objective world.

The first half of the *Critique of Pure Reason* sets out Kant's elaborate theory of the two forms of intuition, i.e., our way of perceiving everything in space and time, and the twelve categories, i.e., the fundamental forms of thought with their associated concepts such as substance and causation. He thus offers an account of how we have three kinds of knowledge. The vast majority of our knowledge is empirical (a posteriori—i.e., it is justifiable only by perceptual experience), including geography, history, and the sciences. Some knowledge (in logic and mathematics) is *analytic*, i.e., provable by pure reasoning, involving definitions. But—and here Kant makes his controversial claim—some fundamental knowledge is *synthetic a priori*, namely, the previously mentioned presuppositions of science. (He later tried to include the fundamental principles of moral and aesthetic judgment under this heading too.) Kant also claimed that most of mathematics, apart from merely logical inferences, belongs in this third box, because he thought geometry and arithmetic involve an appeal to our "intuition" of space and time. However, many other philosophers would locate mathematics in the second (analytic), box.

Kant had a strong sense of the reality of the material world and of the objectivity of the knowledge provided by science. He rejected Berkeley's subjective idealism, according to which matter cannot exist unperceived. For Kant, material things and all the objects of physical science exist independently of being perceived by anyone (see, for example, his talk of "magnetic matter" at A226/B273). But it has to be admitted that he sometimes wrote in a way that seems to deny this doctrine. He felt it necessary to qualify his commitment to realism, and he offered a double-barreled thesis combining "empirical realism" with "transcendental idealism"—an elusive doctrine that has puzzled his interpreters ever since.

One persuasive insight behind Kant's transcendental idealism is his realization that although material objects exist independently of our thought and perception, the *way* we perceive and think of them depends not only on what there is out there to affect our sense organs, but *also* on how those inputs are processed through our minds. (We need not presuppose a dualist theory here; we can think of mental processes as instantiated in the brain.) Some individual differences can be found in perceptual processing, e.g., someone with a defective retina may be color-blind, unable to discriminate colors that most people can; and it has recently been shown that a few people are unable to recognize other people by their faces, due to an abnormality in their brain processing. Kant was more concerned with what is common to all normal humans but may be peculiar to the human *species*. For example, we see colors and hear sounds, but this is due to the way our sensory apparatus processes the incoming light radiation and air vibrations. Other creatures may not experience the same colors and sounds in response to the same input.

Kant conceived of the more radical and mind-boggling possibility that our "a priori forms of intuition," our way of perceiving things in space and time, may systematically distort our representation of what exists, so that we can only know the world "as it appears" to us, not "as it is in itself." Thus—perhaps!—things "as they are in themselves" may not be in space or in time. Maybe only a divine being, endowed with what Kant called "intellectual intuition," can perceive the world as it really is. Another way he expressed this thought is in his proposal for a "Copernican revolution" in philosophy, in which "objects must conform to our cognition" (Bxvi ff.). But that phrase may be misleading, for it seems to imply that some properties of objects are produced by the nature of our human faculties, whereas all that seems justified is that *the ways in which we perceive and conceptualize* objects depend on our cognitive faculties.

Kant sometimes re-expresses his talk of things as they appear and as they are in themselves (i.e., two aspects of the same set of things) as a distinction between appearances and things in themselves (which sound like two sets of things). He also uses the terms "phenomena" and "noumena" for what may or may not be the same distinction. We do not need to plunge any further into these murky waters here, but later we will find Kant making a rather different use of the appearance/thing-in-itself distinction about human action.

In the second half of the *Critique* (the Dialectic), Kant diagnoses how and why human reason tries to go beyond the limits of its legitimate use. We tend to claim illusory metaphysical knowledge of things as they are in themselves (human souls, the universe as a whole, uncaused events, and God). Such claims have long been central to theology and to Western philosophy, but they go beyond the bounds of human knowledge set out in Kant's Analytic. His view is that although we can formulate and understand such metaphysical assertions (they are not meaningless, as the logical positivists of the twentieth century claimed), we can neither prove nor disprove them; we cannot even acquire probable evidence for or against them.

This makes a decisive break with the tradition of natural theology (by no means dead, even now), which tries to offer rational proofs, or empirical, quasi-scientific evidence, for the existence of God. But there has long been a "fideist" vein in religious thinking—exemplified in such different thinkers as Augustine, al-Ghazali, Pascal and Kierkegaard—which says that faith goes beyond reason from the very beginning. At first sight, Kant would seem to fit into that tradition, saying that theological propositions are a matter for faith rather than knowledge. Whether this is the whole story, we shall see.

THEORY OF HUMAN NATURE: REASONS, CAUSES, AND FREE WILL

The overarching agenda of Kant's philosophy was to reconcile the claims of morality and religion with scientific knowledge. He hoped to paint one big (though complicated) picture, giving human nature its appropriate place within physical nature. Let us go back to his account of human cognitive faculties, near the beginning of the first *Critique*:

> Our knowledge springs from two fundamental sources of the mind; the first is the capacity for receiving representations (receptivity for impressions), the second is the power of knowing an object through these representations (spontaneity in the production of concepts). Through the first an object is *given* to us, through the second the object is *thought*. . . . To neither of these powers may a preference be given over the other. Without sensibility no object would be given to us, without understanding no object would be thought. Thoughts without content are empty, intuitions without concepts are blind. (A50–51/B74–75)

Kant was here developing a theory of knowledge that reconciles the one-sided views of his rationalist and empiricist predecessors (above all, Leibniz and Hume). Perceptual knowledge depends on the interaction of two factors: sensory states caused by physical objects and events outside the mind, and the mind's activity in organizing these data under concepts and making judgments that are expressible in sentences. Animals have the first capacity ("sensibility"), but they lack the second ("understanding"), for they do not use anything like human language. They perceive prey, predators, mates, and offspring, but they do not have concepts, they cannot *say* that anything is a predator, a lover, or a child. Animals can feel pain, and they can be in states of arousal such as lust or aggression, but they cannot say (or even think) that they are in pain, randy, angry, or afraid.

Kant thus can be seen as building on Aristotle's distinctions between plants, animals, and humans (see Chapter 5). But in the light of recent evidence about animal mentality, we may have to allow that the gulf between ourselves and primates or dolphins may be less absolute than we used to think. (And, of course, human infants and those suffering from dementia lack the mental powers of normal adults.) But the existence of shades of gray does not eliminate the difference between black and white: there remains a very clear distinction between the conceptual, linguistically expressible capacities of normal humans and anything that most other animals can do.

There is a further depth in Kant's account of our cognition, in his stress on "reason." Although he sometimes seems to use this term as just another name for the understanding, a special role for reason emerges when he points out that we do not just make lots of particular judgments about facts in the world; we try to integrate all these bits of knowledge into a consistent and unified system. For instance, we often want to know *why* something happens, so we try to explain one fact, or one regularity, in terms of others. At the beginning of the Dialectic (A299/ B355 ff.), and at the end (A642/B670 ff.), Kant gives an elaborate theory of how our faculty of "reason" leads us toward ever-increasing systematization of our knowledge under general laws or principles. He has in mind the scientific search for a unified theory of all natural phenomena.

There is also a vital *practical* dimension to Kant's conception of reason (again echoing Aristotle). We are not merely perceiving, judging, and theorizing beings; we are *agents*—we do things, we affect the world (and each other, and indeed ourselves) by our actions. In this respect too we resemble but transcend the animals. Obviously they often "act" very effectively—in one sense—in hunting, fleeing, mating, constructing nests, and caring for offspring. But they cannot *say* what they are doing, so we cannot credit them with intentions to bring about such-and-such a state of affairs. We may say that the cat is trying to catch a mouse, of course, but there is nothing in the cat's behavior to justify attributing to it the concept of "mouse" rather than food, or prey, or rodent, or small animal, or something exciting! There will be *causes* of animal behavior in their internal drives and external perceptions, but since animals cannot say what they doing, they cannot give *reasons* for it, let alone discuss reasons for and against doing it.

Kant sketches the general conceptual framework of human actions in Chapter II of the *Groundwork* at 4:413, and in the opening sections of the *Critique of Practical Reason* at 5:19 ff. He makes a famous and crucial distinction between hypothetical and categorical imperatives. Some of our reasons for action involve only our own desires (and factual beliefs). Such reasons can be expressed in the general form:

I want B, and I believe that A is the best way to achieve B (i.e., in the circumstances, it is—probable—that *if* A happens, then B will result), therefore I should do A (i.e., it is rational for me to do A—this "should" is not moral, just rational).

This is what Kant, in his ponderous way, labels a "hypothetical impera-tive" (Aristotle called it a "practical syllogism"). But he insists that not all reasons for action take this form, which involves only the selection of a means to satisfy one's own desire. For we sometimes accept an obligation, a moral "ought," a reason for action that we conceive of as holding irrespective of our self-interested desires (and may even go against them). Examples include: any context in which lying would be to one's advantage but where one thinks one ought to tell the truth never-theless; a "Good Samaritan" situation in which one encounters someone in manifest need of urgent help; and any case in which one admits the claims of justice, e.g., fair shares in cutting the available cake. In such cases, Kant says that we recognize the validity of what he calls a "cate-gorical imperative" taking the form:

In this situation, I ought to do C, whatever my own desires may happen to be.

Such categorical imperatives involve what Kant calls "pure" or "a pri-ori" practical reason. His claim is that morality is fundamentally a func-tion of our reason, not just our feelings (as empiricist moral philosophers like Hume would have it). He gives some very abstract formulations of this claim, but at bottom his appeal is to our experience of moral obliga-tion, our (often uncomfortable) awareness of the tension between our de-sires and what we accept as the demands of morality. Kant had learned from Rousseau a deep respect for ordinary moral feeling, and in the first *Critique*, which contains some of the most abstruse philosophizing ever, he modestly added:

. . . in regard to the essential ends of human nature even the highest phi-losophy cannot advance further than the guidance that nature has also con-ferred on the most common understanding. (A831/B859)

Kant's analysis of human cognitive faculties seems to me basically cor-rect. But the large question that arises is, what metaphysics of human na-ture makes these distinctive mental capacities possible? Here the going gets difficult and controversial. Kant's official line on the issue of dual-ism against materialism was that we *cannot know* what we are "in our-selves." In the "Paralogisms" section of the Dialectic, he argues that the traditional metaphysical arguments of "rational psychology" (e.g., in Plato and Descartes) cannot prove the existence of an incorporeal soul. We can only know ourselves as we appear to ourselves in introspection ("inner sense") and to each other as embodied human beings perceived by "outer sense." But Kant insisted that we cannot prove that we are merely material beings either (A379, B420). In his characteristic fashion, he leaves the metaphysical question open. However, his own preference comes out when he rejects "a soulless materialism" (presumably he had in mind Hobbes or de la Mettrie) and suggests—though as a matter of faith, rather than knowledge—that we can survive death and live on into an infinite future (B424–26).

Kant was a rock solid believer in human freedom and moral responsibility. He saw humans as free, rational beings who can make choices that are not predetermined; above all, we are capable of acting on moral reasons, not just on self-interested desires. He dismissed the "compatibilist" account of free will offered by empiricists such as Hobbes and Hume, according to which a "free" action is simply an action caused by the agent's own desires and beliefs, as "a wretched subterfuge" (second *Critique*, 5:96). Kant's view was that human actions cannot be reduced to physical causation and that they involve choices that are not themselves caused.

His proffered solution to his "Third Antinomy" (the apparent contradiction between free will and determinism) is that insofar as we are "appearances" (i.e., perceptible biological bodies in motion), we are just as causally determined as everything else in the physical world, but insofar as we are rational beings who act for reasons, we can be free (A549/B577 ff.). He backs up this claim with a distinction between our "empirical" and "intelligible "characters:

> . . . for a subject of the world of sense we would have first an empirical character, through which its actions as appearances would stand through and through in connection with other appearances in accordance with constant natural laws . . . second, one would also have to allow this subject an intelligible character, through which it is indeed the cause of those actions as appearances, but which does not stand under any condition of sensibility and is not itself appearance. The first one could call the character of such a thing in appearance, the second its character as a thing in itself. (A539/B567)

It sounds as if he means that all the physical states and changes of our bodies—including the movements of our limbs and lips, the circulation of the blood, the excitation of neurons in the brain, the flow of hormones—would count as our empirical character. Presumably our beliefs, desires, hopes, fears, intentions, and emotions would count as our intelligible character. It is then tempting to say that although the former are subject to universal determinism through the causal mechanisms investigated by physiology, talk about reasons for actions involves a *rational, noncausal* relation between beliefs, desires, and possible actions. For example, if someone wants a beer and believes there is beer in the fridge, that gives the person a reason to go to the fridge. Anyone can see that obvious connection without knowing anything about brain functioning. And it is worth noticing that the rational relation is to a *possible* action, for that belief and desire still constitute *a reason* for going to the fridge, even if the person does not in fact make any such move (perhaps this individual has some *other* reason against doing so, such as laziness, asceticism, or morality—if he or she knows it's someone else's beer).

The distinction between reasons and causes, rational explanation and causal explanation, is surely an essential part of any adequate account of human action, and we are in Kant's debt for opening up this topic (albeit somewhat obscurely). If materialism (in the form sometimes called "physicalism") implies that there is only *one* valid kind of explanation—that of giving physical causes—then Kant gives us good reason to reject such a reductive thesis. But it remains open for us to say that human beings are *made* entirely of matter, and that we have here a dualism of conceptual systems (reasons and causes) rather than a dualism of substances. Kant seems closer to Spinoza than to Descartes—though he might not welcome the comparison!

Making these distinctions does not entirely resolve the free will problem, however. At A534/B562 Kant declares that "freedom in the practical sense is the independence of the power of choice from necessitation by impulses of sensibility" (i.e., bodily based desires). He believes that human choice has this degree of freedom: although we feel the *influence* of our desires, our choices are not *determined* by them. Just before that, he claims that this practical freedom is grounded in the "transcendental" idea of freedom, i.e., an uncaused choice. But the absence of necessitation by *sensuous* impulses is not the same as the absence of *any* sort of cause. Can't we say, in the case of prudentially or morally motivated actions, that *nonbodily* desires are among the causes? Could A's desire not to put on weight cause her refusal of the chocolate cake, or could B's desire to respect A's right to say no cause him to desist from further sexual advances? Can't our choices have *rational* causes—in our combinations of beliefs and desires—while still being free? Whether Kant is prepared to accept that version of compatibilism, is unclear.

Here we surely need to distinguish two senses of reasons, connected with an ambiguity in the notion of beliefs and desires. In one sense, two people can have the same belief and desire—when they believe the same proposition and desire the same thing—and they can thus have the same reason for action. In another sense, only *my* belief and desire—i.e., my present state of believing and desiring—can motivate my action (how could someone else's mental states motivate *me*?). Reasons in the sense of people's mental states can cause action, whereas reasons in the sense of propositions are not the sort of thing that can be causes at all.

Reasons in the latter, propositional sense are not states or events in time—which may help us interpret Kant's puzzling statement that "this acting subject, in its intelligible character, would not stand under any conditions of time" (A539/B567). This may also explain why he thought he could apply his distinction between (temporal) appearances and (nontemporal) things in themselves to the case of causes and reasons. However, the alleged unknowability of things in themselves does not apply in this case, for we surely know our own reasons for action, as Kant acknowledges when he says at A546/B574 that "the human being . . . knows himself through pure apperception, and indeed in actions and inner representations which cannot be accounted at all among impressions of sense." What we have here seems to be a contrast not of the knowable and the unknowable, but of two different ways of knowing.

Does Kant solve the free will problem, then? I cannot answer this question here, except to note that in Chapter III of the *Groundwork* (4:450 ff.) he distinguishes "two points of view," by which we can regard ourselves as belonging to the sensible world of appearances, or to the intelligible world of reasons and laws (he presumably meant moral rather than scientific laws here). A little earlier (4:446), he offers a distinctively practical defense of freedom. When one is making up one's mind what to do, reviewing reasons for and against various options, one cannot at the same time think of one's decision as already determined. However much one may be impressed by theoretical arguments for determinism, there is no escaping the necessity to arrive at a decision here and now, and one is (sometimes painfully) aware that the relevant reasons do not make the decision for one. As Kant puts it, we have to act "under the idea of freedom"—from the practical point of view, we are already free.

DIAGNOSIS: SELFISHNESS AND SOCIALITY

We have seen how Kant emphasizes the distinction between self-interested inclinations and moral duty. He contrasts our human nature with the animals on one side, and with the conception of a "holy will" on the other. Animals feel no tension between desires and duty, for they do not have the concept of duty. A rational being who had no self-interested desires (an angel?) would also not experience any such tension, but for an opposite reason: not being subject to temptation, they would always do the right thing. But we human beings are mixed creatures, mid-way between animals and angels. We are finite beings with our individual needs—and these include not just physical desires, but emotional needs or drives for love, approval, status, and power. Yet we are also rational beings, and for Kant that includes "pure practical reason," the recognition of moral obligations. The tension between these two sides of our nature is an inescapable feature of the human condition. We can never achieve moral perfection.

Some philosophers have asked how anyone can *ever* be motivated to do his or her duty, to fulfil a moral obligation when it goes against self-interested desires. "Why be moral?" the skeptic asks, and seems to expect some justification in self-interested terms. I think Kant does not see such skepticism as a real issue; he just presupposes what he takes to be the universal and necessary fact that we all accept the validity of some moral obligations or other (although we may disagree about what they are in particular cases).

It is relevant here to point out a distinction that Kant makes *within* the class of self-interested reasons—namely, between desires for immediate satisfaction and considerations of prudence, i.e., longer-term self-interest. One can resist the allure of the third glass of wine, an item of designer clothing, or a seductive tempter, for the sake of one's longer-term health, wealth, or happiness. Our mixed nature is also manifested in our ability to recognize prudential reasons and to act on them—at least sometimes! We all need to be able to postpone the satisfaction of desires in the interest of longer-term goals. To be unable to do this, e.g., in addiction, is to be reduced to an almost animal level. Any child needs to start learning at an early age to postpone gratification. But it is a difficult matter, which we each have to negotiate in our own way, what balance to strike between living for the moment and planning for the future.

In his works of ethical theory, Kant tends to present his view in an apparently very severe guise that suggests that the only motivation he really approves of is a grim determination to do one's duty irrespective of one's own inclinations. He may seem to imply that if one is naturally inclined to look after one's children, tell the truth, or help someone in distress, that does not make the actions admirable and might even *detract* from their moral value (*Groundwork* 4:398). But wider and more careful reading of Kant dispels this common misinterpretation. He *is* concerned to encourage virtues as traits of human character: the more that people develop mental dispositions to do the right things, the better. Kant's point is that as rational beings we are not mere bundles of inclinations; we have reasons for our actions, and the general principles presupposed by our reasons can be made explicit as "maxims" and can be morally assessed. It is not enough for us to bring about good states of affairs in the world: virtue depends on inner motivation: we must act for the right reasons. This is what is meant by describing Kant's ethics as "deonto-logical" as opposed to utilitarian ethics, which concentrates on produc-ing good results. As Kant famously put it at the beginning of the *Groundwork*, the only thing that is unconditionally good is a good *will*.

But how can we measure up to the demands of Kantian morality? In his late work, *Religion within the Boundaries of Mere Reason*, Kant wres-tles with the most profound problems of human nature and suggests some new insights, or new versions of old ones. He talks of the "radical evil" in human nature. He acknowledges the "frailty" of human nature—our difficulty in doing what we know we ought to do—and our "impurity," i.e., our tendency to confuse or adulterate moral reasons with other mo-tives. But for Kant, what is radically evil is not our naturally given de-sires, nor is it the tension between these and duty. It is rather the "depravity" of human nature—the freely chosen *subordination* of duty to inclination, the deliberate preference for one's own happiness (as one con-ceives of it) over one's obligations to other people (6:19 ff.).

This is a place where Kant, along with so many other thinkers (such as Augustine and Pelagius), is pulled in two directions. On the one hand, he insists that the evil in us is a result of our own choice, our wrong use of our freedom. But on the other hand (in his version of the doctrine of orig-inal sin), he wants to say that evil is "radical" or innate in us; it is a uni-versal and unavoidable feature of our condition as needy but rational beings:

> There is in the human being a natural propensity to evil; and this propen-sity itself is morally evil, since it must ultimately be sought in a free power of choice, and hence is imputable. This evil is *radical*, since it corrupts the ground of all maxims; as natural propensity, it is also not to be *extirpated* through human forces. . . . Yet it must equally be possible to *overcome* this evil, for it is found in the human being as acting freely. (*Religion* 6:37)

Kant's position is *not* that radical evil must attach to every rational but finite, needy creature: our needs as finite beings involve our animal na-ture, which Kant regards as innocent. Nor does he attribute a predisposi-tion to evil to our rational nature, which would make us devilish beings. Rather he thinks that radical evil attaches to our predisposition to rational self-love as a result of human development under social conditions.

This is another Rousseauian aspect of Kant's doctrine: the "unsocial sociability" of human beings, i.e., our need and inclination to be mem-bers of a human society, combined with our tendency to be selfish and competitive. Paradoxically, Kant's thesis that we are by nature evil amounts to much the same thing as Rousseau's assertion that we are by nature good (there was a rather similar debate within the Confucian tradition; see the end of Chapter 1). For the phrase "by nature" is used by the two philosophers in opposing ways: Rousseau means "prior to the social condition," and he thinks that social development has corrupted original human nature, whereas Kant thinks that our truly human nature can be expressed only in society; he doesn't believe there is such a thing as a presocial, yet *human*, condition.

PRESCRIPTION: PURE RELIGION AND CULTURAL PROGRESS

How are right intentions and virtuous dispositions to be achieved and encouraged? It is not enough just to formulate a theory of what pure practical reason requires, universalizing the "maxims" behind our actions, applying them to all rational beings and treating each person as an end "in himself" (as Kant does in *Groundwork* Chapter II and in the second *Critique*). Nor is it enough to state more specific moral rules or their application in particular cases (as Kant does in his late work *The Metaphysics of Morals*). For as Plato and St. Paul saw, it is one thing to recognize an obligation and another thing to do it. Philosophizing and moralizing notoriously have limited effects on human conduct!

There are very practical problems here for parents, teachers, social workers, legislators, and social reformers about how people can be taught and encouraged to develop virtue. Kant has things to say about such questions (not all of his writing is at the level of abstruse theory). The most obvious response is to offer rewards or threaten punishment, but that does not produce Kantian virtue, for it amounts only to putting new self-interested reasons in place. That may (or may not!) induce outward conformity to rules, but it cannot create the virtuous inner attitude, the will to do the right action *just because it is right*. Kant does not look on moral blame and praise as mere external incentives like a slap or a sweet. Rather they are ways of "sharing in the reason of one another"; they are part of distinctively moral discourse, involved in moral education. They are intended to *convince* or *remind* someone about what is right or wrong.

Kant's answer to the problems of human nature shares the ambiguity of his diagnosis. The preceding quotation from *Religion* suggests that only a religious answer will suffice: for if the evil in us cannot be "extirpated through human forces" yet needs to be "overcome," believers will be quick to say that only God's salvation (in their recommended version) can do the trick. Much of Kant's mature work—including the later sections of all three *Critiques*—touches on religious themes. A first glance may suggest that this might be mere conventional piety, artificially tacked on to his serious philosophical work. But more careful reading shows his understanding of religion to be serious, even if it departs from Christian orthodoxy—which is why the Prussian censorship tried to hinder the publication of his thought.

In Chapter III of the Dialectic of the first *Critique*, Kant classifies all theoretical arguments for the existence of God into three kinds: the ontological (from the very concept of God), the cosmological (from the supposed necessity of a creator), and the "physico-theological" (from what seems to be intelligent design in the world). He examines each argument in detail, and his criticisms of them are clearly and vigorously expressed. Hume had already criticized the design argument in his *Dialogues Concerning Natural Religion*, but an original aspect of Kant's treatment is his claim that the design argument presupposes the cosmological, which in turn depends on the ontological. So if Kant is right, his demolition of the latter brings down the whole house of metaphysical cards.

But Kant destroys only to try to rebuild on a different, practical basis. Although propositions about God, immortality, and free will cannot be proved (or disproved) by the theoretical use of reason, he suggests that they can be justified from a practical point of view. When we are thinking of how to *act*, different sorts of consideration are relevant. The idea of our own freedom is directly presupposed in our deliberations about what to do (as noted earlier). But what about God and immortality— where do they come in (if they have to come in at all)? Kant endeavored to explain his "moral theology" in the Method section of the first *Critique*, in the Dialectic of the second, in sections 86–91 of the third, and in the *Religion*.

At A805/B833 Kant distinguishes three questions that sum up "all the interests of reason, speculative as well as practical":

1. What can I know?

2. What ought I to do?

3. What may I hope?

The first question is discussed in depth in the first *Critique*. The second is treated in the *Groundwork*, the second *Critique*, and other ethical works. The third (glossed as "If I do what I ought to do, what may I then hope?") introduces a new topic, somewhat neglected in recent philosophy, which is both theoretical and practical. Kant's philosophy of history and of religion come under this heading of hope.

In the Dialectic of the second *Critique* he gives his fullest exposition of his practical argument for belief in God and immortality. He is deeply concerned about the relation between virtue and happiness ("If I do what I ought to do, what may I then hope?"). Ancient Stoicism maintained that virtue is the highest good, whereas Epicureanism said that it is happiness. Once again, Kant offers a third, synthesizing, view. We have seen how he holds that we must not be concerned *merely* for our own happiness, yet he is unwilling to disconnect virtue from happiness completely, so he argues that the "highest good," the ultimate end of all moral striving, must be the *combination* of virtue and happiness (rather like Aristotelean *eudaimonia*).

It is painfully obvious, however, that virtue is not always rewarded with happiness in the world as we know it. All too often, the good suffer and evildoers seem to flourish. It is an obvious step—which millions of people have taken—to say that justice requires there to be a God, who knows the secrets of all human hearts, and who will reward everyone appropriately in a future life beyond this world. It may seem that in invoking God and immortality Kant is doing no more than repeating this common human hope for justice and reward in a life after death. But, as we have seen, it is fundamental to his moral philosophy that our motive for doing our duty should *not* be to reap benefit thereby, so it would be quite inconsistent for him to postulate rewards beyond death in order to motivate right action.

And yet, Kant claims, we need to be able to hope that virtue will eventually be rewarded. His case seems to be that our very motivation for moral action would be undermined unless we can at least believe that the highest good, the combination of virtue and happiness, is possible. We are not to aim directly at it for ourselves, but we need to have *hope* for happiness—we have to assume that doing the right thing is not ultimately pointless. But does this really need belief in the traditional metaphysical assertions about God and immortality? In the second Critique, Kant offered some rather shaky arguments for this, but in the *Religion* he tends to back off from such claims, at least in their traditional interpretations, e.g., when he says of the notions of heaven and hell that they are "representations powerful enough . . . without any necessity to presuppose dogmatically, as an item of doctrine, that an eternity of good or evil is the human lot also objectively" (6:69). He writes that "religion is (subjectively considered) the recognition of all our duties as divine commands"; and that "faith needs only the *idea of God* . . . without pretending to secure objective reality for it through theoretical cognition" (6:154, footnote). It seems that we can take the "as" in "recognition of our duties as divine commands" as the entertaining of a certain picture, rather than literal belief in the existence of a super-natural person.

Speaking of the struggle between "the good and the evil principles," by which Kant meant personifications of good and evil in Christ and Satan, he says:

> It is easy to see, once we divest of its mystical cover this vivid mode of representing things, apparently also the only one at the time *suited to the common people*, why it (its spirit and rational meaning) has been valid and binding practically, for the whole world and at all times: because it lies near enough to every human being for each to recognize his duty in it. Its meaning is that there is absolutely no salvation for human beings except in the innermost adoption of genuine moral principles in their disposition. . . . (*Religion* 6:83)

Such "demythologizing" language worried the eighteenth-century Prussian censors, and it unsettles Christian orthodoxy even today. And we are less inclined than Kant (and Plato) to distinguish what is believ-able by an educated elite and by "the common people." Kant's approach is to reinterpret theology in terms of morality. He suggests that the scrip-tures should be interpreted in this way, even if that is not their literal meaning. There is, in his view, no need for belief in miracles or sacra-ments. Yet he saw a need for a radically reformed church, a human in-stitution that will set forth ethical ideals and help its members to live up to them. He hoped that what is rationally and morally acceptable in the various "ecclesiastical" faiths (both Christian and non-Christian) could be gradually separated from what is unnecessary, and formed into a "pure religious faith" (see the *Religion* Parts III and IV).

Kant also expressed more this-worldly hopes in his essays on history, which paved the way for the philosophies of Hegel and Marx in the next century. He envisaged continued progress in human culture through educa-tion, economic development, and political reform, gradually emancipating people from poverty, war, ignorance, and subjection to traditional authori-ties. He was a supporter of the egalitarian and democratic ideals of the French Revolution, though aware of its excesses. In his essay *On Perpetual Peace*, he sketched a world order of peaceful cooperation between nations with democratic constitutions. (He would surely be delighted with the achieve-ments of the European Economic Community, for all its faults.)

The status of Kant's historical hope is rather unclear, however. In his essay "Idea for a Universal History with a Cosmopolitan Purpose" (1784), he appeals to a conception of what "Nature" intends for human progress. He thinks there is an overall trend in history that theorists can discern, although it goes beyond all the specific intentions that people have: they are "unconsciously promoting an end which even if they knew what it was, would scarcely arouse their interest." Thus the "unsocial sociability" of human beings, i.e., our social yet competitive nature, is "the means employed by Nature" to produce a law-governed social order, in which human talents and powers can be fully developed.

But this conception of Nature's design or will is unstably poised between belief in God's providence—which Kant presumably did not mean to endorse (otherwise why wouldn't he have used the traditional theological language?)—and an obscure belief in Nature as having "designs" that are not the conscious intentions of any rational being, divine or human. At any rate, Kant sets out the idea of progress toward an ever-greater fulfilment of human potential as an *ideal* to aspire to. It can encourage our *hopes* and inspire a sort of social *faith*. Its status for Kant thus seems to be like that of the concept of God.

Kant was in all this an Enlightenment thinker, but unlike many others of that time (and since), he had a vivid, realistic sense of the dark side of human nature, our potentiality for evil—which has been amply confirmed since his time. His practical philosophy leaves us with a combination of hope for gradual social progress and a more religious vision that holds out hope for divine grace in the transformation of our fallen, selfish human nature.

FOR FURTHER READING

For a short introduction to Kant's thought, see Roger Scruton, *Kant* (Oxford University Press 2001)—a little gem of compressed insight. A more comprehensive introduction is Otfried Hoeffe, *Kant* (Albany: State University of New York Press, 1994). A still more comprehensive introduction, combined with some judicious critical appraisal, is Paul Guyer, *Kant* (London Routledge, 2006). For a clear introduction to the ethics, see Roger J. Sullivan, *An Introduction to Kant's Ethics* (Cambridge: Cambridge University Press, 1994).

For those brave enough to start reading Kant for themselves, the usual starting points are his two formidably titled shorter works, *Groundwork for the Metaphysics of Morals* and *Prolegomena to any Future Metaphysics*. Some may like to look at Kant's *Religion within the Bounds of Reason Alone*—there is a recent translation by George di Giovanni, with an introduction by Robert. M. Adams, published by Cambridge University Press.

Easier reading for those more interested in the social aspects of Kant's thought can be found in *Kant on History*, edited by L. W. Beck (Indianapolis: Bobbs-Merrill, 1963), or *Kant's Political Writings*, 2nd ed., edited by H. Reiss (Cambridge: Cambridge University Press, 1991).

Allen Wood, in *Kant's Moral Religion* (Ithaca, N.Y.: Cornell University Press, 1970), defends Kant's account of religion. Wood has also contributed a chapter on this topic in *The Cambridge Companion to Kant*, edited by Paul Guyer (Cambridge: Cambridge University Press, 1992). I have a paper comparing Kant's approach to religion with that of Quakers, in *Kant and the New Philosophy of Religion*, edited by Chris. L. Firestone and Stephen. R. Palmquist (Bloomington: Indiana University Press, 2006).

8

Marx: The Economic Basis of Human Societies

Our image of Marxism is strongly colored by our knowledge of the rise and fall of communism in Russia and Eastern Europe in the twentieth century. We may also be influenced by what we have heard about China (where Marx's influence has now dwindled to almost zero), Cuba, and North Korea. However, this chapter will be about the theories that Karl Marx developed in the mid-nineteenth century, rather than Leninist, Stalinist, or Maoist practice. Marx himself cannot be held directly responsible for the failings and atrocities of the communist regimes that came to power after his death.

If Kant was the deepest philosopher of the eighteenth century Enlightenment, Marx was the greatest critical theorist of the Industrial Revolution and nineteenth-century capitalism. Although hostile to religion, Marx inherited an ideal of human equality and freedom from Christianity, and he shared the Enlightenment hope that scientific method could diagnose and resolve the problems of human society. Behind his elaborate historical, social, and economic theorizing was a prophetic, quasi-religious zeal to show the way toward a secular form of human salvation.

MARX'S LIFE AND WORK

Marx was born in 1818 in the German Rhineland, of a Jewish father who, under the discriminatory laws of the time, had to convert to Christianity to be able to practice as a lawyer. The young Karl displayed his intellectual ability early, and in 1836 he enrolled in the Law Faculty of the University of Berlin. There was a ferment of philosophical, aesthetic, and social ideas in the Romantic movement of that time, into which Marx eagerly plunged. He learned languages, wrote poetry, and worked on a dissertation on ancient Greek metaphysics while also getting deeply concerned about social reform.

At that time the dominant influence in German thought was the philosophy of Hegel, and Marx became so immersed in it that he abandoned his legal studies. Hegel's main inspiring idea was progress in human history through stages of mental and cultural development. He interpreted historical progress in terms of his peculiar conception of *Geist*, i.e., Mind or Spirit in the world as a whole, thus reinterpreting theological language with a meaning closer to pantheism or humanism. The whole sweep of human history was seen as the progressive self-realization of *Geist*, with increasing consciousness or self-awareness. Successive eras of human social life involved increasingly adequate ideas of reality; each stage of society contains conflicting tendencies, but lays the basis for a fuller development of consciousness and freedom at the next stage.

Hegel also developed an influential conception of "alienation" in which the knowing subject is confronted with an object other than and unknown to ("alien to") himself. The distinction or opposition between subject and object is supposed to be "overcome" as the subject gets to know the object. According to Hegel, the processes of mental and cultural development will arrive at a stage in which there is "absolute" knowledge: and he seems to have thought that his own era had more or less achieved it! (In that he differed from Kant, who said that we cannot have knowledge of things as they are in themselves, and we never achieve moral perfection either.)

The followers of Hegel split into two camps over how his ideas applied to society, politics, and religion. The "Right" Hegelians held that the processes of history had already led to the full development of human potential, so they saw the contemporary Prussian State as almost ideal and were conservative in politics. But the "Left" or "Young" Hegelians held that the highest form of human freedom had yet to be realized, that European society of the time was very far from ideal, and that it was up to people to help change the old order and bring about the next stage of human development. Accordingly, they looked for radical reform or revolution.

One of the most important thinkers in the latter group was Ludwig Feuerbach, whose groundbreaking book *The Essence of Christianity* was published in 1841. Feuerbach argued that Hegel had gotten things upside down, that far from God or *Geist* progressively realizing Himself in history, religious ideas and beliefs are produced by human beings as a pale reflection or idealization of life in this world, which is the fundamental reality. People become "alienated" in that they project their own human potential into theological fantasies and undervalue their actual lives. Feuerbach diagnosed metaphysics and theology as "esoteric psychology," i.e., the expression of our own feelings in the disguised form of obscure claims about the universe. So he saw religion as a symptom of human alienation, from which we must free ourselves by realizing our destiny in this world. This was a forerunner of the sociological or psychological explanations of religion offered by Marx, Durkheim, and Freud. Marx's reading of Feuerbach broke the spell that Hegel had cast on him, but he retained the idea that Hegelian philosophy contained truth in an inverted form. He saw it as his mission to "put Hegel right way up" by expressing the real, material, truth about human nature and history.

Marx wrote a critique of Hegel's *Philosophy of Right* in 1842–43 and became the editor of a radical journal that was suppressed by the Prussian government, and he fled to Paris. In 1845 he was expelled from France and moved to Brussels. In these formative years Marx encountered the other great intellectual influences of his life: his wide reading included the French socialist Saint-Simon and the Scottish philosopher-economist Adam Smith. The latter had analyzed the workings of capital, wages, and trade in his famous book *The Wealth of Nations* in 1776, written in an earlier generation when Britain was just starting to industrialize. Marx also debated with other pioneering socialist and communist thinkers such as Proudhon and Bakunin, and began his lifelong collaboration with Friedrich Engels.

In the 1840s Marx and Engels began to formulate their "materialist conception of history," which saw the driving force of social change as material rather than mental. The key to human history, they claimed, lay not in mere *ideas*—and certainly not in God or a cosmic Spirit—but in the *economic* conditions of life. Alienation is at root neither metaphysical nor religious, but social and economic. Under the capitalist system labor is something alien to the laborer in that he does not work for himself but for someone else—the capitalist—who directs the process and owns the means of production, and the product, as private property. The capitalist aims to maximize his profits and tends to exploit his employees by paying them only the minimum wage necessary for their physical survival. This conception of human alienation under capitalism is most vividly expressed in the "Economic and Philosophical Manuscripts" that Marx wrote in Paris in 1844, but which remained unpublished for a century. The materialist conception of history was asserted in *The German Ideology* of 1846 (coauthored with Engels) and in *The Poverty of Philosophy* of 1847.

Marx became involved with organizing the international communist movement, for he saw the purpose of all his work as "not just to interpret the world, but to change it." Convinced that history was moving toward the revolution by which capitalism would give way to communism, Marx worked to educate and organize the "proletariat"—the class of industrial workers who had to sell their labor in order to survive, and to whom he thought victory in the class struggle must eventually go. Together with Engels he wrote the *Manifesto of the Communist Party* in 1848, deploying his rhetorical skills to famous effect. In that very year there were abortive revolutions in several European countries, but they were soon defeated, and Marx had to find exile in Britain, where he remained for the rest of his life.

In London Marx lived a life of comparative poverty, existing on journalism and gifts from Engels (who, ironically, came from a factory-owning family himself). He pursued systematic research in the Reading Room of the British Museum, where he was able to use the already extensive documentation about conditions in British industry. In 1857–88 he wrote another extensive set of manuscripts, the *Grundrisse*, sketching a plan of his total theory of history and society, the complete text of which was not available in English until the 1970s. In 1859 he published the *Critique of Political Economy*, and in 1867 the first volume of his magnum opus, *Capital*. These works contain a mass of detail on economic and social history, deployed to support Marx's materialist interpretation of history and the inevitability of communism.

It is these later works (from the *Communist Manifesto* onward) that have become best known. In them we find German philosophy, French socialism, and British political economy—the three main influences on Marx—welded into an all-embracing theory of history, economics, sociology, and politics. This is what Engels came to call "scientific socialism": for Marx and Engels claimed to have discovered the correct *scientific* method for the study of human society, and thus to be able to establish the objective truth about its present workings and future development.

The publication in the twentieth century of Marx's *Economic and Philosophical Manuscripts* of 1844 has shown the origins of his thinking in Hegelian ideas and the early German reactions to them. So the question has been raised whether there were two distinct periods in his thought—an early phase that has been called humanist or existentialist, giving way to "scientific socialism." However, there is a continuity between these two phases: the theme of human alienation under capitalism and the hope for salvation from it is still there in the later "scientific" work.

THE MATERIALIST THEORY OF HISTORY

Marx was an atheist, and the general trend of his thought was materialist and determinist. He presented himself as a social scientist, aiming to treat all human phenomena by the methods of science as he understood them. But this is not peculiar to Marx: the same applies to many thinkers of the Enlightenment, such as D'Holbach, de la Mettrie, and Hume.

What is distinctive of Marx is his claim to have found the truly scientific method for studying the *economic history* of human societies. In his early philosophizing, he looked forward to the day when there would be a single science, including the study of man along with natural science. But any such unified science would obviously have to include many levels, including physics, chemistry, biology, psychology, and sociology. Marx implicitly compared his theory to physics when he said (in the preface to the first edition of *Capital*) that "the ultimate aim of this work is to lay bare the economic law of motion of modern society"; and he wrote elsewhere of the natural laws of capitalist production "working with iron necessity towards inevitable results." But these are verbal flourishes (Marx was a great rhetorician); the detail of his theorizing does not show that he was a *reductionist* materialist, or a strict determinist. He did not expect every single fact about human individuals or societies to be explained in terms of physics (or brain science). Rather, he looked for general socioeconomic laws applying to human history. The most fundamental feature of Marx's worldview is this "materialist" theory of history. He applied this both synchronically, as an explanation of social structure and functioning, and diachronically, as an explanation of social change.

Synchronically, the economic base is supposed to determine the ideological superstructure. Marx would dismiss what rich and powerful people say in defense of capitalism as mere "ideology," consciously or unconsciously motivated by their own economic interests. He would say that liberal economic philosophy, with its rhetoric of "freedom" of enterprise and trade, is merely an expression of the self-interest of those fortunate enough to possess land, property, and capital. (In a strictly "liberal" system, those without such advantages would be left "free to starve" if the labor market does not provide them with a job.)

But even if we think there is something in this suspicion of capitalist "ideology," we should not allow Marx to have things all his own way.

As we saw in the introduction to this book, we cannot rationally allow any theorist to assume the truth of his own theory when he tries to diagnose irrational motives behind those who disagree with him—that is a circular procedure. If Marx himself is allowed to offer what he claims to be good, rationally persuasive, reasons for his own theory, others must have an equal chance for theirs. A liberal economic philosophy (which many inaccurately ascribe to Adam Smith,) deserves a proper, rational hearing and critique. Ideas and opinions may well be *biased* by economic influences (and many others), but it does not follow that they are totally determined by them.

Marx tended to say that legal and political systems were in the hands of the capitalists, who controlled the economic processes of production. But that leaves it unexplained how government regulations have limited at least the worst excesses of early capitalism—for example, by banning child labor and passing laws about the health and safety of workers. Marx would have to retreat to saying that law and politics are affected, but not totally controlled, by the capitalist class. (This is not an empty or out-of-date claim, considering the influence of industrial lobbyists.)

Diachronically, there are long-term processes of technological and economic development that eventually result in large-scale social, political, and ideological change. Marx divided history into epochs identified by their different economic bases. First there were primitive tribes, then the Asiatic system of absolute monarchy, the ancient world of Greece and Rome (with slavery), the feudal system of the Middle Ages (with peasants tied by obligations to their feudal lord), and most recently, the bourgeois or capitalist phase (with industrial workers having to sell their labor). Marx held that each stage had to give way to the next when the technological and economic conditions were ripe. (Adam Smith had already distinguished four main stages: hunters, shepherds, farmers, and manufacturers.)

The best-known summary of the materialist theory of history is in the preface to Marx's *Critique of Political Economy* (1859):

> In the social production of their life, men enter into definite relations that are indispensable and independent of their will, relations of production which correspond to a definite stage of development of their material productive forces. The sum total of these relations of production constitutes the economic structure of society—the real basis, on which rises a legal and political superstructure, and to which correspond definite forms of social consciousness. The mode of production of material life conditions the social, political, and intellectual life process in general. It is not the consciousness of men that determines their being, but, on the contrary, their social being that determines their consciousness. . . .

In some expositions of Marxism, this has been taken as saying that the economic basis of a society determines *everything* else about it. But Marx writes here only of the foundation "conditioning" social life (or, as another translation puts it: "determining its *general* character"), not of the determination of every detail. He could admit the influences of nationalism, religion, wars, and of particular charismatic characters such as Caesar, Napoleon, and Lenin. There is no realistic prospect of treating history as an exact, quantitative science like physics, and Marx was under no illusion about that.

Everyone now recognizes that economic factors are hugely important, and no serious study of history or social science can ignore them. Marx can take much of the credit for the fact that we now acknowledge this. However, the preceding quotation is difficult to interpret, for there is an ambiguity about where to make the dividing line between foundation and superstructure. Careful attention to the whole passage suggests that Marx meant to distinguish *three* levels rather than two. He talks (a) of "the material powers of production," which would include natural resources (land, climate, plants, animals, minerals), technology (tools, machinery, communication systems), and human resources (labor power and skills). He talks (b) of the "economic structure" as including "relations of production," which presumably means the way in which work is organized, e.g., the division of labor, hierarchies of authority in the workplace, the legal powers of ownership, the systems of rewards and payments. The description of these relations of production, at least in modern societies, involves both the legal concept of property and economic concepts like money, capital, and wages. And he talks (c) of the ideological superstructure of a society, i.e., its beliefs, morality, laws, politics, religion, and philosophy.

What, then, did Marx mean by "the real basis" or "foundation"? Is it (a) alone or (a) plus (b)? Is he saying that (a) determines (b), and thereby (c)? Or that (b) alone determines (c)? Or that (a) plus (b) together determine (c)? If he meant that the basis includes only (a), the strictly material powers of production, he would be committed to a thesis of "technological determinism." But this seems implausible, since similar natural resources and technologies can surely be used in societies with different ideologies or legal systems, e.g., Christian, Islamic, or secular capitalist, socialist, or communist. If the basis is (a) plus (b), which is said to determine (c), there is the difficulty that the legal concept of property seems to belong in (c), yet it also seems to be part of (b).

An answer to the latter objection may be that Marx could have given an account of level (b), the social relationships involved in economic production, in terms of actual relations of physical power and effective control without using legal concepts of property, contracts, etc. After all, he wants to apply his theory to primitive societies that lack the formalities of law, but where it may be very clear who has control over resources and people! Even in our own society, there are times and places where personal power, asserted with force or the threat of it, is stronger than legal niceties.

It is also open to Marx to maintain a double-barreled determining or "conditioning" thesis: first, that (a), the material powers of production, condition or limit (b), the relations of production (e.g., the hand-mill fits into the feudal structure, but large machinery such as the steam mill requires capitalism); secondly, that (a) and (b) together ("the economic structure") condition or limit (c), the ideological superstructure. If talk of "conditioning" or 'limiting" does not mean the determining of every last detail, then Marx can avoid the objection that the same technology can be used in different societies; he can just say that those societies must have some relevant features in common. A modern example would be that widespread use of computer technology requires a certain standard of education for most members of society, with all the social and political implications of that.

But this raises the question of what Marx's talk of "conditioning" or "corresponding to" really amounts to. How much determinism did he wish to assert, synchronically or diachronically? Obviously, any society has to produce the necessities of life, to provide for individual survival and reproduction. We have to eat if we are to act or think, but it does not follow that how we produce what we eat determines everything that we do or think. The plausible thing to say—and it seems to be what Marx did say, when he was careful—is that the economic basis has a very significant influence on everything else: it sets limits within which the other factors play their part. The way a society produces the necessities of its life *may* influence how its people characteristically think. But the trouble is that this is *vague*, for it is left open what counts as "significant" or "important" influence. In the end, we seem to have merely a recommendation to seek out the economic factors in each particular case, and to examine how far they influence the rest. But that has proved an immensely fruitful methodology in historiography, anthropology, and sociology.

History is an empirical study in that its propositions must be tested by evidence of what actually happened. But it does not follow that it is a *science*, in the sense of involving *laws of nature*, i.e., generalizations of unrestricted universality. For history is after all the study of what has happened in human societies on this particular planet, in a finite period of time. The subject matter is one *particular* series of events. We know of no similar histories elsewhere in the universe—nor can we do experimental reruns of historical events!

Now for any particular series of events—even the fall of an apple from a tree—there is no limit to the number of different laws and contingent facts that may be involved in its causation—e.g., the laws of gravity and mechanics, the weather and gusts of wind, the decay of wood and the elasticity of twigs, shakings of the tree by animals or birds, or tweaking by human fingers. If there is no closed system of influences (and hence no overall determinism) governing even the fall of a single apple, how much more implausible it is to say that the course of human history is predetermined. There are some long-term and large-scale *trends*, e.g., the increase of human population and the development of ever more complex technology. But trends are not laws of nature: their continuation is not inevitable, but may depend on conditions that can change. (Population growth and technological development may be reversed by war, disease, famine, or environmental catastrophe.)

From his general understanding of history Marx predicted that capitalism would become more and more unstable, that the class struggle between the owners of capital and the proletariat would increase, with the latter getting both poorer and larger in number, until in a major social revolution they would take power. However, he did not make any definite predictions of communist revolution in the countries where capitalism was most developed, namely, Britain, France, and the United States. In the *Communist Manifesto* he pointed to Germany, still semifeudal at the time, as a place where he expected a bourgeois revolution to be shortly followed by a proletarian one. In some of his journalism, he suggested that communism might be first achieved in China. And he saw that communist ideas could be imported into countries where a relatively small proletariat, allied with impoverished peasantry, could seize power from the traditional ruling class. In a war-ravaged Russia, the Bolsheviks under the leadership of Lenin did just that in October 1917, half a year after a bourgeois revolution had deposed the last Czar.

About Russia and China, Marx seems to have been roughly right in predicting communist revolution, if not its subsequent vicissitudes. (We can hardly count the imposition of Soviet rule in Eastern Europe by the Red Army at the end of the Second World War as a proletarian revolution.) But there has been no revolution in the advanced capitalist countries. The capitalist economic system has on the whole become more stable (with notable exceptions, such as the Great Depression of the 1930s; we have yet to see what the twenty-first century holds in store). Conditions of life for most people have improved vastly on what they were in Marx's time, and class divisions have blurred rather than intensified. There are now large numbers of white-collar workers such as office staff, government employees, medical staff, teachers, and lawyers, and these are neither manual laborers nor industrial owners.

The nonoccurrence of communist revolutions in Western Europe and the United States would seem to be a major falsification of Marx's theory of history. It cannot be explained away by saying that the proletariat have been "bought off" by concessions of higher wages—for Marx predicted their lot would get *worse*. Unrestrained nineteenth-century capitalism as Marx knew it, with its dreadful conditions for the working class, including child labor, epidemic diseases, and shortened life, has largely ceased to exist in the West (though it is a different story elsewhere). Through indirect investment, e.g., in pension funds, many people now have some small share in the ownership of capital (though not in its control).

It may be suggested that colonies and underdeveloped countries have in effect formed the proletariat vis-à-vis the industrialized countries, and that even now we are benefiting from the exploited agricultural labor and sweatshops of the third world. Some countries (e.g., in Scandinavia) have not had colonies, but their economies have presumably benefited from the patterns of world trade. Perhaps Marx should have paid more attention to slavery. In Britain and America it was not just those who owned slaves who profited from them; the system of slavery contributed to economic development, and we are still benefiting from that.

THEORY OF HUMAN NATURE: ECONOMICS, SOCIETY, AND CONSCIOUSNESS

Except in his early studies of Hegel and the Greeks, Marx was not interested in questions of academic philosophy, which he would later dismiss as idle speculation compared to the vital task of changing the world. So when he is labeled a materialist, this refers to his materialist theory of history rather than to a position in the philosophy of mind about the relation between the mind and the brain. Even if we take him as saying that all states of consciousness are determined by the economic foundations of society, this could be an "epiphenomenalist" position, saying that our mental states, although nonphysical, have their *contents* determined by material events. Marx was not interested in any metaphysically materialist view that consciousness is to be literally identified with brain processes.

What is more distinctive of Marx's concept of humanity is his view of our essentially *social* nature. In one place he even wrote that "the real nature of man is the totality of social relations." Apart from obvious biological facts such as our bodily makeup, our need to eat, and our urge to reproduce, Marx would say that there is no such thing as a fixed human nature—for what is true of people in one society or period may not be true in another place or time. Indeed, he remarked that "all history is nothing but a continuous transformation of human nature." Whatever a person does is an essentially social act, which presupposes the existence of other people. Even the ways in which we produce our food and bring up our children are socially learned. Economic production typically requires cooperation. This does not mean that society is an abstract entity that mysteriously affects individuals: rather, what kind of things one does are affected by one's interactions in the society one lives in. What seems "instinctive" or "natural" in one society or epoch—for example, a certain role for women—may be quite different in another.

We can summarize this crucial point by saying that sociology is not reducible to psychology. Not everything about human beings can be explained in terms of facts about individuals; the kind of society they live in must be considered too. This methodological point is one of Marx's most distinctive contributions, and one of the most widely accepted. For this reason, he is recognized as one of the founding fathers of sociology. And this method can be accepted whether or not one agrees with the particular conclusions he came to.

But there is at least one universal generalization that Marx does offer about human nature. This is that we are *active*, productive beings, we are different by nature from the other animals because we *produce* our means of subsistence. And we do not do this like bees producing honey, for we make conscious plans for how to produce our livelihood in new situations: it is natural for human beings to plan and work for their living. No doubt there is a factual truth here, but (as with so many assertions about what is "natural" for human beings) Marx also associates a value judgment with it, namely, that the kind of life that is *appropriate* for us involves purposive productive activity. This is implicit in his diagnosis of alienation in industrial labor, and in his prescription for a future society in which everyone can be free to cultivate his or her own talents.

What does Marx's theory imply about the female sex? If there is a point in his concentration on production, there is surely also a truth about the necessity for *reproduction*. Obviously no society can survive unless it can produce new members to carry it on. But we must recognize that that includes not just sexual intercourse, pregnancy, and childbirth ("labor" in *that* sense of the word!), but the longer processes of child care, education, and socialization—which are laborious in their own way and can involve men! In *The Origin of the Family, Private Property and the State*, Engels (writing, for once, without Marx) argued that economic production determines *both* kinds of production: labor and the family. But on the whole Marx was a man of his time, assuming that the traditional division of family roles has a "purely physiological foundation," with women being almost totally responsible for child care. It seems he did not realize that what he thought of as biologically determined differences between the sexes are themselves affected by socioeconomic factors. Technical developments like reliable contraception, formula milk for babies, and economic changes that require mental skills more than manual labor have transformed the question of male and female "nature" in ways that Marx himself did not foresee, but which his theory has resources to deal with.

DIAGNOSIS: ALIENATION AND EXPLOITATION UNDER CAPITALISM

Marx's diagnosis of what is wrong with people and society was expressed in his early writings in terms of his concept of alienation or estrangement, derived from Hegel and Feuerbach. This involved both a description of certain features of capitalist society and a value judgment that they are wrong. But Marx does not make it clear exactly *which* features he is criticizing. He was not, after all, totally condemnatory of capitalism: he acknowledged that it leads to a great increase in productivity and would thus make communism economically possible. He believed that capitalism is a necessary stage through which society has to go, but he thought that it will be (and ought to be) surpassed.

Logically, alienation is a relation—it must be *from* somebody or something; one cannot be just "alienated," any more that one can be married without being married to someone. Marx wrote in one place that alienation is "from man himself and from Nature." For him, "Nature" seems to mean the *humanly made* world (the opposite of its usual meaning!), so presumably he thought that people are not what they should be because they are alienated from the products they create and from the social relations involved in production. They do not care about either, except as a means to earning a wage. People without capital have to sell their labor in order to survive and can therefore be exploited by the captains of industry, who can dictate the terms of their employment.

Sometimes it sounds as if it is private property that Marx primarily condemns: in one place he wrote that "the abolition of private property is the abolition of alienation." But elsewhere he said, "Although private property appears to be the basis and cause of alienated labor, it is rather a consequence of the latter." Marx describes this alienation of labor as consisting in the fact that the work is not part of the worker's nature; he does not fulfil himself in his work, but feels miserable, physically exhausted, and mentally debased. His work is forced on him as a means for satisfying his basic needs, and at work he does not "belong to himself"— he is under the control of other people. Even the materials he uses and the objects he produces are alien to him because they are owned by someone else.

Sometimes Marx seems to be blaming alienation on the use of money, as a means of exchange that reduces all social relationships to a common commercial denominator—"callous cash payment," as he put in the *Manifesto*. In that context he was making a contrast with feudal society, in which there were nonmonetary economic relationships—though no doubt those could be callous in their own way! Elsewhere he suggests that it is the division of labor that makes work an alien power, preventing people from switching from one activity to another at will (as Marx implausibly suggested everyone will be able to do in future society).

What then *is* Marx diagnosing as alienation? It is hard to believe that anyone can seriously advocate the abolition of money (and a return to a system of barter?), the end of all specialization in work, or the communal control of everything (even toothbrushes, clothes, books, etc.?). It is the private ownership of *industry*—the means of production and exchange—that is usually taken as the defining feature of capitalism. The practical program of the *Communist Manifesto* includes the nationalization of land, factories, transport, and banks. But it seems unlikely that state control of these can cure the alienation of labor that Marx describes in such psychological terms in his early works. (Were not people just as alienated under communist rule in the Soviet Union?) If it is the *state* that is the basis of social evils (or one main cause of them), nationalization might make things worse by increasing the power of the state.

The competitiveness of life under capitalism conflicts with the ideal of solidarity with other human beings. So we might try to understand Marx as saying that alienation consists in a lack of *community*, so that people cannot see their work as contributing to a group of which they are members, since the state is too large to be a real community. Such a diagnosis may suggest decentralization into "communes," in which the abolition of money and private property might look more realistic. But the feasibility and desirability of this is contentious on economic grounds, for how could the kind of worldwide production and distribution on which we have now come to depend be organized in a society of independent communes? The technologies of the Internet, however, may offer some new opportunities here.

In his later work, Marx offered a more direct diagnosis of the evil of capitalism (though the notion of alienation did not entirely disappear from his writing). He developed a "labor theory of value" and a concept of "surplus-value" appropriated by the owners of industry. Using these more technical terms, he condemned the exploitation of the class who have to sell their labor by the much smaller class of people who own capital. These concepts have been much discussed in economic theory, and I will not go into them here. Marx's main diagnosis was always a moral one, about the *injustice* of the economic structure of capitalism.

Surprisingly perhaps, there is some agreement here between Marx and Adam Smith. The pioneering Scottish economist has often been hailed as the apostle of capitalism and economic liberalism, advocating unfettered competition as not merely the most efficient but also the most moral foundation for modern society. But Smith was a moral philosopher at least as much as an economist, and he too was alarmed about the tendency for the developing capitalist economy to impoverish its working class:

> No society can surely be flourishing and happy, of which the far greater part of the members are poor and miserable. It is but equity, besides, that they who feed, cloath and lodge the whole body of the people, should have such a share of the whole produce of their own labour as to be themselves tolerably well fed, cloathed and lodged. (*The Wealth of Nations* 96)

And even when material needs *were* met, mental or spiritual needs were not. Human potential remained sadly unrealized:

> We find that in the commercial parts of England, the tradesmen are for the most part in this despicable condition: their work thro' half the week is sufficient to maintain them, and thro' want of education they have no amusement for the other but riot and debauchery. (*Lectures on Jurisprudence* 540)

So Smith was also worried about alienation—though not under that name. And we are hardly free of these worries, even now (*plus ça change. . .*).

There is a more general diagnosis here, which would perhaps command universal assent: that it is wrong to treat any person as only a means to an economic end (remember Kant's formulation of the moral law always to treat rational beings as ends in themselves). Human beings were treated as mere means of production in the unrestrained capitalism of the early nineteenth century, when adults and children worked long hours in filthy conditions and died early deaths after miserably unfulfiled lives. This still happens in some countries; and even in the advanced nations where capitalism is so often trumpeted as a stunning success, there is a constant tendency for managers to try to extract the greatest possible profit from the labor of their employees, driving down wages, cutting the workforce, or extending working hours. The latest trend is to relocate business to a country where labor is much cheaper and legal regulations weaker.

The idea that remains significant is that capitalist society restricts the full development of human potential and encourages the exploitation of the masses by those who own or control capital. These days Marx could well say that "alienation" affects not merely manual laborers, but all those who have to work under competitive economic pressures. The average employee, whether in small businesses, large corporations, or government agencies, whether cleaner, machine minder, pen pusher, keyboard clicker, software programmer, salesperson, or middle manager, may feel "alienated" from his or her human potential by the conditions of the workplace, and is liable to exploitation by the system. Even the self-employed businessperson and those at the top of the economic system, such as the executives, bank officers, and government administrators, may feel constrained by forces outside their control. Sometimes the most worrying thought is not so much that the wrong people are in control, but that nobody is in control.

Perhaps we can express Marx's main point in a paraphrase of Jesus' saying about the Sabbath: human beings do not exist for the purpose of production, rather production is supposed to be for human benefit. And this should apply to *all* the people involved—employers, employees, consumers, and anyone affected by side effects such as pollution. The huge practical difficulty is, of course, how to give social effect to this ideal.

PRESCRIPTION: REVOLUTION AND UTOPIA

"If man is formed by circumstances, these circumstances must be humanly formed." If alienation and exploitation are social problems caused by the nature of the capitalist economic system, then the solution is to abolish that system and replace it by a better one. Marx thought that this was bound to happen anyway: capitalism would burst asunder because of its inner contradictions, and the communist revolution would usher in the new social order. Rather in the way that Christianity claims that God's salvation has been enacted for us, so Marx claimed that the resolution of the problems of capitalism is already on the way in the movement of history, and our responsibility is to align ourselves with it.

His view on the metaphysical question of free will is rather ambiguous. His overall view obviously sounds determinist, yet there seems to be an irreducible element of human freedom left, since Marx appealed to people both to realize the direction in which history is moving and to *act* accordingly and help bring about communism. Within the Marxist movement there were controversies between those who emphasized the need to wait for the appropriate stage of economic development before expecting revolution, and those (like Lenin) who proposed to act decisively to bring it about. But perhaps there is no contradiction here, for Marx could say that while the revolution is bound to occur sooner or later, it is possible for prescient individuals and organized groups to hasten its coming and "ease its birth pangs."

Marx held that only a complete revolution of the capitalist economic system could properly solve its problems. Limited reforms such as higher wages, shorter hours, pension schemes, etc., may be welcome ameliorations of the harshness of capitalism, but they do not alter its basic nature. Hence the basic difference in aim between the Communist Party and most trade unions and democratic socialist parties. But again, followers of Marx have disagreed about political strategy. Some thought that working to reform the system may distract attention from the class struggle and the need to *overthrow* the existing order. Others said the very process of arousing workers to combine together to fight for reform will "raise their consciousness," create class solidarity, and thus hasten revolutionary change.

In fact, a long series of piecemeal reforms *have* modified capitalism very considerably, beginning with the British Factory Acts in the nineteenth century, which limited the worst exploitation of workers and children, continuing with national insurance schemes, unemployment benefits, and national health services (in Europe, though not in the United States). Trade unions have made steady progress in increasing real wages and improving working conditions. In fact, many of the specific measures proposed in the *Communist Manifesto* have long since come into effect in the so-called capitalist countries—namely, graduated income tax, free education in state schools, centralization of considerable economic control in the hands of the state, and nationalization of major industries in some countries. The unrestrained capitalist system as Marx knew it in the mid-nineteenth century has ceased to exist in the developed countries—and not by revolution. This is not to say that what we have now is perfect, but it does imply that contempt for gradualist reform is mistaken; and reflection on the violence and suffering involved in revolutions elsewhere may confirm this.

Like Christianity, Marx envisaged a total regeneration of humanity—but he expected it within this world. He described communism as "the solution to the riddle of history," for the abolition of private property is supposed to ensure the disappearance of alienation and exploitation, and the coming of a genuinely classless society. He was extremely vague on how all this would be achieved, but he saw the need for an intermediate period before the transition to true communism, which will require what he called "the dictatorship of the proletariat." Alienation cannot be overcome on the day after the revolution. In a phrase that sounds ominous in the light of twentieth-century history, he wrote that "the alteration of men on a mass scale is necessary"—but in his defense it may be said that he had in mind an alteration of consciousness, not the forcible methods of Soviet Russia. In the higher phase of communist society, the state is supposed to wither away, and the realm of true human freedom will begin. Then human potentiality can develop for its own sake, and the guiding principle can be "from each according to his ability, to each according to his needs."

Much of this utopian vision must surely be judged unrealistic. Marx gave us no good reason to believe that communist society will be genuinely classless, that those who exercise "the dictatorship of the proletariat" will not form a new governing class with many opportunities to abuse their power and develop new forms of exploitation. No set of economic changes can be expected to eliminate *all* conflicts of interest and all feelings of boredom or "alienation" at work. States have not withered away—they have become more powerful; although these days we must also recognize the power of the big corporations and the increasingly global nature of the market, which restricts the power of any one corporation or government.

Yet with other elements in Marx's vision, we can surely agree. The application of science and technology to produce the necessities of life for everybody, the shortening of the working day and the provision of universal education so that all human beings can develop their potential, the vision of a decentralized society in which people cooperate in communities for the common good, and of a society in balance with nature—these are ideals that most people now share, though it is no easy matter how they can be compatibly realized. Probably it is because Marxism has offered this kind of hopeful vision of a human future that it was able to win the allegiance of so many people. Like religions, Marxism has been a secular faith, a prophetic vision of social salvation.

Even now, despite the disputability of some of Marx's theoretical assertions and the failures of the communist regimes of the twentieth century, his ideas are far from dead. But his diagnosis is a good deal more convincing than his prescription. Social reforms and technical developments have altered the face of the capitalist system for the better in many ways, but many people see the need for some limitation on or transformation of global capitalism, to make it serve widespread human needs and not just enrich those who are already rich.

However, the Marxist emphasis on *economic* factors directs our attention to only one of the obstacles in the way of human fulfilment. Sexuality and family relationships are obviously vital, too, as are our existential/religious attitudes to the noneconomic limitations of life, such as moral failure, illness, and mortality. And human conflict—from tribalism to nationalism, nuclear confrontation, and terrorism—seems to involve something more (and darker) in human nature than economic competition. We must look elsewhere—to psychology, existentialism, evolutionary theory, and perhaps to religious conceptions—for deeper insights into the problems of human individuals and societies.

FOR FURTHER READING

There is no one main text by Marx that one can recommend as basic. The *Communist Manifesto* is an obvious starting point, but it is stronger on polemics than on theory, and its third section is dated; the *German Ideology* is deeper and longer, but fairly readable.

There are several useful selections from Marx's extensive writings, such as *Karl Marx: Selected Writings in Sociology and Social Philosophy*, translated by T. B. Bottomore, edited by T. B. Bottomore and Maximilien Rubel (London: Penguin, 1963; New York: McGraw-Hill, 1964)—which is helpfully organized under themes; *Marx and Engels: Basic Writings on Politics and Philosophy*, edited by Lewis. S. Feuer (New York: Anchor Books, 1959); and *Karl Marx: Selected Writings*, 2nd ed., edited by David McLellann (Oxford University Press, 2000).

There are biographies of Marx by Isaiah Berlin, *Karl Marx: His Life and Environment* 3rd ed. (Oxford University Press, 1963); and Francis Wheen, *Karl Marx* (London: Fourth Estate, 1999).

A classic criticism of Marxism was presented by Karl Popper in *The Open Society and Its Enemies*, Vol. 1, 5th ed. (London: Routledge, 1966). There is an in-depth discussion of Marx on human nature in John. Plamenatz, *Karl Marx's Theory of Man* (Oxford University Press, 1975). The religious dimension of Marx's thought is brought out by Robert Tucker, in *Philosophy and Myth in Karl Marx*, 2nd ed. (Cambridge: Cambridge University Press, 1982). For a sophisticated defense of Marx's materialist theory of history using the methods of analytical philosophy, see G. A. Cohen, *Karl Marx's Theory of History: A Defence* (Oxford University Press, 1978). On the relation of Marxist theory to feminism, see Friedrich. Engels, *Origin of the Family, Private Property and the State*; and Alison. Jaggar, *Feminist Politics and Human Nature* (Totowa: Rowman & Littlefield, 1983), Chapter 4. A postcommunist defense of Marx's ideas is given by Keith Graham in *Karl Marx Our Contemporary: Social Theory for a Post-Leninist World* (Toronto: University of Toronto Press, 1992).

There is a very readable recent reevaluation by Jonathan Wolff, *Why Read Marx Today?* (Oxford University Press, 2002); the author addresses the labor theory of value, not discussed in this chapter.

For an introduction to the thought of Adam Smith, see D. D. Raphael, *Adam Smith* (Oxford University Press, 1985); and Athol Fitszgibbons, *Adam Smith's System of Liberty, Wealth and Virtue* (Oxford University Press, 1995).

9

Sartre: Radical Freedom

Jean-Paul Sartre (1905–1980) was a philosopher in two senses. He had a brilliant student career, in his thirties he wrote some strikingly original books, and after the publication of *Being and Nothingness* he was widely recognized as France's leading philosopher. But he was also a very public intellectual who expressed his ideas in novels, plays, and biographical studies, and applied them to the great social and political issues of his time, taking controversially radical stances against the conventional wisdom of the day.

Let me first put Sartre in the context of the development of existentialist thought. Three main concerns are central to existentialism. The first is with *individual* human beings: existentialists tend to think that general theories about human nature leave out precisely what is most important— the uniqueness of each individual and his or her life situation. Second, there is a concern with the *meaning* or purpose of human lives rather than with scientific or metaphysical truths, even if the latter are about human beings. Inner or "subjective" experience is at the center of existentialist attention, rather than "objective" truth. Third, there is a strong emphasis on *freedom,* on the ability of each individual to choose not just particular actions, but his or her attitudes, projects, purposes, values, or lifestyles. And the typical existentialist concern is not just to assert this, but to persuade people to *act* on it, to exercise their freedom.

These themes can be found in a wide variety of contexts, in descriptions of the concrete detail of particular characters and situations in biography or fiction. But to be an existentialist *philosopher* involves some general analysis of the human condition; and the most obvious division is between theist and atheist accounts.

The Danish Christian thinker Søren Kierkegaard (1813–1855) is generally recognized as the first modern existentialist, though there is, of course, an existential dimension to all religions—notably in Paul, Augustine, Luther, and Pascal in the Christian tradition. Like his contemporary Karl Marx, Kierkegaard reacted against Hegel's philosophy, but in a very different direction. He rejected the abstract Hegelian system, likening it to a vast mansion in which the owner does not actually live; Kierkegaard concentrated instead on what he thought supremely important; namely, the individual person and his or her life choices. He distinguished three basic attitudes to life: the aesthetic (the search for pleasure), the ethical (commitment to marriage, family, work, and social responsibility), and the religious (seeing everything in terms of the eternal, the transcendent, the divine). He held that the religious (more specifically, the Christian) way is the "highest," although it can be reached only by a free, nonrational "leap into the arms of God."

The other great nineteenth-century existentialist was a crusading atheist. The German writer Friedrich Nietzsche (1844–1900) argued that since "God is dead" (i.e., the illusions of religious belief have now been seen through), we will have to rethink the whole foundations of our lives and find our meaning and purpose in human terms alone. In this, he had much in common with his earlier compatriot Feuerbach. What is most distinctive of Nietzsche is his emphasis on our radical, unsettling freedom to change the basis of our values. As in other existentialist thinkers, there is a tension between a "relativist" tendency to say that there is no objective basis for choosing or valuing one way of life more than another, and a recommendation of a particular choice. In Nietzsche's case, the latter is expressed in his vision of the "Superman," who will reject our conventional, meek, religiously based values and replace them by the "will to power" (a phrase that acquired sinister connotations in the light of subsequent Nazi history).

In the twentieth century too, existentialism included both religious believers and atheists. There were existentialist theologians such as Marcel in France, Bultmann in Germany, and the Jewish thinker Martin Buber. Existentialist philosophy developed mainly in continental Europe. In the hands of Heidegger and Sartre existentialism became a more academic, jargon-ridden, and system-building style of philosophy. Another source of this was "phenomenology": the philosophical movement started by

Edmund Husserl (1859–1938), who hoped to find a new method for doing philosophy, namely to describe the "phenomena" as they appear to human consciousness. This concern with human experience rather than scientific truth is characteristic of existentialist philosophers (but a less dramatic version of it was also a feature of "ordinary language" philosophy in the English-speaking world, stemming from Wittgenstein's later thought).

The most original and influential of twentieth-century existentialists was Martin Heidegger (1889–1976), whose *Being and Time* was published in 1927. Heidegger's language is strange and difficult: in his attempt to question the fundamental concepts of Western philosophy since Plato, he invented hyphenated neologisms in the German language to try to express his distinctive insights. Although he often seems to be doing abstract metaphysics (like Aristotle), it emerges that he has a central existential concern with the meaning of human existence, our relation to "Being"; and he points to the possibility of "authentic" life through facing up to one's real situation in the world, especially to the inevitability of one's own death. "Being" in Heidegger's writing sounds like an impersonal substitute for God—the ultimate reality of which we can become aware if we attend in the right sort of way. In his later philosophy, there is an emphasis on quasi-mystical kinds of experience that may be expressed in poetry or music but cannot be formulated in literal scientific or philosophical statements.

SARTRE'S LIFE AND WORK

Sartre's philosophy is indebted to Heidegger, but his writing (some of it, at least!) is rather more accessible. He rapidly absorbed the thought of the three German *H*s: Hegel, Husserl, and Heidegger. Many of the obscurities of Sartre's writing can be traced to the influence of those purveyors of ponderous abstractions. Themes from Husserl's phenomenology are prominent in Sartre's first books, the remarkable philosophical novel *Nausea* of 1938 and his studies in the philosophy of mind, *Imagination* (1936) and *Sketch for a Theory of the Emotions* (1940). The centerpiece of his early philosophy is the lengthy and difficult *Being and Nothingness* (1943), strongly influenced by Heidegger's *Being and Time,* but written with Sartre's own French flair.

At the beginning of the Second World War Sartre served as a meteorologist in the French army and soon became a prisoner of war (he spent the time reading Heidegger!). After release he was sympathetic to the French Resistance to Nazi occupation, but devoted himself to writing *Being and Nothingness.* Something of the atmosphere of that time can perhaps be detected in the pessimistic conception of the human condition that he presents in that work. The choice that confronted each French citizen of collaboration, risky resistance, or quiet self-preservation was a very obvious example of what Sartre saw as the ever-present necessity for individual choice. Similar themes are expressed in his trilogy of novels *Roads to Freedom* and in the plays *No Exit* and *Flies*. After the liberation, he gave a stylish account of his atheistic existentialism in *Existentialism and Humanism,* a lecture delivered in 1945 to much public acclaim—but his treatment there is brief and popular, and does not express the depth of his thought.

Sartre rejected the academic career that was then open to him and became a freelance writer and a leading French intellectual for the rest of his life. As time went on, he began to modify the very individualist approach of his early writings, and devoted more attention to social, economic, and political realities. He asserted the need for a classless democratic society if genuine human freedom was to be possible for everyone, and he came to espouse a form of Marxism that he described as "the inescapable philosophy of our time," though needing refertilization by an existentialist account of individual human freedom. He joined the French Communist Party at the time of the Korean war, but left it a few years later when the Soviets invaded Hungary.

The later phase of Sartre's philosophy started with *Search for a Method* (1957) and continued with his second magnum opus, the *Critique of Dialectical Reason*, the first volume of which (concentrating on the French Revolution as a historical case study) appeared in 1960; the second volume (about the Russian Revolution) was published posthumously in 1985. Sartre developed a strong sympathy for the oppressed, both the workers under capitalism and the population of third world countries suffering from colonialism or imperialism. He supported Algeria's violent struggle for liberation from French rule and he campaigned against the American war in Vietnam. He gave a notable lecture on his new approach to ethics in Rome in 1964, and toward the end of his life, unable to write because of his blindness after a stroke, he gave interviews that have since been published. His funeral was attended by some fifty thousand people.

Like that of any other serious philosopher, Sartre's thought was never at rest and cannot be captured in a single system. There is a fairly clear distinction between his early philosophy, which focuses almost obsessively on individual freedom, and the second main phase, which explores the social and economic limitations on human freedom. The former is that for which Sartre became most famous, but now that so much of the latter has been published, we can begin to appreciate him as a more rounded whole. This presents a problem for writing an introduction. I propose to concentrate on *Being and Nothingness* (making page references to the English translation), but I will add a final section giving an outline of Sartre's second phase.

It is only fair to warn the reader that *Being and Nothingness* is far from easy reading. This is a matter not just of length and repetitiousness, but of a word-spinning delight in the technical term, the abstract noun, and the unresolved paradox. Sartre seems to enjoy teasing his readers with obscure, apparently contradictory, or grossly exaggerated statements. The influence of Hegel, Husserl, and Heidegger may explain this, but can hardly excuse it. One does wonder whether he could not have said what he had to say more clearly—and a lot more briefly. Sartre had an extraordinarily self-confident facility to pour out philosophical verbiage onto pages (in Parisian cafés, at the dead of night, so the story goes), but he does not seem to have been so good at self-criticism or editorial revision (legend has it that his manuscripts were delivered straight to the printers from the café tables). There are passages of relative lucidity and insight, however, and the effort to understand his system reveals a view of human nature that has a certain compelling fascination. (At the end of this chapter, I suggest some sections of *Being and Nothingness* to excerpt for a first—or only!—reading.)

METAPHYSICS: CONSCIOUSNESS AND OBJECTS, ATHEISM

The most basic feature of Sartre's system is his radical distinction between consciousness or "human reality" (*etre-pour-soi,* being-for-itself) and inanimate, nonconscious reality (*etre-en-soi,* being-in-itself). These terms are derived from Hegel, but are given new definitions by Sartre in the introduction to *Being and Nothingness*. This distinction may sound like the dualism of mind and body of Sartre's French predecessor Descartes, but it is important to see how different it is. Sartre affirms that a human being is a unified reality ("the concrete is man within the world," p. 3): what he is distinguishing are not two substances or beings, but two modes of being—the way that conscious beings exist is different from the way that inanimate things exist. Sartre understands consciousness as "intentional" in the sense made famous by the Austrian philosopher Franz Brentano: states of consciousness are *of* something conceived as distinct from the subject (p. xxvii), though they also involve an implicit awareness of self (pp. xxviii–xxx). In contrast, being-in-itself (e.g., the mode of existence of rocks, oceans, and tables) involves no awareness *of* anything, and no conception of itself (pp. xxxix–xlii). (What Sartre would say about animal perception and intention is not clear.)

Sartre also distinguishes between reflective (positional, "thetic") consciousness and prereflective (nonpositional, nonthetic) consciousness. All consciousness is "positional" consciousness of something taken to be distinct from the subject. But "every positional consciousness of an object is at the same time a non-positional consciousness of itself" (p. xxix). For example, if I am counting the cigarettes in my case, I am conscious of the cigarettes, and that there are a dozen of them; and I am *prereflectively* conscious that I am counting them (as is shown by the answer I can immediately give when asked what I am doing); but I am not *reflectively* conscious of my activity of counting until someone asks such a question.

Sartre's second most important metaphysical assertion is his denial of the existence of God. (He does not take over the mystical or quasi-religious dimension of Heidegger's concept of "Being," though a posthumously published work called *Truth and Existence* remains closer to the spirit of Heidegger.) Sartre claims that we all fundamentally desire to be God in the sense that we want to "be our own foundation," that is, we would like to be perfectly complete and self-justifying: as he puts it, we aspire to become "in-itself-for-itself" (p. 566). But this ideal, which he identifies with the idea of God, is self-contradictory (pp. 90, 615).

Like Nietzsche, Sartre holds the absence of God to be of the utmost significance; the atheist does not merely differ from the theist on a point of metaphysics, he holds a profoundly different view of human life. In the worldview of *Being and Nothingness*, there are no transcendent objective values set for us—neither commandments of God nor a Platonic Form of the Good. Nor is there any intrinsic meaning or purpose in human existence (no Aristotelean *telos*). In this sense, our life can be described as "absurd": we are "forlorn" or "abandoned" in this world. There is no heavenly Father to tell us what to do or help us do it; as grown-up people, we have to decide for ourselves and look after ourselves. Sartre repeatedly insists that the only foundation for values lies in our own choices; there can be no external or objective justification for the values, projects, and way of life that anyone chooses to adopt (pp. 38, 443, 626–27).

THEORY OF HUMAN NATURE: EXISTENCE AND ESSENCE, NEGATION AND FREEDOM

In one sense, Sartre would deny that there is any such thing as human nature for there to be theories about. This is a typical existentialist rejection of generalizations about human beings and human lives. Sartre expresses it in his formula "man's existence precedes his essence" (pp. 438–39). He means that we have no "essential" nature, we have not been created for any particular purpose, either by God or evolution or anything else, we simply find ourselves existing by no choice of our own and have to *decide* what to make of ourselves, so each of us must create his or her own nature or "essence." Of course, Sartre cannot deny that there are some true generalizations about our bodily nature, for instance; the necessity to eat, our metabolism, and our sexual impulses. But as we noticed when discussing Marx, there is room for dispute about what count as *purely* biological facts. Sartre thinks there are no general truths about what human beings *want* to be: the project of becoming God is only the abstract form of our particular desires, which are many and various (pp. 566–67). Certainly, he holds that there are no general truths about what we *ought* to be.

An existentialist *philosopher*, however, has to make *some* general statements about the human condition. Sartre's central assertion is human freedom. We are "condemned to be free"; there is no limit to our freedom except that we cannot cease being free (p. 439). He derives this conclusion from his understanding of consciousness as *of* something conceived of as distinct from oneself. (Even if one is mistaken in a particular case, as Macbeth was about the illusory dagger, one is thinking of something that one *believes* to exist objectively at a particular position in space.) Sartre sees a connection between consciousness and the mysterious concept of "nothingness" that appears in the title of his book. The subject is aware in a *non*reflective ("nonthetic") way that the object is *not* the subject (pp. xxvii–xxix, 74–75). That is one way in which negation enters into the nature of conscious awareness.

Another way is that many of our judgments about the world are negative in their content; we can recognize and assert what is *not* the case, as when I look unsuccessfully for my friend in the café where we arranged to meet and say "Pierre is not here" (pp. 9–10). If we ask a question, we understand the possibility of the reply being "No" (p. 5). A related point is that we perceive the world as full of *possibilities* for our actions, and this involves our conceiving of states of affairs that are *not* already the case (they are "nothingnesses," in Sartre's rebarbative language), but that we might decide to make real. Desire also involves recognition of the *lack* of something (p. 87), as does intentional action (p. 433 ff.). Thus, conscious beings who can think and say what *is* the case can also conceive of, and act to bring about, what is *not* the case.

Sartre indulges in verbal play with his concept of nothingness, in paradoxical phrases such as "the objective existence of a non-being" (p. 5)—which presumably means that there are true negative statements— sometimes in dark metaphorical sayings like "Nothingness lies coiled in the heart of being—like a worm" (p. 21). The concept of nothingness makes a conceptual connection for him between consciousness and freedom. For the ability to conceive of what is not the case involves the freedom to imagine other possibilities (pp. 24–25) and to try to bring them about (p. 433 ff.). As long as one is alive and conscious, one can always conceive of something being otherwise than it is, and one may desire it to be otherwise (we can never become "in-itself-for-itself"). The mental power of negation thus involves both freedom of mind (to imagine new possibilities) and freedom of action (to try to actualize them). To be conscious is to be continually faced with choices about what to think and what to do.

Sartre contradicts two fundamental Freudian claims. His view is plainly incompatible with complete psychic determinism (p. 458 ff.). He also rejects the postulate of unconscious mental states, for he holds that consciousness is necessarily transparent to itself (p. 49 ff.). But the latter point sounds like mere verbal legislation: of course *consciousness* cannot be unconscious, but Sartre has not shown that it is illegitimate to talk of unconscious states that are *mental* in some wider sense.

Every aspect of our mental lives is, in Sartre's view, in some sense chosen and ultimately our own responsibility. Emotions are usually thought to be outside the control of the will, but Sartre maintains that if I am sad it is only because I choose to make myself sad (p. 61). His view, explained more fully in his *Sketch for a Theory of the Emotions,* is that emotions are not just moods that "come over us," but ways in which we apprehend the world: emotions typically have objects—one is fearful of some possible event, angry with someone about something. But what distinguishes emotions from other ways of being aware of things is, in Sartre's view, that they involve an attempt to transform the world by magic—when one cannot reach the bunch of grapes, one dismisses them as "too green," attributing this quality to them even though one knows quite well that their ripeness does not depend on their reachability. We are *responsible* for our emotions, for they are ways in which we choose to react to the world (p. 445).

There is something right about this, in that emotions presuppose both beliefs and evaluations; for example, anger with someone involves belief that they have done something wrong. If one ceases to believe that they did it, or to see it as wrong, one's anger disappears. (Thus, the Stoics tried to cure us of emotion by persuading us to stop caring about anything other than our own virtue.) But much of what we care about, whether our own health and freedom from pain, the sexual attractiveness of others, or the well-being of our children, does not seem a matter of choice but more like a biological given. On emotion and care, Sartre seems to overstate his case.

Sartre holds us responsible for longer-lasting features of our personality or character. He argues that one cannot just assert "I am shy" (or a great lover, or unfit for work) as if these were unchangeable facts about oneself like "I am male, or black, or six feet tall," for the former descriptions depend on the way we behave in certain situations—and we can always try to behave differently. To say "I am ugly" (or attractive, persevering, or easily discouraged) is not to assert a determinate fact already in existence, but to anticipate how one will act and how people will react in the future, and one has choices about that (p. 459). But, again, we need to integrate what truth there is in this with the increasing evidence of genetic influences on personality and sexuality.

Sartre tries to extend our freedom and our responsibility to everything we think, feel, and do. He suggests there are times when this radical freedom is clearly manifested to us. In moments of temptation or indecision (e.g., when the man who has resolved to give up gambling is confronted with the gaming tables once again), one realizes, painfully, that no motive and no past resolution, however strong, determines what one does *next* (p. 33). Every moment requires a new or renewed choice. Following Kierkegaard and Heidegger, Sartre uses the term "anguish" to describe this consciousness of one's own freedom (pp. 29, 464). Anguish is not fear of an external object, but the uneasy awareness of the ultimate unpredictability of one's own behavior. The soldier fears injury, pain, or death, but he feels anguish when he wonders whether he is going to be able to "hold up" courageously in the coming battle. The person walking on a cliff top fears falling, but feels anguish when she realizes that there is nothing to stop her from throwing herself over (pp. 29–32). Fear is common, but anguish is rare because it is "the *reflective* apprehension of freedom by itself" (p. 39).

DIAGNOSIS: ANGUISH AND BAD FAITH, CONFLICT WITH OTHERS

Anguish, the consciousness of our freedom, is mentally painful, and we typically try to avoid it (pp. 40, 556). Sartre thinks we would all like to achieve a state in which there are no choices left open for us, so that we would "coincide with ourselves" like inanimate objects and would not be subject to anguish. But such escape from responsibility is illusory, for conscious beings are necessarily free, and without justifications for our choices. Such is Sartre's metaphysical diagnosis of the human condition. Hence his gloomy description of our life as "an unhappy consciousness with no possibility of surpassing its unhappy state" (p. 90), "a useless passion" (p. 615).

A crucial concept in Sartre's diagnosis is that of "bad faith" (*mauvaise foi*, sometimes translated as "self-deception"). Bad faith is the attempt to escape anguish by trying to represent one's attitudes and actions as determined by one's situation, or one's character, one's relationship to others, employment or social role—anything other than one's own choices. Sartre believes bad faith is the characteristic mode of most human life (p. 556).

He gives two famous examples of bad faith, both of them scenes from the Parisian cafés that were his favorite haunts (pp. 55–60). He pictures a young girl sitting with a man who, she has every reason to suspect, would like to seduce her. But when he takes her hand, she tries to avoid a decision to accept or reject his advances by seeming not to notice: she carries on their intellectual conversation while leaving her hand in his as if she were not aware of his holding it. In Sartre's interpretation, the girl is in bad faith because she somehow pretends—not just to her companion, but *to herself*—that she can be distinguished from her body, that her hand is a passive object, a mere thing; whereas she is, of course, a conscious embodied person who knows perfectly well what is going on and is responsible for her actions—or lack of reaction, in this case.

The second example is of the café waiter who is doing his job a little too keenly; his movements with the trays and cups are flourished and overly dramatic, he is "acting the part" of being a waiter. If there is bad faith here at all (and there need not be), it would lie in his identifying himself completely with the role, thinking that it determines his every action and attitude, whereas the truth is, of course, that he has chosen to take on the job and is free to give it up at any time, even though he might face unemployment. He is not *essentially* a waiter, for nobody is essentially anything. Sartre writes: "the waiter cannot be immediately a café waiter in the sense that this inkwell *is* an inkwell"; "it is necessary that we *make ourselves* what we are" (p. 59). An employee's actions are not literally *determined* by company policy, for he or she can always decide to object or to resign. Even a soldier can refuse to fight, at the cost of court martial or execution. Anything we do, any role we play, and (Sartre wants to add) any value we respect (pp. 38, 627) is sustained only by our own constantly remade decision.

Sartre rejects any explanation of bad faith in terms of unconscious mental states (pp. 50–54). A Freudian might try to describe Sartre's café cases as examples of repression into the unconscious: the girl might be said to be repressing the knowledge that her companion has made a sexual advance to her. But Sartre points out an apparent self-contradiction in the very idea of repression. We must attribute the act or process of repressing to some element within the mind ("the censor"); yet this censor must be able to make distinctions between what to repress and what to retain in consciousness, so it must be aware of the repressed idea, but supposedly in order *not* to be aware of it. Sartre concludes that the censor itself is in bad faith and that we have not gained any explanation of how bad faith is possible by localizing it in one part of the mind rather than in the person as a whole (pp. 52–53).

He goes on to argue that "good faith," or "sincerity," presents just as much of a conceptual problem. For as soon as one describes one's role or character in some way (e.g., "I am a waiter," "I am shy," "I am gay"), a distinction is involved between the self doing the describing and the self described. The ideal of complete sincerity seems doomed to failure (p. 62), for we can never be mere objects to be observed and described like any external matter of fact. An example Sartre offers here is of someone with a clear record of homosexual activity, but who resists description of himself as gay (p. 63). He is in bad faith because he refuses to admit his inclinations and tries to offer some other explanation of his homosexual encounters. His friend, "a champion of sincerity," demands that he acknowledge that he is gay. But in Sartre's view nobody just *is* gay in the way that a table is made of wood or a person is red-haired. If the person were to admit that he is gay, and thereby imply that he *cannot* cease his homosexual activity, he would also be in bad faith—and so would any "champion of sincerity" who demanded such an admission (p. 63).

Sartre is touching here on the deep difficulties of self-knowledge. But his account threatens to make these matters unnecessarily perplexing, for he displays an inordinate fondness for the paradoxical formula that "human reality must be what it is not, and not be what it is" (pp. xli, 67, 90). This is, of course, a self-contradiction, so we cannot literally believe it. Did Sartre enjoy provoking his philosophical readers? Did he deceive himself into thinking that by its incantation he had achieved insight? Or did he just present the paradox, while shirking the difficult task of explaining in clear, consistent terms what it is about the concept of consciousness that generates the possibility of bad faith? He leaves us some hints about how to resolve the paradox, however. I suggest that we take it as misleading shorthand for "people are not *necessarily* what they are, but must be *able* to become what they are not yet" (which is my variation on something he says on p. 58). The crucial point is that we are always free to *try* to become different from what we are.

In Part Three of *Being and Nothingness,* entitled "Being-for-Others," Sartre gives his philosophical analysis of interpersonal relations, and comes to another pessimistic conclusion. He throws some new light on the philosophical problem of other minds, arguing by appeal to common experience that we often have an immediate, noninferential awareness of other people's mental states. When one sees a human (or even an animal) face with two eyes directed at oneself, one immediately knows one is being observed, and one knows it with as much certainty as anything about physical events in the world. The "look" of another human can have a special power over us. If we are engrossed in doing something not normally approved of, such as spying on someone through a keyhole—or picking our nose—and we hear (or think we hear) a footstep of someone approaching, we suddenly feel *ashamed,* for we become aware of someone else who might be critical of our actions. Conversely, when witnessed doing something admirable, we can feel pride. Many of our emotions involve in their conceptual structure the existence of other people and their reactions to oneself.

Sartre goes on to argue for the more disputable thesis that the relationship between any two conscious beings is necessarily one of conflict. Supposedly, another person represents a threat to one's freedom by his or her very existence, in that the person's perception of one "objectifies" oneself as a mere object in the world. According to Sartre, one has only two strategies to ward off this threat: one can treat the other as a mere object without freedom, or one can try to "possess" the person's freedom and utilize it for one's own purposes (p. 363). He gives a persuasive version of Hegel's famous discussion of the relation between master and slave in which, paradoxically, the slave ends up with more psychological power because the master needs the slave to *recognize* him as master. Sartre applies this analysis to some forms of sexual desire, especially sadism and masochism (p. 364 ff.). He demonstrates that human sexual relations raise deep philosophical issues about human nature. But he goes on to allege that genuine respect for the freedom of other people, in friendship or in erotic love, is an impossible ideal (p. 394 ff.). At this stage of Sartre's writing, the outlook seems bleak indeed.

But is there not a contradiction between Sartre's insistence on our freedom and his analysis of the human condition as determined in these respects? He asserts that we all aspire to fill the "nothingness" that is the essence of our existence as conscious beings; that is, we aspire to become a Godlike being that would be the foundation of its own being, an "in-itself-for-itself" (pp. 90, 566, 615). And as we have just seen, Sartre also claims that any relationship between two people always involves conflict, in the form of an attempt to deny or to possess the freedom of the other (pp. 363, 394, 429). In these two ways, he represents human life as a perpetual striving for the logically impossible. But *must* it be like that? Can't someone choose *not* to aspire to become an object, and not to make other people into objects?

PRESCRIPTION: REFLECTIVE CHOICE

In view of his rejection of objective values, Sartre's prescription has to be a somewhat empty one. There is no *particular* project or way of life that he can recommend. What he condemns is bad faith, the attempt to think of oneself as not free. Bad faith may be the usual attitude of most people, but Sartre implies that it is possible reflectively to *affirm* one's own freedom. It looks as if all he can praise is the making of our individual choices with fully self-conscious, "anguished" awareness that nothing determines them. We must accept our responsibility for everything about ourselves—not just our actions, but our attitudes, emotions, and characters. The "spirit of seriousness," namely the illusion that values are objectively in the world rather than sustained by human choice—which Sartre ascribes especially to "the bourgeois" who are comfortable with their situation—must be decisively repudiated (pp. 580, 626).

In *Existentialism and Humanism*, Sartre illustrated the impossibility of prescription by the case of a young Frenchman at the time of the Nazi occupation who was faced with the choice of joining the free French forces in England or staying at home to be with his mother, who lived only for him. The former course would be directed to the nation, though it would make little difference to the total war effort. The latter would be of immediate practical effect, but directed to the good of only one person. Sartre holds that no ethical doctrine can arbitrate between such incommensurable claims. Nor can strength of feeling settle the matter, for there is no measure of such feeling except in terms of what the subject actually does—which is precisely what is at stake. To choose an advisor or moral authority is only another sort of choice. So when Sartre was consulted by this young man, he could only say: "You are free, therefore choose."

It has to be admitted, however, that no system of objective ethical values (whether Platonic, Aristotelian, Christian, or Kantian) can claim to offer a single, determinate answer to *every* individual human dilemma in each concrete situation. Often, there are difficult dilemmas, in which more than one course of action may be morally permissible; but this is not to say that *anything* is permissible, that *no* moral question ever has a right answer, which seems to be what Sartre implies.

Sartre does commit himself to the intrinsic value of "authentic," self-conscious choice. His descriptions of particular cases of bad faith are not morally neutral, but implicitly condemn any refusal to face the reality of one's freedom and affirm one's own choices. He thus offers another perspective on the ancient virtue of self-knowledge put before us by Socrates, Spinoza, Freud, and many others. For all its obscurities and exaggerations, there is something important to learn from Sartre's analysis of how the very notion of consciousness involves freedom. His view is not a mere misuse of language. For we commonly reproach each other not just for our actions, but for our attitudes, reactions, and emotions: "How *could* you feel like that, when you know that p?" "I don't like your attitude to X"

"Must you be so selfish? So impatient?" Such reproaches—and more neutral psychotherapeutic interventions—are not without effect, for to make someone *aware* that they are feeling or behaving in a certain way can make a difference. The more they are aware of their own anger or pride or self-centeredness, the more they may become capable of change.

Sartre's understanding of the nature and possibility of self-knowledge differs from Freud's, however. Sartre rejects the very idea of unconscious causes of mental events; for him everything is supposed to be already available to consciousness (p. 571). But in view of how much has been discovered about the operation of the brain, we have to see this as assertion rather than argument. There is now an overwhelming empirical case for the existence of unconscious processes that deserve to be called mental.

In what Sartre calls "existential psychoanalysis" we have an interpretative, hermeneutic program rather than a scientific one. We are to look not for the *causes* of a person's behavior, but for the *meaning* of it; that is, for intelligible *reasons*, which will involve the person's beliefs and desires. For Sartre, desires are based on fundamental value choices rather than biological drives or instincts (pp. 568–75). (Some psychiatrists have adopted this methodology, seeking to understand how patients see their world, rather than looking for unconscious drives, or brain states, behind their behavior.)

Sartre holds that because a person is a unity, not just a bundle of unrelated desires or habits, there must be for each person a fundamental choice (the "original project") that gives the ultimate meaning or purpose behind every aspect of his or her life (pp. 561–65). The biographies he wrote of Baudelaire, Genet, and Flaubert are exercises in "existential psychoanalysis," applied to the whole of a life. But it is not at all obvious that for each person there must be a *single* fundamental choice. Sartre himself allows that people can sometimes make a sudden "conversion" of their original project (pp. 475–76). And need there be just one such project even in each period of someone's life? Can't someone have two or more projects that are not derived from any common formula (e.g., family and career, plus perhaps sport, or art, or politics)?

If no reasons can be given for fundamental choices, they would seem to be unjustified and arbitrary. It looks as if on his own premises Sartre would have to commend the man who "authentically" chooses to devote himself to exterminating Jews, seducing women, abusing children, or playing computer games, provided that he makes such choices with full reflective awareness. Could Sartre find within his own philosophy any reason to criticize a Nietzschian *Ubermensch* who resolutely and reflectively developed his own freedom at the cost of other less-than-super human beings? Conversely, if someone devotes himself or herself to bringing up his or her children, helping the poor, or playing music, but deceives himself or herself (in Sartre's view) into thinking that these are objective values, would Sartre condemn the person as living in bad faith?

In some intriguing footnotes to *Being and Nothingness*, Sartre uses quasi-religious language to suggest that it is *possible* to "radically escape bad faith" in "a self-recovery of being which was previously corrupted." He calls this redemption "authenticity" (in the footnote on p. 70), and he talks of "an ethics of deliverance and salvation" and of "a radical conversion" (p. 412). And in the middle of some of his most obscure theorizing in Part Two, Sartre identifies what he calls "pure" or "purifying" reflection as opposed to "impure" or "accessory reflection" (pp. 155, 159 ff.). He seems to attribute a peculiarly moral power to the former, which can, he says, only be attained as the result of a "katharsis" or cleansing. But he says that these suggestions cannot be developed in a work of ontology, and he end with a promise to write another book on the ethical plane (p. 628). Sartre never published any such work, presumably because as he worked toward it his view began to change. His conception of human nature became less abstract and individualistic, more concrete and social.

THE "FIRST ETHICS": AUTHENTICITY AND FREEDOM FOR EVERYONE

Sartre's *War Diaries* and *Notebooks for an Ethics* have been published posthumously, so we can now see in what direction his ethical thought was heading. Here I will rely on the useful summary in Chapters 4 and 5 of Thomas C. Anderson's book *Sartre's Two Ethics* (which saves us wading through hundreds of pages of notes, which are, Anderson says, "of uneven clarity and significance").

Sartre came to recognize more explicitly how human freedom is situated in the midst of what he calls "facticity," the facts about oneself and one's situation that constrain the ways in which one can express one's freedom. One kind of facticity depends on the vulnerability of the human body; for example, one's freedom is importantly limited or "contaminated" if one contracts a serious illness such as tuberculosis. Another kind of facticity is one's situation in a given society at a certain stage in history. A slave, a manual laborer, a worker on an assembly line, a sales assistant, a cleaning lady, or a "sex-worker," may have some limited choices about how to act in his or her socioeconomic situation, but it would be a cruel deception to assure the person that he or she really is as free as every other human being. In the abstract terms of *Being and Nothingness*, perhaps they are—but in concrete, realistic terms they are not. Sartre now begins to acknowledge the obvious—that socioeconomic factors limit human freedom, even if they do not determine every individual choice. And he rejects "abstract morality" in favor of an ethics that takes account of bodily, economic, and social factors, and places its hopes in social (perhaps revolutionary) change, at least as much as in individual psychological transformation.

In the *Notebooks*, Sartre says some interesting things about pure reflection and the authentic human existence it is supposed to give rise to. Pure reflection enables us to give up the project of becoming Godlike beings, which *Being and Nothingness* represented as our inevitable but useless passion. We can, after all, come to accept the contingency of our existence, and in a creative, generous spirit we can give meaning and purpose to our lives, and thereby to the world:

> . . . authentic man never loses sight of the absolute goals of the human condition . . . to save the world (in making there be being), to make freedom the foundation of the world, to take responsibility for creation, and to make the origin of the world absolute through freedom taking hold of itself. (Notebooks, p. 448)

It seems we are to give up the project of becoming Godlike in one sense by becoming Godlike in another sense; namely, recognizing ourselves as the only sources of meaning and purpose in the world.

In authentic existence, relations with other people can also be transformed. Another person's perception of me, although "objectifying" in that they perceive my body as one object among others, is not necessarily a threat:

> . . . It only becomes so if the Other refuses to see a freedom in me *too*. But if, on the contrary, he makes me exist as an existing freedom as well as a *Being/object* . . . he enriches the world and me, he *gives a meaning* to my existence *in addition to* the subjective meaning that I myself give it. (*Notebooks*, p. 500)

Sartre thus allows that sympathetic comprehension of another person, and assistance in pursuing his or her goals, is possible after all. He even talks of "authentic love" (reminiscent of Christian *agape*) that "rejoices in the Other's being-in-the-world, without appropriating it" (*Notebooks,* p. 508).

The freedom of the individual thus becomes Sartre's basic value. But this has to be understood as asserting not merely the necessary truth that every conscious being is free in the abstract sense, but the value judgment that every person ought to be able to *exercise* his or her freedom in concrete ways, and thus that human society should be changed in the direction of making this a reality for everyone. Authenticity, the lucid assuming of responsibility for one's own free choices, must involve respecting and valuing the freedom of all other conscious, rational beings.

Sartre had made a suggestion in this Kantian direction in *Existentialism and Humanism* (p. 29), where he said that in choosing for oneself one chooses for all men and thereby creates an image of man as one believes he ought to be. In the *Notebooks*, he uses the phrase "a city of ends" to express this goal, which he now sees as "absolute" or objectively valid. This choice of words carries echoes of two previous ideals, namely Augustine's "City of God" (the heavenly ideal, distinct from all earthly societies), and Kant's formula of the "Kingdom of Ends" (that we should treat every rational being never merely as a means, but always as an end). Sartre tends, however, to interpret the goal in more down-to-earth terms as a socialist, classless society—invoking the same sort of utopian ideal as Marx's envisioned "truly communist" state of future society in which all human beings will be able to express their freedom.

THE "SECOND ETHICS": SOCIETY
AND HUMAN NEEDS

In Sartre's later period, from about 1950 onward, he acknowledged the power that social circumstances have over individuals and he began to analyze the social conditions that restrict freedom. In his *Critique of Dialectical Reason*, he presented a frankly materialist view of human nature, in both the ontological and the Marxist senses. He now defines man, not as a free consciousness, but as a material organism, an embodied animal—though endowed with the power of rational thought and action. And he adopts an explicitly Marxist standpoint on the processes of history, accepting that the material, economic foundations of any stage of human society place definite limits on the possibilities for individuals in that culture. There is "a dialectical relationship"; that is, a mutual interaction between human beings, the natural world, and the social world. Sartre now rejects his earlier view that man is fundamentally free in all situations; rather, we are strongly influenced by the past of our culture, by the social class we are encultured into, and by the idiosyncrasies of our family. In emphasizing the influence of the family on the early development of the individual personality (as he does in his biographical studies of Genet, Baudelaire, and Flaubert), Sartre incorporates a strong element of Freud.

Accordingly, there is now no question of individual salvation through pure reflection and authentic self-choice; rather, Sartre looks to social action, in particular to organized, "pledged" groups committed to social and political change, trying to achieve real, concrete human freedom for the oppressed. While he was a member of the Communist Party Sartre was notoriously unwilling to criticize the horrors of Stalinism, apparently because he had placed his faith in the communist movement as the only realistic vehicle of progress toward the worldwide, classless, radically democratic society that he envisaged. As he later said, he "sent ethics on a vacation," thinking it had to give way to political realism. But we may protest that it is always dangerous—and wrong—to suspend ethical constraints in the name of some supposedly greater good; and in the 1960s Sartre changed his view once more, realizing the need for a moral philosophy even in the midst of political struggles. He presented his new view of ethics in a lecture at the Instituto Gramsci in Rome in 1964, and in parts of his lengthy study of Flaubert, *The Family Idiot*. I rely again on Thomas Anderson (Chapters 7–9) for an account of this "second ethics."

Sartre hoped to find a level of ethical thought about society that is not merely conditioned by the prevailing economic structure, yet not totally abstract and unrelated to social reality. He notes, with Kant, that we conceive ethical obligations as having a peculiarly categorical force, they call us toward a "pure future," something that we accept *ought* to exist, even if it has not been the case so far. The oppressed (and those who identify with their cause) are strongly aware that human life ought to be quite different from the reality for so many people under colonialist or capitalist exploitation. There is thus an implicit conception of what Sartre calls "integral humanity," human life as it should be, when freely developed and fulfilled. This, he says, is the "true ethics," the proper goal of human history. And, like Kant, he seemed to find some grounds for hope that history is moving in the right direction, with people becoming more aware of this ideal.

At this point, Sartre, who had once firmly rejected the idea of an essence of humanity, is in fact presupposing some general conception of human potentiality and its ideal fulfilment. His thought begins to move in an Aristotelean direction (much as he might hate to admit it!). He focuses on human *needs*, as setting us objective values that "demand" to be fulfiled. This notion of need is flexible enough to cover several levels, though Sartre does not seem to list them systematically. First, there are physiological needs, things we need to maintain life and health, such as air, water, carbohydrates, proteins, vitamins, medicines. But beyond mere bodily growth and maintenance, there are psychological needs— most fundamentally the needs of infants and children for loving care if they are to grow up feeling valued and believing that life is worth living

(Sartre brings this out vividly in *The Family Idiot*). We might add here the typical adult needs for friendship and for sexual fulfilment (ideally, for both together in a partnership of equals), and for children of one's own.

Beyond the individual and the family, there is always the wider society: the meeting of even our bodily needs depends on our membership in an economic structure. We can talk here of needs for education and culture, to have one's voice and individuality recognized, to contribute one's work to society, to take part on a basis of justice and equality. Finally, Sartre recognizes a need that all humans have for a meaning and purpose to their lives. But he puts his own particular gloss on this when he says that we desire the absolute, that "finitude makes us mad for an unattainable infinite." This picks up a theme from his early period, but he now identifies this "religious instinct" not as the aspiration to *become* God, but the desire for a justification for our lives that could only come from an almighty loving God. However, Sartre continues to hold that this is an illusion and that only we ourselves can confer meaning and purpose on our lives and on the world.

Sartre hoped that some such list of human needs would provide a basis for ethics that is not tied to any particular stage of socioeconomic development, while still being concrete and realistic enough to justify ethical and political value judgments. He listed a series of conditions under which, he thought, violence on behalf of the oppressed could be morally justified—conditions that bear some resemblance to those in the traditional Christian doctrine of "just war" (although Sartre does not explicitly rule out targeting the innocent).

He does not seem to have faced up to the question of how to decide what is a universal human need and what is relative to a given stage of society or a social role (e.g., contemporary "needs" for a car, a TV, a computer, or a mobile phone), or merely created artificially by advertising or fashion (such as a need for a new car every year, for cosmetic surgery, or for the latest brand of designer-label jeans). Sartre ended up appealing to a general conception of human nature or the human condition ("nude man" as he ludicrously put it), as opposed to what is characteristic of a particular stage of society.

What Sartre was arriving at is a synthesis of themes from Aristotle, Kant, Marx, and Freud, without the transcendent metaphysics of Plato or Christianity. The vast verbiage of his philosophy issues in a challenge to us all: first, to become more truly self-aware and to use our freedom to change ourselves for the better; and second, to do what we can to work toward a worldwide society in which all people have equal opportunity to exercise their freedom.

FOR FURTHER READING

For thought-provoking introductions to existentialism generally, see William Barrett, *Irrational Man: A Study in Existential Philosophy* (New York: Anchor Books/Doubleday, 1962); and David E. Cooper, *Existentialism: A Reconstruction* (Oxford: Blackwell, 1990).

For admirable short guides to important existentialist thinkers, see Patrick Gardiner, *Kierkegaard* (Oxford University Press, 1988); Michael Tanner, *Nietzsche* (Oxford University Press, 1994); George Steiner, *Heidegger* (London: Fontana, 1978); Arthur C. Danto, *Sartre* (London: Fontana, 1975).

Those who want to read Sartre for themselves might start with his novel *Nausea* and his lecture *Existentialism and Humanism* (London: Methuen, 1948); then perhaps his short books, *The Transcendence of the Ego* (New York: Farrar, Strauss & Giroux, 1957) and *Sketch for a Theory of the Emotions* (London: Methuen, 1962).

Rather than attempting to plough straight through the huge, dense forest of *Being and Nothingness* (English translation by Hazel Barnes, London: Routledge, 2002; Secaucus, N.J.: Citadel Press, 2001), I suggest starting with Part 4 (itself nearly 200 pages!), then the second chapter of Part 1 ("Bad Faith"), the concluding pages ("Ethical Implications"), plus some of Part 3—at least Chapter 1, section III ("The Look").

Francis Jeanson, *Sartre and the Problem of Morality* (Bloomington: Indiana University Press, 1980, first published in French in 1947) is an interpretation of the early philosophy that was enthusiastically endorsed by Sartre himself.

In *Sartre's Two Ethics; From Authenticity to Integral Humanity* (Peru, Ill.: Open Court Publishing Company, 1993), Thomas C. Anderson has given a very useful account of both Sartre's "first ethics" (from the period immediately after *Being and Nothingness*) and his "second ethics," especially as presented in the Rome Lecture of 1964.

Gregory McCulloch, *Using Sartre: An Analytical Introduction to Early Sartrian Themes* (London: Routledge, 1994), is a very clear interpretation of fundamental themes from *Being and Nothingness*, relating them to analytical philosophy of mind and epistemology.

10

Darwinian Theories of Human Nature

Some readers may be wondering whether it has been worth giving so much attention to the religious traditions, philosophies, and speculative theories of previous centuries. Now that the scientific method has established itself as the proper way of understanding everything in the world, including living beings like ourselves, surely we should look to science for the truth about human nature?

In fact, this program is nothing new; it inspired many thinkers in the seventeenth and eighteenth centuries, notably Hobbes, Hume, and the *philosophes* of the French Enlightenment. But it has found new strength since Darwin propounded his theory of evolution in the mid-nineteenth century. Most people have come to accept that humans share a common descent with all other creatures on Earth. But this claim is still resisted by some religious believers, although most mainstream Christian denominations have accommodated to it. The status of evolutionary theory has been at issue in legal contests about science education in the United States in the 1920s and again more recently. There have been a number of stages of scientific theorizing and public controversy since Darwin's day. In this chapter I will examine three main waves of evolutionary thinking about human nature.

Most biologists, psychologists, and social scientists have been chary of talking about something as vague and publicly controversial as "human nature" and have concentrated on making their professional reputations by specialized technical studies. A few of them, however, have made bold to offer some sort of diagnosis and prescription for human problems, i.e., a "theory" of human nature in the sense used in this book. But as we will see, when would-be scientists of human nature offer their secular schemes of salvation (or progress), their claims go beyond their area of scientific expertise and become just as controversial as those of the older theories considered in previous chapters. So along with my exposition of various types of evolutionary theorizing, I will offer some conceptual and ethical critique.

EVOLUTIONARY THEORY, STAGE I:
DARWIN AND HIS CONTEMPORARIES

Metaphysical Background

Before Darwin came on the scene, scientists were beginning to realize that the world had a vastly longer history than previously thought. Most people in the Judeo-Christian tradition had assumed the biblical stories to be literally true, and it had been widely believed that the Creation (shortly followed by the Flood) had occurred only about four thousand years ago. But in 1755 the youthful Kant propounded a theory of how the solar system had "evolved" by the gradual accretion of the planets from dust swirling around the sun. And in the early nineteenth century, geologists were coming to realize that the observable rock strata have been formed and molded by familiar processes of eruption and sedimentation, earth movement and erosion, acting over vast periods of time. This "uniformitarian" account was authoritatively propounded in Charles Lyell's *Principles of Geology* (1830–33), and it strongly influenced Darwin's thought. (In fact, Darwin made his own early reputation more as geologist than biologist.)

The most famous use of the word "evolution" is, of course, for the process of formation and change in biological *species*. The hypothesis of long-term species change was already in the air in Darwin's time. The discovery of fossilized bones in the rocks showed that there had once been creatures very different from those that exist now. The idea that the manifold kinds of organism found on Earth have been "transmuted" from their predecessors by a series of small changes was propounded by various thinkers, including Darwin's own grandfather Erasmus Darwin and the French biologists Comte Georges-Louis Leclere de Buffon and Jean-Baptiste de Monet de Lamarck.

Darwin on Natural Selection

It is a significant further step from the overall *fact* of the transmutation or evolution of species to understanding how the process could really work. The great contribution of Charles Darwin (1809–1882) was to realize the *causal mechanism* for adaptive evolution, the process that he came to call "natural selection."

There had been previous speculations about the means by which species might change, and Lamarck had suggested in 1809 that creatures can pass on to their offspring certain physical traits that they had developed during their own lifetimes. According to this theory of the "inheritance of acquired characteristics," an individual herbivore that had stretched its neck to eat leaves off tall trees might produce children with longer necks— and thus, perhaps, giraffes might have evolved! Yet it seemed implausible that all changes in species could be accounted for in this way.

As a student, Darwin developed a passionate interest in biology and geology, neglecting his university curricula in medicine at Edinburgh and in theology at Cambridge, yet managing to impress the professors in his unofficial studies. At the age of twenty-two, he had a lucky break when he was offered the position of naturalist on the British naval surveying ship the *Beagle* (even then, it took the persuasiveness of his uncle to overcome the objections of his father).

During the voyage, which took nearly five years, Darwin spent most of the time in and around South America and on various islands along the way. He also seized the opportunity to make extensive inland explorations of little-known territories. He found bones of enormous extinct animals and fossilized remains of sea creatures high in the Andes Mountains; he also witnessed an earthquake in Chile that noticeably uplifted the earth. All this was clear evidence of long-term and continually acting processes of geological change. He made extensive collections of flora and fauna previously unknown to science, sending many boxes of them back to London for study. He was especially puzzled by the birds and animals of the Galapagos Islands in the Pacific Ocean, which resembled those of South America, but differed in detail from island to island. The youthful Darwin was thus blessed with a unique opportunity to gather vast quantities of new evidence. But what was it evidence *for*?

After his return from this epic voyage, Darwin settled down to marriage (to his cousin Emma Wedgwood), a large Victorian family, and a life of science (supported by inherited wealth). The basic idea of natural selection came to him quite soon, and he wrote down a sketch of his theory in 1844. But he did not publish it for fifteen years, for he was painfully aware just how controversial the idea of species change was. It was incompatible with the biblical story of God's creation of animals and humans in Genesis if the latter is read literally—not that that worried Darwin himself, but he was very reluctant to get embroiled in religious controversy. There had already been some notoriously amateurish books about evolution, and he wanted to document his theory in fully scientific fashion by assembling all the evidence he could find, from all sources.

Publication of Darwin's long-gestated theory was provoked by the sudden arrival in 1858 of a paper from Alfred Wallace, a young English naturalist then researching in the East Indies, who had independently hit on the idea of natural selection. Darwin hurriedly wrote up his years of research in his most famous, epoch-making book, *The Origin of Species*, published in 1859. Wallace, who shared the initial scientific credit at a meeting of the Royal Society, did not have nearly as much evidence as Darwin and could not match him in detail. (He later compromised his biological insights when he became a convert to spiritualism and tried to exempt the human mind from evolution.)

The heart of the Darwinian argument for natural selection is an elegant logical deduction from four large empirical generalizations. The first two are as follows:

1. There is variation in the traits of individuals of a given species.
2. Traits of parents tend to be passed on to their offspring.

These two general facts emerge from a wide variety of observations of plants and animals, and they had long been put to practical use in the selective breeding of new varieties of plants and farm animals, dogs and pigeons. Hence, Darwin's talk of natural "selection" as a process that, analogously to human selection, modifies species—but unintentionally, of course. The other premises of the overall argument are as follows:

3. Species are intrinsically capable of a geometric rate of increase of population.
4. The resources of the environment typically cannot support such an increase.

The truth of (3) consists in the fact that any pair of organisms can produce considerably more than two offspring—in many species, thousands of seeds or eggs are produced. It follows from (3) and (4) that only a small proportion of seeds, eggs, and young reach maturity. In effect, there is competition to survive and to reproduce, both between members of the same species and between different species. This does not always involve bodily confrontation, as when individuals scrabble with each other for food or males fight for females: in Darwin's sense, plants compete for light and nutrients, and animals compete to avoid being detected and eaten by predators.

From the inevitability of such competition, and from (1), we can deduce that at any stage there will be some individuals in the population that, because of their differences from others, will have the best chance of surviving long enough to leave offspring. They can be described as the "fittest" in their environment or ecological niche, which includes all the factors relevant to their life, including other species of plants and animals. Given (2), their traits will tend to be passed on to the next generation, and less advantageous traits will not.

Thus, over many generations the typical characteristics of a population can change significantly. And given the immense periods of past time proved by geology, and the distribution of plants and animals into the wide variety of environments around the world, different species can evolve from common ancestors. All that is needed is the constant pressure of natural selection acting on the variations within the populations, in different environments. There is no need to postulate any Lamarckian inheritance of acquired characteristics, although Darwin did some backsliding on this point, partly because he not know the genetic basis of the patterns of inheritance summed up in (1) and (2).

Besides natural selection—or rather as a special case of it—Darwin recognized the operation of what he called "sexual selection," treated at length in his double-barreled work of 1871, *The Descent of Man, and Selection in Relation to Sex*. The heavy antlers of the stag and the elaborate tail of the peacock would seem to be encumbrances to the ordinary business of their lives, such as getting around in search of food and fleeing from predators. Surely natural selection would give the advantage to deer with smaller antlers and to peacocks with more modest tails? But that would be to ignore the biologically crucial business of sexual reproduction. Stags use their antlers in the "rut" when they fight with each other to get access to the hinds, while peacocks display their gloriously colored tails to prospective mates, who then exercise their privilege of female choice of the most impressive partner. Thus, there is competition not just to survive, but to breed as well. Individuals with the more highly developed traits that lead to sexual success are most likely to pass them on to their offspring, and this presumably outbalances any disadvantage experienced outside the mating season.

The Origin of Species was that rare thing—an original work of science written in a vivid style that was intelligible to most educated readers. Darwin was able to document his case with a virtuoso display of evidence from selective breeding, worldwide natural history, and paleontology. The book was an immediate best-seller and was translated into many languages. Of course, it aroused controversy and in some quarters it still does.

Darwin on Human Evolution

With characteristic caution, Darwin did not at first make explicit his view that human beings are descended from apelike ancestors. At the end of the *Origin*, he allowed himself only a typically English understatement—that "light will be thrown on the origin of man and his history." But to his readers, the cat—or should we say *the apeman*?—was already out of the bag, and Thomas H. Huxley, his most forthright scientific supporter, produced a book on the evolutionary origins of man only four years later. In 1871 Darwin at last published his own thoughts on human evolution in *The Descent of Man*. With his usual thoroughness, he reviewed the anatomical, medical, embryological, and behavioral evidence for our kindred with other animals, calling attention to telltale "rudiments" such as the little feature in our outer ears that he argued is the result of the infolding of the pointed ears of our distant ancestors.

The evolution of species, including ourselves, from simpler forms of life is now acknowledged by biologists to be not just a theory but a *fact*. There is direct empirical evidence for our common ancestry with other animals. Comparative anatomy shows the human body to have the same plan as other vertebrates: four limbs with five digits on each. Our close bodily similarity to monkeys, and especially to the great apes, is obvious. The human embryo goes through stages of development in which it resembles those of lower forms of life. In the human body there are remnants of lower forms, e.g., a vestigial tail. The biochemistry of our bodies—cells, proteins, blood, DNA—is very similar to that of other creatures. And in recent years many thousands of fossil remains of various hominoid species intermediate between apes and humans have been unearthed. That we have evolved from more primitive creatures is thus now as well-established a fact as anything else in science. (I will address the religious resistance to this fact in the concluding chapter.)

"Social Darwinism"

I have been presenting Darwin's theory of evolution of species on its own terms as a strictly scientific hypothesis, to be evaluated by the relevant empirical observations. And I have concurred with the general scientific judgment that it is overwhelmingly confirmed by all the available evidence and may therefore be said to be true in all essentials (though no doubt some details remain to be sorted out, even now).

Contemporary readers (like those of Darwin's own day) will be keen to debate the ethical or political or religious implications of this theory.

But we should first ask ourselves whether and how a scientific theory can have implications for what we ought to do. Science is supposed, by definition, to find out truths about the physical world, it is often described as "dealing only with *facts*." How, then, can a scientific theory say or imply anything about *values*? As David Hume put it, how can we deduce an "ought" from an "is" or from any number of factual statements? The answer is surely this: only if we include at least one value judgment in the premises, explicitly or implicitly. For example, medical science tells what we "ought" to do, by showing us what means we need to use to prevent or cure various diseases. It is taken for granted on all sides that it is a Good Thing to reduce human suffering whenever we can—that is the underlying value judgment in this case. Less attractively, science has made possible new kinds of weapons—but it does not tell us whether to deploy them or use them. Science does not change our basic values; it just gives us new means of promoting them.

So the theory that humans are evolved creatures does not in itself tell us how we ought to live. Yet there is a common tendency to go beyond this "purely scientific" view and to suggest that evolution in some sense creates its own values. After all, the basic point of Darwinian theory is that the biologically fittest individuals are those that survive longest and leave the most progeny; and the successful species, in a given environment are those that survive over many generations, maintaining and perhaps increasing their numbers. And, it may be alleged, isn't biological *success* the ultimate value? Among humans, the strongest, the cleverest, the sexiest are the most successful—so aren't *they* the most valuable, to be most admired and emulated? Some may jump to the conclusion that the ethical message of Darwinian evolution is that it is every man (and woman) for himself (or herself), and perhaps even that "greed is good" after all. But if there were any such Darwinian ethic, it would recommend those with the biggest families, or more exactly, those who bring the most offspring to adulthood—which is not always the same thing as being strong or clever or sexy, though those traits obviously help at certain life stages!

The phrase "survival of the fittest" tends to suggest this view that those who survive and reproduce best are, quite simply, the *best* in some wider sense. In fact, these words and the associated outlook were around before the publication of Darwin's *Origin*, notably in the writing of the influential Victorian social philosopher Herbert Spencer (1820–1903). He, like Darwin, had been strongly influenced by Thomas Malthus's 1798 *Essay on the Principle of Population*, which argued that population has a natural tendency to outstrip resources, with the result that the weakest get weeded out. The questionable implication was drawn that charitable aid to the starving is pointless (a principle notoriously followed by the British government during the Irish potato famine in the 1830s). Spencer was above all a philosopher of social progress, the general idea of which had taken firm root in European and American thought since the Enlightenment, Kant, and Hegel. (Marx put his own economic and political spin on it.) Spencer had developed an elaborate theory about the "evolution" of human society, seeing the "civilized" society of nineteenth century capitalism as the inevitable—and *best!*—outcome of all preceding human history.

Many thinkers in the second half of the nineteenth century, including E. L. Youmans and W. G. Sumner in America, eagerly took up the theme. It seemed to them that there was a straightforward inference from the fact of biological evolution by natural selection to the need for severe competition within human society. So they thought they saw a justification for unrestrained laissez-faire capitalism, and even for the most extreme disparities between rich and poor. There was also an easy transition to racialist attitudes, even trying to excuse the near-extermination of the aboriginal populations of North and South America and Australia as the inevitable victory of the supposedly advanced peoples over the primitive races of mankind. At both the individual and the social level, might was pretty well identified with right.

But surely an "ought" has been smuggled in somewhere, in trying to derive such ethical and political consequences from the purely scientific theory of evolution? It does *not* follow that those who are the fittest in the biological terms of survival and reproduction are the *best* in any other sense: they may not be morally, artistically, intellectually, or spiritually the best. Conversely, the richest in modern human societies are not always the best at reproduction! As we will see, Darwin himself did not fully endorse "social Darwinism." The phrase has stuck as a label for this kind of ethical and political thought, but it might be more historically accurate to call it "social Spencerism." Darwinian evolution is a strictly scientific biological theory about the origin of species; Spencer's brand was a speculative interpretation of human history, set in a background of metaphysical theory about "cosmic" evolution.

Marx was a contemporaneous political theorist at the opposite extreme from Spencer. Whereas Spencer glorified those who did well out of capitalism, Marx saw them as an exploiting class who would be dispossessed in the coming communist revolution cross-reference goes before period (see Chapter 9). Marx had his own speculative theory of the historical development of human societies through economic stages, and he too hailed Darwin in his own support. The fact that such opposing social thinkers could both try to hitch their bandwagons to evolutionary theory should alert us to the large logical gulf between scientific theories and political programs.

Darwin's Own Values

In *The Descent of Man*, Darwin, after reviewing the physical evidence for our common ancestry with the apes, went on to offer some interesting suggestions about how our intellectual and moral faculties might have evolved from more primitive antecedents. Against the common objection that our human language, intelligence, emotions, morality, and religion make us different in kind from even the most advanced ape, Darwin insisted that there was no barrier in principle to a gradual mental as well as physical evolution over huge periods of time. He had acquired an encylopedic knowledge of animal behavior and was able to demonstrate primitive analogues and possible antecedents for most human behavior. Percipiently, he picked out our social nature and our facility for language as crucial to human mentality.

Darwin was aware that many of his ideas in *The Descent of Man* were speculations rather than proven facts (as he took natural selection to be). He was suggesting how human evolution might have proceeded, rather than demonstrating the path it must have taken (later evolutionary theorizers have done the same, without always being aware of it). And in two respects he argued in ways that biologists have since questioned. He tended to appeal to the theory of the inheritance of acquired characteristics, but subsequent theory decisively rejected this (as we shall see later). And he postulated a time when natural selection operated on our ancestors by competition between human groups as well as between individuals. For instance, a tribe whose members were willing to sacrifice their lives in warfare might survive better than other more pacific tribes. But it is unclear how such "group selection" could operate. After all, the self-sacrificing warrior may not survive to propagate his genes, whereas the draft dodger has a better chance of doing so, so surely selection would favor the latter?

As for value judgments in aesthetics, morality, or religion, Darwin offered various suggestions about how our capacity for them may have evolved. But he did *not* take the kind of reductionist line outlined in the section on social Darwinism earlier. He confidently made his own judgments about beauty and morality. He was inclined to attribute the origin of our sense of beauty to sexual selection. And he remarked how standards of beauty differed between societies, contrasting the "hideous" ornaments and music of "savages" with the "refined" tastes of the "civilized races."

In *The Descent of Man*, Darwin described our conscience or "moral sense" as "the most noble of the attributes of man," and he paid homage to Kant's concept of Duty as the highest human motivation of all, quite distinct from biologically based "appetite." He did not see any incompatibility between this philosophical endorsement of morality and his

evolutionary account of it as emerging from a combination of social instincts and intellectual powers. For instance, while speculating about evolutionary struggles between tribes or races, he also talked of the "great
sin" of slavery and of the treatment of wives like slaves (p. 94).

About history and politics, Darwin, insofar as he expressed any views,
was on the liberal or progressive side. He wrote that "man has risen, though
by slow and interrupted steps, from a lowly condition to the highest standard as yet attained by him in knowledge, morals, and religion." Admittedly,
he did in one place offer a prescription tending toward social Darwinism:

> The advancement of the welfare of mankind is a most intricate problem:
> all ought to refrain from marriage who cannot avoid abject poverty for their
> children. . . . Man, like every other animal, has no doubt advanced to his
> present high condition through a struggle for existence consequent on his
> rapid multiplication; and if he is to advance still higher he must remain
> subject to a severe struggle. . . . There should be open competition for all
> men; and the most able should not be prevented by laws or customs from
> succeeding best and rearing the largest number of offspring. (p. 403)

But he was wise enough to recognize the limits of natural selection and
the crucial importance of human culture and ethics:

> Important as the struggle for existence has been and even still is, yet as far
> as the highest part of man's nature is concerned there are other agencies
> more important. For the moral qualities are advanced . . . much more
> through the effects of habit, the reasoning powers, instruction, religion, etc.,
> than through natural selection. (p. 404)

Darwin voiced some worry about the multiplication of inferior types
of people being "injurious to society," but he immediately went on so to
say that we could not check our sympathy for the weaker members of our
society "without deterioration in the noblest part of our nature" (pp.
168–69). So the ethic of universal compassion and respect, or "love thy
neighbor as thyself," should take precedence over any hardheaded biological calculations about theoretical benefits to society as a whole. Such
arguments would be based on scientific hypotheses that might be far from
certain. As Darwin put it, they "could only be for a contingent benefit,"
whereas there would be "a certain and great present evil" if we inten-
tionally neglect the weak and helpless.

These humane remarks can encourage us to reply to the "social
Spencerist" tendency as follows: since our human evolution has given us
both the sympathy to care for our fellow humans and the intelligence to in-
stitute laws and social programs to help them, shouldn't we use those mental

capacities to try to steer human society in the direction of greater equality? Isn't that more "natural" to us than unflinching adherence to "the survival of the fittest"? It would be dangerous, however, to rest our case on the extremely slippery concept of what is "natural." It would be clearer to appeal directly to explicit ethical principles about human dignity, equality, needs, and rights (as in Kant or Sartre, and indeed in the New Testament) that cannot be derived from any factual statements about evolution.

About religion, Darwin was more circumspect. He talked of the "ennobling" belief in an omnipotent God, but remarked that it is not present in all cultures, though the belief in unseen spiritual agencies of some sort is universal. He said that the existence of a Creator and Ruler of the universe has been affirmed by "the highest intellects that have ever lived," but he refrained from directly endorsing it himself—presumably not just from modesty! He described the feeling of religious devotion as a complex mixture of "love, complete submission to an exalted and mysterious superior, dependence, fear, reverence, gratitude, and hope," yet he suggested a distant antecedent for it in the love of a dog for its master! Privately, he admitted that his early belief in conventional Christianity had gradually faded away, without pain. But he shied away from controversy on the matter; his wife, Emma, was a believer, and their children were brought up in the Church of England. It seems that Charles Darwin was a rather typical specimen of the Victorian age—an ethically serious, politically liberal closet atheist.

Further Reading on Darwin

Darwin's classic, *The Origin of Species*, is reprinted in Pelican classics and in a Mentor paperback (New York: New American Library). The full title of the book is *The Origin of Species by Means of Natural Selection: Or the Preservation of Favored Races in the Struggle of Life*. Steve Jones has updated the *Origin* for today in *Almost Like a Whale* (New York: Doubleday, 1999)

Darwin's second major book, *The Descent of Man and Selection in Relation to Sex*, first published in 1871, is now available in a facsimile edition with a useful introduction by John Tyler Bonner and Robert M. May (Princeton: Princeton University Press, 1981). What is in effect the third volume of one lengthy work was published separately as *The Expression of the Emotions in Man and Animals* in 1872 (Chicago: University of Chicago Press, 1965).

There is an excellent critical discussion of many sides of Darwin's thought by Tim Lewens in *Darwin* (London: Routledge, 2007), with separate chapters on mind, ethics, knowledge, politics, and philosophy.

EVOLUTIONARY THEORY, STAGE II:
THE REACTION AGAINST BIOLOGICAL
ACCOUNTS OF HUMAN NATURE

The Genetic Basis of Heredity

Darwin could not himself explain the facts about heredity expressed in the generalizations (1) and (2) set out earlier in summarizing his theory of natural selection. It was sufficient for his basic argument that they were true, but he did not have any explanation of *why* they were true. The source of the variations within a species and the mechanism of inheritance were obvious fundamental questions for biology, on which Darwin later offered his own speculative theory which he called "pangenesis."

According to this theory, inside the organs of every plant and animal were small particles called "gemmules" that developed through the life of the organism and somehow encapsulated or represented the nature of the organs. For example, a strong muscle would produce gemmules for strong muscles, and a clever brain might generate corresponding particles for intelligence. Supposedly, these gemmules circulated around the body and collected in the reproductive organs, from where they would be passed on to the offspring. This would have provided a mechanism for the inheritance of acquired characteristics.

It was not a bad guess for its time, but soon after Darwin's death, the theory was shown to be wrong. There is a useful lesson here: that even the most distinguished scientists are fallible. (Einstein, for instance, never accepted quantum mechanics.) Fallibility is all the more likely when a scientist ventures outside his or her special field. (Newton, for example, dabbled in alchemy.) Publicly verifiable evidence is the ultimate test of scientific theories. Let us hasten to add that the falsity of Darwin's theory of gemmules does nothing to disprove his main theory of evolution of species by natural selection, which does not depend on any particular account of the mechanisms of variation and inheritance.

In the 1880s the German biologist August Weismann argued that the "germ plasm" of an organism, i.e., the parts of the reproductive system that carry the hereditary information, such as the eggs and sperm, remain quite independent of the other organs, contrary to Darwin's idea of migrating gemmules. So no matter what happened to an animal in its own lifetime, the changes were not reproduced in its offspring. For example, the descendants of many generations of mice whose tails had been systematically docked in the laboratory were born with just as long tails as ever.

The theoretical explanation of the patterns of biological inheritance had been first offered by the Austrian monk Gregor Mendel in Darwin's own lifetime, but the crucial importance of his work was not recognized until after 1900. Mendel's theory postulated distinct indivisible causal factors (now called "genes"), which are passed on from parents to offspring in a process of random mixing of genes from the two parents in sexual reproduction. As Weismann said, the genes carried by the reproductive organs remain unaffected by changes during the lifetime of an individual. Mendel's distinction between "dominant" and "recessive" genes explains how traits of grandparents that do not develop in the parents can reappear in a grandchild, if the individual inherits from each parent a recessive gene for the relevant trait.

A certain mystery remained about the sources of the variations between genes within populations of organisms. It was concluded that genes occasionally change or "mutate" for no biological reason, and these mutations were described as "random." (Natural or artificial radiation is now known to be one cause of mutations.) In the 1920s and 1930s, it was realized that a full account of natural selection operating over time on large populations of slightly varying organisms required considerable use of statistics. Mathematically trained biologists such as Sewell Wright and R. A. Fisher transformed the theory of evolution into a sophisticated "modern synthesis." (Though Darwin's original argument involved arguing informally about probabilities, his own mathematical abilities were modest, so he would not have understood the modernized version of his own theory!) The biochemical basis of the copying of genes through the unwinding of the elegant "double helix" structure of the DNA molecule was discovered by James Watson and Francis Crick in 1953.

Eugenics, Racism, and Sexism

While that post-Darwinian synthesis was being worked out, its apparent social implications were also eagerly discussed. If there is no such thing as the inheritance of acquired characteristics, some thinkers were quick to jump to the contentious conclusion that there are innate differences between individuals, or races, or sexes, which make some of them innately inferior. The "gold standard" for humanity was usually assumed to be set by intelligent, white, "civilized" males.

Darwin's cousin Francis Galton, a statistician well versed in his relative's biology, picked up on worries that Darwin himself had expressed about civilized societies being undermined because they allowed the physically weak and the mentally retarded to breed. Legal rights, charity, vaccination, health care, and social programs seemed to mean that natural selection, operating by the elimination of the unfit, or at least the restriction of their reproduction, no longer applied to human society. That, it was feared, was a Very Bad Thing. Galton coined the word "eugenics" for the study of how to produce fine offspring. The practical implication was that society ought to take care of its own genetic future. The antidote to "the multiplication of the reckless and the improvident" (Darwin's all-too-evocative phrase) seemed to be a program analogous to the selective breeding of animals. The state should prevent "inferior" humans being born (negative eugenics) and perhaps encourage the production of "superior" types of people (positive eugenics).

The eugenics movement gathered widespread support across the political spectrum, from reformers at least as much as conservatives—though it was opposed by the Roman Catholic Church. In the early decades of the twentieth century, many U.S. states and Scandinavian countries passed laws for the compulsory sterilization of confirmed criminals and the "feebleminded." Germany joined in, even before Hitler's accession to power. Under the Nazis, the production of "pure-blood Aryan" children was encouraged, and "defectives" of various kinds were not just sterilized, but killed.

The basic ethical objection to positive or negative eugenic programs is that they involve the state intruding on one of the most basic human rights of individuals, namely, to form sexual relationships and produce children as they choose. There is also an important genetic difficulty in trying to eradicate defects or diseases that are carried by recessive genes, since many of the population may carry one such gene, yet the problem will show up only in those who inherit two. To prevent reproduction by *all* those who carry the gene would be practically impossible, even if it were ethically acceptable. And its effects on the overall population would be very unpredictable.

Eugenics depended on making discriminatory judgments about who was to be treated as "inferior." It was thus easily associated with racism. Racial prejudice was deeply entrenched in European culture, affecting even world-famous philosophers of the Enlightenment such as Hume and Kant. Black slaves were imported into the Americas by the early European colonists, and the social and economic aftereffects of that system of slavery persist, so that race has remained a social issue even to the present day.

Darwin wrote a chapter about "the races of man," trying to assume a naturalist's classificatory point of view. Some of the physical differences are obvious, but he pointed out that *within* each race there is a great deal of variety. And despite the differences in skin color and physiognomy, we all have enormous similarities in body and psychology. (Darwin remarked that he had once been intimate with "a full-blooded Negro," which must have been at some point on his epic voyage.) All human beings can interbreed, and the offspring tend to display a graduating blend of characteristics. So there is often no sharp distinction between black and white. The fact that some people with light brown skin are labeled "black" and that many different peoples count as "white" shows that our everyday classifications are more sociological than biological. Darwin concluded that the so-called races of man were, for him, "varieties" that had arisen under long periods of geographical separation, perhaps by sexual selection at least as much as natural selection. But he was quite clear that races are not separate species.

It has to be admitted, however, that Darwin was not entirely free of the prejudices that were commonplace in his time. He talked of "civilized" and "barbarous" races. He was made vividly aware of the differences between himself and the natives of Tierra del Fuego that he encountered on his world tour, but he hoped that individuals he met such as Jeremy Button could be "improved" by English education. He thought of such "savages" as examples of how our own distant ancestors had been. The archaeological evidence showed that many ancient cultures had become extinct. And he expected—alas, all too truly—that the remaining primitive peoples would tend to die out in the worldwide competition for resources.

Darwin's speculative theory that natural selection in human prehistory had operated on tribes as much as on individuals seemed to license people to conclude that the presently dominant tribes (or races, cultures, or nations) had been successful because they were innately superior. Many people already believed this, or wanted to believe it, and eagerly latched on to what looked like scientific backing for their prejudice. Weismann's refutation of the inheritance of acquired characteristics seemed to leave little hope for the advancement of "innately inferior" races by education and social programs.

In the United States, the Harvard psychologist William McDougall pronounced in 1921 that the races differ in intellectual stature, just as they do in physical stature. Social and political thinkers who were inclined to racism thought they had a justification for continued discrimination and exploitation of the black population. In the early years of the twentieth century, there was considerable worry about an alleged weakening of the American population through the immigration of supposedly inferior peoples from southern and eastern Europe, including many Jews. Psychologists such as Carl Brigham of Princeton claimed that the evidence showed "Nordics" to be superior to all other groups. The U.S. Immigration Act of 1924 displayed clear racial and ethnic bias against Chinese, Japanese, and non-Nordic Europeans.

Another conspicuous way of dividing and discriminating was by sex. On this topic, too, Darwin's legacy was somewhat ambiguous. No naturalist could fail to notice the differences in physique, coloration, and behavior between the sexes in many species of animals and birds. Darwin had argued that sexual selection was often an important factor in natural selection. When it came to humans, his remarks about alleged mental differences would raise hackles now. He said that "man is more courageous, pugnacious, and energetic than woman, and has a more inventive genius" (p. 316). Worse, he wrote:

> The chief distinction in the intellectual powers of the two sexes is shewn by man attaining to a higher eminence, in whatever he takes up, than woman can attain—whether requiring deep thought, reason, or imagination, or merely the use of the senses and hands. . . . We may also infer . . . the average standard of mental power in man must be above that of woman. (p. 327)

However, he went on to say:

> In order that woman should reach the same standard as man, she ought, when nearly adult, to be trained to energy and perseverance, and to have her reason and imagination exercised to the highest point. (p. 329)

So Darwin could not be numbered among the opponents of higher education for women, who tried to argue that women's place was in the home and that they were innately incapable of benefiting from advanced education.

The Reaction in Favor of Culture and Education: Intelligence Tests, Sociology, and Anthropology

By what criteria were these invidious distinctions between the races and the sexes drawn? That there are some physical differences in both cases is obvious. The controversial point is whether these correlate, on average, with mental differences, and especially with intelligence. We have just seen Darwin himself asserting this. But what was his evidence? It fell below his usual high scientific standard, being nothing more than an impressionistic survey of the achievements of the sexes in history so far (and the same applies to his estimates of mental differences between the races). But from achievement to potential, from difference in mental performance to difference in innate mental power, is not a valid inference unless the conditions are equal for the individuals or groups being compared. So it is perfectly reasonable to object that the social conditions and educational opportunities for nonwhites, and for women, had been very far from equal to those for white men, in the period we are talking about, up to about 1900.

In comparing the intelligence of different groups, psychologists and social scientists in the next half century or so tended to assume that in each individual there is some fixed, innate factor that they called "intelligence," which they thought could be measured by "intelligence tests." Such tests were used in 1917 to assign U.S. Army recruits to different roles and to classify criminals. They were also employed to diagnose "mental deficiency" or "feeblemindedness," and thus identify candidates for sterilization under eugenic laws. And they could be applied, controversially, to compare men and women. Indeed, some of the early IQ tests showed women in the lead, so the content of the tests was changed to include more spatial reasoning, which "corrected" the "imbalance"! This vividly illustrates just how contentious the very definition of "intelligence" is.

But the significance of such tests was hotly debated. Obviously, there are mental differences between individuals, but it does not follow that there is a single thing that we can call "intelligence." Some people are good at mathematics, some at carpentry, music, languages, cooking, business, hunting, child care, politics, and so on. It is not obvious that all these kinds of ability can be amalgamated onto a common scale, so that each person can be labeled with an "intelligence quotient" (IQ). Some psychologists have talked of "social intelligence" and "emotional intelligence," thus widening the debate about the concept.

And for any particular test performance, we can always ask how much of it is due to innate "intelligence" (or better, to innate abilities for specific activities) and how much is due to opportunities, need, encouragement, and training. Of course, it is often difficult to say. There are *individual* differences, to be sure, but it certainly does not follow that they are correlated with distinctions of race, ethnicity, or sex. If someone is categorized as "mentally deficient" as a result of certain tests, how far are we to put that down to innate factors and how much to lack of opportunity, especially perhaps to early experience in a dysfunctional family? The whole business of intelligence testing, and the supposed scientific basis of intergroup mental comparisons, became thoroughly controversial.

In this same period (roughly, 1875–1925), what we now call the "social sciences" were emerging as academic disciplines, the main contenders being anthropology, sociology, social psychology, economics, and "political science." The founding fathers of social science, such as Karl Marx, Max Weber, and Emile Durkheim, held that apart from a few obvious biological universals like eating, defecating, sleeping, copulating, giving birth, and breastfeeding, most human behavior depends more on culture than on biology. The claim for a distinctive subject matter was based on a threefold division between facts about human beings:

1. the physical facts—studied by anatomy, physiology, and evolutionary theory

2. the (individual) psychological facts—studied by individual psychology

3. the social/cultural facts—studied by the social sciences

The French sociologist Emile Durkheim (1858–1917) argued strongly for the irreducibility of social facts (e.g., about what is legally or morally required) to any ensemble of individual psychological facts. He insisted that social facts are "things," in the sense that their existence is just as independent of human will as anything in the physical world. (Disobey a moral or legal rule, and you are likely to find yourself faced with very real sanctions or penalties!) Such social facts are "emergent" in the same way that many facts about other wholes cannot be derived from the nature of their parts—e.g., the wetness of water cannot be deduced from the properties of hydrogen and oxygen.

Society is not a mysterious abstract entity: social rules can only affect people via other people's actions, such as law enforcement by police officers and judges, or reminders about etiquette from mothers-in-law. But police officers have to be appointed by social institutions, and they are supposed to have some understanding of the legal powers they are given. Mothers-in-law stand in specific social relationships to their family, and their ideas often have a distinctively social content (revealed in comments like, "What will the neighbors say?"). So there seems to be no reduction of social facts to purely psychological facts.

Durkheim was an evolutionary theorist only in the most general nonbiological sense, in that he believed in law-governed processes of change and development in human societies. He saw some analogy between the evolution of species and the social trend toward increasing division of labor, and hence he talked of the differentiation of "species" of economic and social roles. But he was under no illusion that this was Darwinian natural selection; rather he held that it is subject to distinctively sociological laws.

In the United States, Alfred Kroeber (1876–1960) of the University of California arrived at a very similar conception, expressed through his concept of the "superorganic," by which he meant the variable element of culture that is superimposed on common biological human nature and is irreducible to it. "Civilization and heredity," he wrote, "are two things that operate in separate ways." Kroeber had been a pupil of Franz Boas (1858–1942), the founding father of anthropology in the United States. From the very beginning of his academic career, Boas relentlessly opposed the idea that cultural differences were based on innate racial differences in mentality. He almost single-handedly persuaded social scientists (in the United States at least) that culture is irreducible to biology, thus introducing the modern conception of *cultures*, in the plural.

Boas's influence was due not just to a priori arguments, but to a striking empirical study (the results of which surprised even himself!). At the time the most widely accepted measure of innate biological differences between peoples was the "cephalic index"—the ratio of the length to the width of the human head. Boas's 1911 study showed that the cephalic index of the children of immigrants to the United States had changed significantly within ten years of arrival. This must have been caused by some kind of environmental change, for there was obviously no change in genes. In a quite different study of auditory perception, Boas argued that our inability to hear certain crucial differences in sounds in foreign languages is a result not of innate differences but of our early training in our native language. Such evidence provided a direct counter to racist assertions that the different races had innately different mental capacities. Boas was very happy about that, for he was a resolute opponent of the prevailing racism in American society and academia. He had been born into a liberal Jewish family in Germany, but emigrated to the United States because of rising anti-Semitism. His liberal convictions drove his theoretical claims, but there is no evidence that they distorted them.

It is clear that certain *values*—equality of opportunity, equality before the law, and equal respect for human dignity in every person—were deeply involved in the reaction of so many twentieth century social thinkers against what they saw as the insidious influence of evolutionary biology toward racism and sexism. The concept of "culture" as independent of biology in explaining human nature was the linchpin of this whole generation of thought. "Culture" was not merely a theoretical concept, but was strongly associated with an ethical/political outlook that wanted to treat all people (in the singular) and all peoples (in the plural) as equal.

It should be noted, however, that there is an important distinction here. It is one thing to insist that all human *individuals* should be given equal opportunities, but quite another to say that all human *cultures* are of equal value. Boas, for example, thought (for better or for worse) that the best future for Afro-Americans and for Amerindians was to assimilate to the dominant culture of European origin. Talk of individual human rights has a clear meaning and authority in many contexts, but it is less clear that talk of the rights of cultures makes similar sense. After all, some alleged cultural "rights"—to suttee, foot binding, or female circumcision, for instance—come into obvious conflict with individual rights. Anthropologists in this period made it their task to describe the variety of human cultures all around the world. Indeed there was a rush to catalog the remaining "primitive" societies before they died out or became homogenized into the global economy. Whether such extinction or assimilation is a Good or Bad (or Indifferent) Thing is another question.

Differences between the sexes was a quite different issue, which brought people closer to home (quite literally). There have been several generations of feminist thought since Darwin's time, and no complete survey can be given here. But from the beginning, feminists have differed among themselves, sometimes hotly. There have been "equality feminists," who tend to argue that apart from the obvious physical differences, the human sexes are innately very much the same in mental endowment, so that any average differences in performance are due to the different sets of expectations, education, and social role that societies or cultures impose. The policy implication was usually drawn that all such differential social treatment should be eliminated, and strict equality aimed at. On the other hand, "difference feminists" argued that there are, on average, innate mental differences between men and women, and that society should therefore treat them differently to some extent (to be much debated!). Some of the difference feminists have been prepared to claim that women are innately *morally superior* to men because they are more caring, sympathetic and cooperative.

The Reaction against Instinct Theory: Behaviorist Psychology

Within psychology there was a similar pattern of early influence of Darwinian (or supposedly Darwinian) ideas, followed by a strong reaction against them. The thought of Sigmund Freud (1856–1939) can be described as an attempt to put psychology on a biological basis. He postulated "*Triebe*," or instincts, as the fundamental driving forces in the human mind, but he was somewhat vague in his account of them. He admitted we can distinguish an indeterminate number of "instincts," yet he suggested that they can all be derived from a few basic ones. Freud is notorious for emphasizing the ubiquitous influence of sexuality, but he always held that there was at least one *other* basic drive. In his early theorizing he talked of "self-preservative" instincts, for eating and self-protection. But in later works he radically changed his classification, ascribing libido and hunger to one "life" instinct (Eros), and referring sadism, aggression, and self-destruction to a biologically implausible "death" instinct (Thanatos).

In the United States, the concept of instinct was also very freely deployed in the psychologies of William James (1842–1910) and William McDougall (1871–1938). James defined "instinct" as "the faculty of acting in such a way as to produce certain ends, without foresight of the end, or without previous education in the performance," and he included as instincts standing, walking, rivalry, anger, resentment, hunting and fear— a notably longer and more diverse list than Freud's! James was a deep philosopher and a founding father of scientific psychology, but it was inevitable that there would be a reaction against the vagueness of this talk. After all, if we are to recognize instincts in the plural, there ought to be a determinate way of counting just how many there are, in any given species.

The "behaviorist" movement initiated by John B. Watson (1878–1958) proposed to put psychology on a newly rigorous methodological basis by defining it as the study of the observable behavior of animals and humans, and forbidding it to invoke any suspiciously mentalistic notions such as instinct, intention, or consciousness in the explanation of behavior. Watson also proclaimed a naive faith in the power of environmental influences over individual differences, as when he overboldly claimed that any healthy child could be trained or "conditioned" to become a world-class athlete, a physicist, a captain of industry, or a thief. (Perhaps it is no surprise that he ended up in the advertising industry!)

The behaviorist program was carried further at Harvard by B. F. Skinner (1904–1990), one of the most influential experimental psychologists of his generation. Skinner liked to draw an analogy between his theory of behavioral conditioning and Darwinian natural selection, saying that the environment "shapes" or "selects" behavior, rewarding or "reinforcing" some behaviors so that they tend to be repeated. Skinner hoped to find "laws of behavior" and "schedules of reinforcement" that would hold good across all, or many, different species. To this end he conducted elaborate experiments mainly on rats and pigeons, and he tried—very contentiously—to extrapolate his findings to human beings in popular books such as his *Science and Human Behavior* of 1953.

Skinner tended to assume that animal and human behavior can be explained in terms of *environmental* causes. He could not deny the differences between species, but he assumed that there are no significant innate differences between individuals. However, the fact that identical twins brought up apart usually turn out so similar in personality and mental ability is clear evidence for inherited individual differences. Human behavior manifestly depends on innate factors as well as environmental input. Much of what is innate is our common human biological, gene-based nature, which is distinct from other animals, even from our nearest relatives, the great apes. But there are also innate individual differences, as all parents know.

Because of the strength of the mid-twentieth century political/cultural/environmental/behavioral reaction against supposedly Darwinian ideas, these general facts were rather obscured from view for a generation or more. Both the racist and sexist prejudices, and the equality-of-opportunity rejection of them, were based on social values rather than biology. We may continue to applaud and endorse the equal rights values, but we should not confuse them with scientific facts.

For Further Reading

In the Very Short Introduction series published by Oxford University Press, there are relevant titles on Darwin, evolution, evolutionary psychology, psychology, and social and cultural anthropology.

My structuring of the post-Darwinian debates has been influenced by Carl N. Degler's book, *In Search of Human Nature: The Decline and Revival of Darwinism in American Social Thought* (Oxford University Press, 1991).

A brief survey of Darwinian thought and its wider implications is given by John Dupre in *Darwin's Legacy: What Evolution Means Today* (Oxford University Press, 2003).

EVOLUTIONARY THEORY, STAGE III: THE RETURN TO HUMAN NATURE

Genes and Memes

After the "modern synthesis" of evolutionary theory in the 1930s and 1940s, a further depth of biological understanding was attained by a new generation of pioneering thinkers in the 1960s and 1970s. George Williams, Robert Trivers, William Hamilton, and John Maynard Smith offered new mathematically based insights into adaptation, kin selection, reciprocal altruism, and the relevance of game theory to evolving populations.

Given all this, it became possible to re-express Darwin's basic insights in terms of genes, as Richard Dawkins did in his famous book *The Selfish Gene* in 1976. That title is a brilliantly chosen metaphor, inviting us to take "a genes'-eye-view" of evolution. Philosophers diagnosed a category mistake, since genes cannot literally be selfish: only whole people can be thus described. But Dawkins's point was to see biological evolution not so much as species gradually changing because of competition between individuals, but as genes competing with each other for a place in the next generation. Animals are born and die, but genes are passed on through the generations: compared to individual organisms, genes are relatively immortal (though they are lost when a species goes extinct).

In a more speculative chapter at the end of his book, Dawkins suggested that human culture could be seen as a field of analogous, but much faster, evolution. This would involve identifying fundamental items of human culture (ideas? beliefs? practices? fashions?) for which Dawkins proposed the neologism "memes." His idea was that memes, like genes, can be transferred from person to person; some "catch on" and survive (with modifications) over many generations, but others die out rather quickly. Even here, there was an anticipation by the far-seeing Darwin, when he compared the survival of words in human languages to that of organisms in environments. However, it is unclear what, if anything, can count as a "unit of culture" or "meme." Discussion continues among biologists over exactly what should be seen as the units of selection: genes, packages of genes, individual organisms, memes, or perhaps (after all!) groups of individuals such as human tribes. Perhaps indeed there are *multiple* levels of simultaneous selection. Things are getting complicated in biological theory!

The Rise of Ethology

In the mid-twentieth century, a new discipline was emerging that came to be called "ethology," the scientific study of animal behavior in its *natural* environment. This discipline had roots in the work of earlier naturalists, including Darwin himself, who published *The Expression of the Emotions in Animals and Man* in 1872, in which he argued that much of the behavior of animals, and ourselves, is as innate as physiological structures. Niko Tinbergen (a Dutchman who became a professor at Oxford) was one of the founding fathers of ethology, other pioneers and Nobel Prize winners being Konrad Lorenz and Karl von Frisch, who studied the communicative dances of bees.

The ethologists argued that many patterns of animal behavior (mainly those that we colloquially describe as "instinctive") could not be explained in the behaviorist way, since they appear spontaneously in all individuals of the species (or in all males or all females), almost independently of previous experience or learning. In many birds, for example, the typical patterns of feeding, courtship, nest building, and care of the young answer to this description. During the rutting season, male deer start to fight with other males and to pursue the females. Seagull chicks peck at the red spot on the beak of their parent to stimulate the disgorging of food. Male stickleback fish react aggressively to the distinctive coloration of another male on their territory. Such behaviors seemed to Lorenz to be instinctive or "fixed," in that they cannot be eliminated, however much the environment is varied. (But it was soon realized that the story was not so simple.) To explain such apparently instinctive behavior, ethologists appealed not to the past experience of the *individual* animal, but to the process of evolution that has given rise to the *species*.

Tinbergen distinguished four kinds of questions that can be asked about any particular item of behavior, or equivalently, four senses of the question "Why did that creature perform that behavior in that situation?":

1. What was the *internal physiological cause* of the behavior? To this the answer may be given in terms of muscle contractions, nervous impulses, hormone secretions, and so on.

2. What in the *development* or *experience* of the individual prepared the way for that behavior? Here the answer may appeal to the development of the fetus in the womb and to the normal growth pattern in the species (e.g., the hormonal changes involved in reaching sexual maturity). But there is also room for particular experiences of the individual to make a difference to later behavior (e.g., the detail of adult birdsong may depend on what songs the individual has heard; primates have developed different kinds of tool use that are passed on by teaching and imitation).

3. What is the *function* of the behavior? That is, what is it *for*, what goal does it typically achieve for the individual? Here the answer is sometimes obvious, and the behavior is described as feeding, predator avoidance, mating, or care of the young. But in other cases it is not clear what the function of a certain behavior is, although it may be quite distinctive in terms of the bodily movements involved—e.g., is it threat, or courtship, defense against predators, or reinforcement of a bond between a "married" pair? Prolonged observation of such a behavior pattern in various contexts may enable ethologists to interpret its function, as contributing in some particular way to passing on the individual's genes.

4. What is the *evolutionary history* of this pattern of behavior? Sometimes this seems hardly distinguishable from (3); for example, the bodily movements involved in feeding have presumably always had the same function. In other cases, however, a distinctive behavior pattern in a species may not have had the same function in the ancestors as it has now. For example, some of the "signaling" postures of birds that now function as threats or courtship seem to have resulted from a "ritualization" of what were once merely "intention movements" preparatory to flight. The evolution of behavior, as of bodily features, often involves "jerry-building," the adaptation of inherited items to new uses in changing conditions. We cannot press rewind buttons and observe the past, but in some cases ethologists can make reasonable inferences about a pathway of evolutionary history, and thus distinguish (4) from (3).

Obviously, answers of these four kinds are perfectly compatible with each other; they are all part of the overall complicated truth about animal behavior. If there is such a thing as a complete explanation of any single act, it would have to include the relevant facts at all four levels.

Konrad Lorenz (1903–1989) made his reputation with his studies of animal behavior, notably the "imprinting" of ducklings on the first moving thing they see. He also wrote engagingly for the general public and tried to apply his biological understanding to human problems. In *On Aggression* in 1963 he offered a diagnosis of human problems based on our allegedly innate aggressive tendencies. He suggested that humans have an innate drive to aggressive behavior toward our own species, and he sought an evolutionary explanation for this, speculating that at a certain stage of our ancestors' evolution, the main threat to life may have come from other hominoid groups. So those groups that banded together best to fight other groups would tend to survive longest.

But Lorenz tended to fall into a trap that awaits such attempts at popular evolutionary explanation of human traits—namely, to assume too readily that a certain pattern of observed human behavior is innate rather than culturally learned or encouraged, and then to imagine, without much attempt at testing, a hypothesis about what selection pressures were at work in a long-distant era of our ancestors' evolution. There is then a strong temptation to infer that since a given sort of behavior is (supposedly) innate in humans, it is inevitable—or at least very difficult to eradicate or discourage. This pattern of argument has been applied, just as dubiously, to aggression, warfare, and rape. Biologists also criticized Lorenz for appealing to "group selection," which, as we have seen, was appealed to by Darwin himself, but was rejected by his successors. However, debate continues about the possibility of group selection in certain conditions, so perhaps we can say that the jury is still out on the defensibility of some version of Lorenz's hypothesis about an innate human tendency to group aggression in certain circumstances.

Chomsky and Cognitive Psychology

One especially distinctive feature of human behavior is our use of language. In his 1957 book *Verbal Behavior*, B. F. Skinner proposed to show that all human speech can be explained in terms of the conditioning of speakers by their early social environment: the speech of surrounding humans and their reactions to noises by the child. Thus, a baby in a Spanish-speaking family is subjected to samples of the Spanish language in use, and when its responses are reasonably accurate reproductions of what it has heard, they are reinforced by approval and reward, and thus the child learns to speak Spanish.

The crucial defects in Skinner's account of language were pointed out by Noam Chomsky, a professor of linguistics at MIT whose research has been fundamental to the cognitive revolution in psychology since the 1960s. Chomsky argued that Skinner's account of *how* language is learned pays no attention to the question of *what* it is that we learn. The *creative* and *structural* features of human language—the way in which we can all speak and understand sentences we have never heard before—make it quite different from any known kind of animal behavior. There is also the matter of innate learning capacities. Obviously, the social environment decides which language is learned. But all normal children learn at least one language, whereas no other animal learns anything resembling a human language in the crucial respect of the formation of indefinitely many complex sentences according to rules of grammar. Experiments on teaching chimpanzees signing systems have been said to show some approximations to human language use, but it still seems that the capacity to learn and use a full range of human language is peculiar to the human species.

Chomsky argued that the amazing speed with which children learn their native language, from exposure to a very limited and imperfect sample of it, can be explained only by the assumption that there is in the human species an *innate* capacity to process language according to grammatical rules of a form common to all human languages. So behind their impressive variety there must be a certain basic systematic structure in common, and we have to suppose that children do not *learn* this structure from their environment, but process whatever linguistic input they receive in terms of it.

Given that we are an evolved species, this peculiar linguistic ability that we have—this "mental organ"—must surely be what evolutionists call an adaptation, i.e., a feature that has been bred into human genes by natural selection operating on hominoid populations in the distant past. At least, that is what recent evolutionary psychologists have argued, though Chomsky himself has expressed some skepticism about such evolutionary speculations about language. Further research is being pursued at three levels: in linguistics, into more detailed specification of just what is characteristic of human languages; in brain science, into how language is processed and how the brain of the language-learning infant develops; and in hominoid evolution, into how our language ability may have evolved.

Speech is not the only human activity, but it is especially important as representative of the higher human mental abilities. This opens up the possibility that other important determinants of human behavior are not learned from the environment but are innate. Much research in psychology has concerned innate mechanisms in perception, an influential paradigm being the work of David Marr on perception. We must reckon with the thought that the evolution of our ancestors may have produced other genetically based "modules" in humans.

Wilson and Sociobiology

Can the theory of evolution, the biochemical understanding of genes, and the study of innate capacities and behavior patterns be brought together and applied to the study of human nature? The Harvard biologist Edward O. Wilson boldly claimed to do just that in his 1975 book, *Sociobiology:*

The New Synthesis. He outlined a newly unified approach to biology that would apply the rigorous methods of population biology and genetics to complex social systems. Building on his earlier technical studies of social insects such as ants, Wilson applied a similar method to other social creatures, and in his final chapter he sketched how it might be extended to humans. Here is the first paragraph of that controversial chapter:

> Let us now consider man in the free spirit of natural history, as though we were zoologists from another planet completing a catalog of social species on Earth. In this macroscopic view the humanities and social sciences shrink to specialized branches of biology; history, biography, and fiction are the protocols of human ethology; and anthropology and sociology together constitute the sociobiology of a single primate species.

Wilson was suggesting that the humanities and social sciences should become subdepartments of biology, and that other areas of biological study would be absorbed into his envisioned superscience of sociobiology. One reason for the controversy that arose was academic turf wars: the various specialists in the humanities and the sciences defending their professional territories against this takeover bid.

The section headings of Wilson's chapter on humans indicate the tremendous range of material that he hoped to bring within his explanatory ambitions: Plasticity of Social Organization; Barter and Reciprocal Altruism; Bonding, Sex, and Division of Labor; Role Playing and Polytheism; Communication; Culture, Ritual, and Religion: Ethics; Esthetics; Territoriality and Tribalism; Early Social Evolution; Later Social Evolution; and—wait for it!—The Future. Nothing, it seems, was to be beyond the bounds of sociobiology!

In his next book, *On Human Nature* (1978), Wilson argued in more detail that the only way toward understanding human nature is to study it as part of the natural sciences. Disarmingly, he said early on that this book was not a work of science, but a work *about* science, "a speculative essay about the profound consequences that will follow as social theory at long last meets that part of the natural sciences most relevant to it." The central chapters are more empirical, making claims about innate factors in human aggression, sexuality, altruism, and religion. But the beginning and end of the book are about "spiritual dilemmas" consequent on the truth of evolution. The biological scientist was turning philosopher! (I will touch on some of these issues in the concluding chapter.)

Wilson has gone on to write several other wide-ranging, popular-level, philosophizing books. Clearly he is a man of tireless energy, an omnivorous intellectual appetite (in both the sciences and the arts), an eloquent flow of words, and a certain missionary zeal. In *The Diversity of Life* and *Biophilia* he campaigned to try to stop the human-caused extinction of so many species on this planet. In *Naturalist* he has given us his auto-biography, including his own account of the great controversies over sociobiology. And in *Consilience* (1998) he argued again for the unification of all legitimate knowledge—social sciences and humanities included—under the scientific banner. The kind of unity he envisages sometimes sounds very extreme—namely, the reduction of all other scientific principles to the laws of physics. But in other places he backs off from that stance and admits that genuine emergence of new properties irreducible to those of lower levels may be found. He asserts that the Enlightenment belief in the possibility of unlimited human progress is being confirmed by scientific evidence—which suggests an element of (perhaps naive) secular faith underneath all the scientific sophistication.

Wilson has been a man with a mission: to apply the theories of evolution, population biology, genetics, and neuroscience to *all* aspects of human existence—and perhaps to save the world! His sociobiological program, seeking to explain human social phenomena in terms of selective pressures (and thus in terms of genes—and maybe ultimately in term of physics?), goes flatly against Durkheim's postulate of the irreducibility of social facts. It threatened the self-images of anthropology and sociology, and seemed to ignore the distinctively cultural aspects of human life.

This explains the moral and political objections that were brought against sociobiology—some of them from Wilson's distinguished colleagues in the biology department at Harvard, Richard Lewontin and Stephen Jay Gould. There was a strong feeling that in emphasizing the biological factors in human life and apparently neglecting the role of culture, Wilson was giving (presumably unintentional) aid and comfort to reactionary tendencies in American and British society. If nature is more influential than nurture in forming human individuals and societies, it seemed that there would be much less possibility than many social theorists had liked to think of improving individuals and society by education, social programs, and political change. Moralists and politicians of conservative tendency could say (erroneously) that if the differences between individuals, the races, and the sexes are innate, there is no point in trying to reduce or eliminate them. Socialists, antiracists, and feminists therefore tended to assume that the only "politically correct" position was that, apart from our bodily physiology and a few general-purpose learning devices, human nature is basically a "blank slate" to be written on by society.

Hot though the controversy was following the publication of Wilson's 1975 manifesto for sociobiology, it now looks to have been the last big throw of the antibiological, pro-culture movement that dominated academic social thought in the middle years of the twentieth century. In fact, any moderately careful reading of Wilson's work, particularly his later writings, shows that, far from denying the influence of culture, he sees biology and culture as *both* contributing essentially to the development of individuals and of human societies. His main point remains that our biology limits the range of variety of human cultures; as he put it, "genes hold culture on a leash." When the blur of ideological prejudice and journalistic oversimplification has cleared away, it is obvious enough that there is no overall choice to be made for or against nature or nurture, since *both* are crucial to the formation of each individual. The empirical question with respect to each aspect of human behavior is *how much of it* is due to nature and how much to nurture (and that is often very difficult to answer!). The value question is how far, if at all, we should treat people differently when they appear to have different innate abilities.

Chomsky's approach to language remains a paradigm here: the common grammatical form of human languages is due to our biology, hardwired in the brain, whereas the enormous variety of human languages is due to culture. Similarly, the human propensity for athletic sports is universal across cultures, but the popularity of different kinds of games is culturally specific (e.g., baseball in the United States, cricket in England— and if the Mayan ball games involved human sacrifice, that was going a bit beyond sport as we understand it). And the whole business of being a successful parent—from courtship and sexual union, through to babycare and child rearing up to the stage when one's offspring can leave home and perhaps become a parent in turn—is the most complex of life's challenges, involving both our most deeply biological behaviors and the helps and hazards of the culture we inhabit.

Very roughly, we can see the dialectic of stages of post-Darwinian evolutionary thinking as follows:

Part I: emphasis on biology, on what is in our nature, innate, "in the genes"

Part II: emphasis on culture, on what is due to nurture, education, and society

Part III: recognition that genes and culture, nature and nurture, are *both* crucial

Away from the oversimplifications of popular thought, the cutting edge of biological theory has now become highly mathematical. This trend started with the statistical treatment of genetics and population biology, and it has proceeded apace. Physicists have long been used to the fact that the only way they can try to explain their highly technical, mathematical theories to the public is to talk in metaphors that are all too easily misunderstood (e.g., space being curved, time starting with a big bang). Biologists are now having to get used to a similar situation in their own discipline.

In *Genes, Mind and Culture* (1981), Wilson and his physicist collaborator Charles Lumsden offered a mathematical theory of how genes and culture coevolve, but it was too esoteric to affect the controversies of the time. However, other biological theorists, such as Robert Boyd and Peter Richerson in their book *Culture and the Evolutionary Process* (1985), have followed up on this line of research.

Cosmides/Tooby and the Integrated Causal Model

Because of the controversy that Wilson's program aroused, his term "sociobiology" has rather fallen out of favor, and "evolutionary psychology" has become the preferred phrase for many of those who persist in applying a Darwinian approach to the human mind. In 1992 there appeared an influential collection of research papers entitled *The Adapted Mind: Evolutionary Psychology and the Generation of Culture*. The first 150 pages or so consist of densely argued programmatic statements of the approach favored by Leda Cosmides and John Tooby, backed up by Donald Symons and Jerome Barkow. (The first three were at the University of California at Santa Barbara, so they have been labeled "the Santa Barbara school."

The basic premise of this school of thought is that there is indeed a universal human nature, but more at the level of evolved *psychological mechanisms* than of specific patterns of behavior. To be sure, there are some bodily movements that are distinctively and universally human, such as walking, talking, and face-to-face sexual intercourse. But culture produces marked variations in most of what we do; it affects what language we use, what we use it to say (on all sorts of occasions), what music we sing, play, or listen to, and all that goes before and after copulation (and perhaps even the styles of sexual congress itself!).

The second main premise is that our evolved psychological mechanisms are "*adaptations*" that have been selected for over many generations of our ancestors. It is important here to make a distinction between what is an adaptation and what is merely "adaptive." Adaptive behavior is what leads to better survival and reproduction in *present* circumstances. For example, going to college is supposed to lead to an economically better life, and hence (perhaps!) to more descendants; if so, it is adaptive in present circumstances. But it has obviously not been selected for in the prehistory of humans! Conversely, if something is an adaptation, that does not imply that it is still adaptive now. Perhaps a male predisposition to anger and aggression in frustrating circumstances has been selected for (*perhaps*—it is controversial), but it does not follow that such a character is conducive to survival and reproduction in present-day societies in which knives and guns are readily available and police are on call.

A third premise of the Santa Barbara school is that the evolved human mind contains a number of adaptations to the way of life of our distant ancestors—*the hunter-gatherers of the Stone Age*, i.e., the Pleistocene era of the last 1.7 million years or so (cumbrously labeled "the Environment of Evolutionary Adaptedness"). If that is the case, we should not be surprised if our psychological inheritance is not particularly well adapted to our contemporary cultures in the skyscrapers of New York, the suburbs of Glasgow, or the shantytowns of Rio. Cosmides and Tooby think it unlikely that there have been any significant changes in the human gene pool since the beginning of agriculture, let alone industrial or postindustrial economies. But other evolutionists have pointed out that they are on debatable empirical ground here. Since the spread of dairy farming, over only a few thousand years, many humans have evolved to be able to digest the lactose in cows' milk. Is it possible that certain aspects of our psychology have also evolved in response to major economic/social/cultural developments? The question would appear to be interestingly open. Recent data from the Human Genome Project are said to support the argument for rapid recent evolution of genes expressed in the human brain.

Cosmides and Tooby give a very thorough exposition and critique of what they call the "standard social science model," which has been typical of the social sciences for most of the twentieth century (see Part II of this chapter). They argue that because of the intensity of its associated antiracist and antisexist ideology, this approach has ignored the evidence for many innate, evolutionarily produced cognitive mechanisms in the human mind, and has misleadingly concentrated on culture as the major creator of each individual. They propose instead (like Wilson) that the biological, the psychological, and the social or cultural should be seen as interlocking parts of a complex causal web behind human nature:

> The rich complexity of each individual is produced by a cognitive architecture, embodied in a physiological system, which interacts with the social and nonsocial world that surrounds it. Thus humans, like every other natural system, are embedded in the contingencies of a larger principled history, and explaining any particular fact about them requires the joint analysis of all the principles and contingencies involved. To break this seamless matrix of causation—to attempt to dismember the individual into "biological" versus "non-biological" aspects—is to embrace and perpetuate

an ancient dualism endemic to the Western cultural tradition: material/spiritual, body/mind, physical/mental, natural/human, animal/human, biological/social, biological/cultural. This dualist view expresses only a pre-modern version of biology, whose intellectual warrant has vanished.

According to this "integrated causal model," behind any human phenomenon—even a single action—there is a complicated set of chains of causation, involving:

1. natural selection operating on our ancestors over many thousands—indeed millions—of years to produce a variety of innate mental modules in the human species;
2. the historical development of a variety of human economies and cultures over many centuries;
3. the mixing of genes in sexual reproduction that gives every human being their own unique set of genes (except in the case of identical twins);
4. the effects of the physical and social/cultural environment on bodily and mental development over the lifetime of each individual;
5. the information processing involved in perception and speech recognition, the results of which ("beliefs") join with motivational factors ("desires") to be the immediate cause of particular actions.

The picture is of "a seamless matrix of causation," and the only kind of explanation that is here recognized is scientific, *causal* explanation. Where that leaves our giving of *reasons* for our actions and for our beliefs (which I touched on in Chapter 7 on Kant) is a philosophical issue to be taken up in the concluding chapter.

All this, the Santa Barbara school argues, makes it very likely that there are a number of innate human mental modules produced by natural selection operating on our hominoid ancestors. And that these have to do with matters that were relevant to the reproductive fitness of our ancestors—such as perception, social communication and language use, cooperation and trade, mate selection, pregnancy, and parental care—is no surprise. The human mind has thus been compared to a Swiss army device, i.e., a compendium of specialized tools rather than a single all-purpose device.

But the issues here are empirical, and in many cases open. The role of culture may be dangerously underemphasized in (4). The cultural influence is dynamic, constantly changing, and socially transmitted. And besides mental modules designed by evolution to perform specific tasks, it seems obvious that humans (and perhaps many animals) also have a general, flexible kind of intelligence that enables them to solve unpredictable problems encountered in experience. It requires detailed argument and elusive empirical evidence to establish exactly what the mental modules are and what the selection pressures were. It is not sufficient to invent plausible evolutionary speculations from the armchair, "just-so stories" that say: this is how it must have been back in the days when we were evolving, so this is why it is as it is now, and must evermore be so. Much empirical work is being done, and evolutionary psychology (in a general sense, not confined to the approach of the Santa Barbara school) now promises to enter on the secure path of an empirical science.

Yet a word of caution still seem appropriate, for it is extremely difficult for us to know how the postulated selective processes may have panned out in the long-vanished Pleistocene era, or indeed in the ten thousand years or more since then. And let us not forget that while today's evolutionary psychologists are committed to putting a good deal of the causation down to culture, their conception of culture would probably be rejected as inadequate by social anthropologists. The Santa Barbara brand of evolutionary psychology is not the only game in the scientific town. There are ongoing research programs in human behavioral ecology and in gene culture coevolution, reviewed by Laland and Brown in *Sense and Nonsense: Evolutionary Perspectives on Human Behaviour* (2002).

In conclusion, dare I say that there is still such a thing as individual choice! Our hormones can affect our behavior, but it is also true that our behavior can affect our hormones—by taking pills or by taking exercise. We may yearn for scientific guidance on how to solve our personal or social problems, but solid scientific knowledge is an elusive commodity, above all on a topic as complicated as human nature. And as we have just seen, it is applicable to social problems only in conjunction with values, which we must get from somewhere else. Useful scientific knowledge is welcome when it comes, as in medicine, but often we have to get on with our lives without it; and even when it comes, it cannot answer all the questions of life.

FOR FURTHER READING

Two thought-provoking histories of psychology are George. A. Millar and R. Buckout, *Psychology: The Science of Mental Life*, 2nd ed. (New York: Harper & Row, 1973); and L. S. Hearnshaw, *The Shaping of Modern Psychology: An Historical Introduction* (London: Routledge, 1987), which covers the whole story since ancient times. In *Acts of Meaning* (Cambridge, Mass.: Harvard University Press, 1990), Jerome Bruner reviews the progress of psychology and recommends "cultural psychology."

Edward. O.Wilson's main ideas are to be found in *Sociobiology: The New Synthesis* (Cambridge, Mass.: Harvard University Press, 2000), *On Human Nature* (Cambridge, Mass.: Harvard University Press, 1978), and *Consilience: The Unity of Knowledge* (Boston: Little, Brown, 1998).

Opposition to sociobiology was vigorously expressed by Steven Rose, R. C. Lewontin, and Leon J. Kamin in *Not in Our Genes: Biology, Ideology and Human and Nature* (New York: Penguin, 1984). The controversy is examined in detail by the sociologist Ullica Segerstrale in *Defenders of the Truth: The Sociobiology Debate* (Oxford University Press, 2000).

For philosophical critiques of sociobiology, see Michael. Ruse, *Sociobiology: Sense or Nonsense?* (Dordrecht: Reidel, 1985); Mary Midgeley, *Beast and Man: The Roots of Human Nature* (London: Methuen, 1980); and Philip Kitcher, *Vaulting Ambition: Sociobiology and the Quest for Human Nature* (Cambridge, Mass.: MIT Press, 1985). Kitcher's book is the most technically demanding; he gave a useful précis in *Behavioral and Brain Sciences* 10 (1987): 61–100.

Robert Wright, *The Moral Animal: Evolutionary Psychology and Everyday Life* (New York: Random House 1994) cleverly interweaves Darwin's theories, his life, and modern evolutionary psychology.

Steven Pinker has written very readable accounts of evolutionary psychology in *How the Mind Works* (New York: W. W.Norton, 1997) and *The Blank Slate: the Modern Denial of Human Nature* (New York: Viking, 2002).

The Santa Barbara school's manifesto is in *The Adapted Mind: Evolutionary Psychology and the Generation of Culture*, edited by J. H. Barkow, L. Cosmides, and J. Tooby (Oxford University Press, 1992).

Recent textbooks of evolutionary psychology include David M. Buss, *Evolutionary Psychology: The New Science of the Mind* (Allyn & Bacon 2007); Louise Barrett, Robin Dunbar, and John Lycett, *Human Evolutionary Psychology* (Princeton: Princeton University Press 2002); K. L. Laland and G. R. Brown, *Sense and Nonsense: Evolutionary Perspectives on Human Behaviour* (Oxford University Press, 2002); and *The Oxford Handbook of Evolutionary Psychology*, edited by Robin Dunbar and Louise Barrett (Oxford University Press, 2007).

Philosophical issues arising from evolutionary psychology are discussed by Anthony O'Hear, *Beyond Evolution: Human Nature and the Limits of Evolutionary Explanation* (Oxford University Press, 1997); Janet Radcliffe Richards, *Human Nature after Darwin: A Philosophical Introduction* (London: Routledge, 2000); and John Dupre, *Human Nature and the Limits of Science* (Oxford University Press, 2001), and *Humans and Other Animals* (Oxford University Press, 2002).

Conclusion:
A Synthesis of the Theories?

To hope to conclude this (or any) book with some complete truth about human nature would be foolish. Final truths do not seem to be given to us fallible human beings (except perhaps in mathematics), and least of all about a topic as broad and controversial as human nature. I have no eleventh theory to offer, only an invitation to begin putting together what seems most acceptable from those already considered (and from any other sources of knowledge and wisdom).

Readers may tend to think of the ten theories as rivals (and admittedly, we rather encouraged this in the introduction), but they are not incompatible with each other on all points. Each of them can surely make some positive contribution to our understanding of ourselves and our place in the universe. So we can see each theory as emphasizing (though perhaps *over*emphasizing) different aspects of the total, complicated truth. In this way they can begin to add up to a more adequate understanding of human nature.

In this concluding chapter, I will try to sketch how the main lines of such a composite picture might go, using our familiar four-part structure of metaphysical background, theory of human nature, diagnosis, and prescription. For this irenical project, I suggest that Kant's system of thought (with some modernization) provides a comprehensive framework for integrating elements from the other theories into an overall view.

METAPHYSICAL BACKGROUND

Theism or Darwinism—or Both?

We cannot avoid facing up to the continuing clash between biological science and some fundamentalist forms of religious belief. As we saw in Chapter 10, there is now overwhelming evidence that human beings have evolved from simpler forms of life. Indeed, it seems that *all* living things on this planet have evolved by natural selection from a common origin. Whether the first forms of life emerged from inanimate matter remains as yet unknown, though it is thought probable by many scientists. Yet some Christian believers feel constrained to stick to a literal interpretation of the Bible; so they want to exempt humans from the process of Darwinian evolution and to insist that we have been specially created by God. (A literal reading of Genesis 1:11–12, 20–25, and 2:19 would suggest the same for each species of plant and animal.) Some Muslims may similarly insist on a literal reading of the accounts of God's creation in the Qur'an.

In recent years it has been suggested (notoriously in American courtrooms) that evolution is "only a theory" and that another theory, namely, "special creation" or "intelligent design," is at least equally worthy of belief and should be given equal time in schools. But that, I suggest, is mixing science with religion, to the detriment of both. Scientific theories, and the evidence for and against them, develop over time. What at one point was only a speculative hypothesis may become so well confirmed by all available evidence that it becomes legitimate to say it is not just a theory, but a fact. We do not say it is "only a theory" that the earth is spherical, though people once believed it was flat. The Catholic Church in Galileo's time (the early seventeenth century) tried to retain the belief that the sun goes around the earth, but we do not say it is "only a theory" that the earth revolves around the sun. The papacy has long since changed its mind on that issue and does not see anything in astronomy as a threat to Christian faith. Most mainstream Christian denominations, including the Catholic Church, now take a similar attitude to biological evolution.

In fact, ever since Darwin first published his theory, there have been theists who say that the talk in Genesis of God creating or forming creatures "out of the dust of the ground" does not have to be understood as saying that on one particular day in past history, God quite literally got his hands dirty and miraculously and instantaneously fashioned living things out of soil and mud. Those passages can instead be interpreted as saying that living beings are made of the same matter as the rest of the universe, though combined in distinctive ways. And God's creativity can be seen as a continuous process rather than a single event, or the work of one week. The six "days" of creation in Genesis 1 do not have to be taken literally: scientifically informed theists can say that God's process of creation extends from the big bang, through stellar evolution and planetary formation, through all the eras of geology, paleontology, and human history down to the present "day"—and beyond. It is thus perfectly possible for believers in God to say that evolution by natural selection is the way He has brought us into being. Evolution can thus seen as progressive, as the process intended by God to lead up to the emergence of creatures made in His own image, and endowed with rationality and free will.

I would therefore invite anyone who comes from a religious tradition that has taught them to reject the theory of evolution (at least as applied to human beings) to consider whether what is spiritually valuable in that tradition really requires that rejection. There is perhaps an associated fear that accepting Darwinian evolution would bring us down to a merely animal level and deny our "higher" nature. And indeed there are people around, both in bars and in seminars, who delight in taking such a reductionist line, which offers a plausible way of diagnosing selfish, biologically based motivations behind most of what people do, thus appearing to deflate all human pretensions to aspire to anything beyond the biological imperatives of survival and reproduction. But rather than reacting to this approach by relapsing into religious dogma, *both* kinds of attitudes need to have their intellectual credentials carefully scrutinized.

It is worth noting that Darwin himself, though he was in no doubt whatsoever that his theory of evolution applies to ourselves, did not see this as "reducing" us to a merely animal level. As we have seen in Chapter 10, he did not cease to apply ethical and aesthetic standards to human actions and artifacts, and to make political judgments about society. Admittedly, he himself was agnostic or atheist, but he was never tempted to think that people are *just* like other animals and have no uniquely human abilities and aspirations. Of course, a cynic may snort that this was just Darwin's mental hangover as an upper-class English gentleman of the Victorian age, and that he was unwilling to face up to the truly bleak implications of his own theory. And of course it is true that nothing can be proved by appeal to the authority and attitudes of any one person, however distinguished. I will suggest some more systematic considerations in the section on human nature later on.

It is worth noting here that the post-Kantian but pre-Darwinian German philosopher Arthur Schopenhauer expressed a reductionist view of human motivation in his conception of unconscious, biologically based "will" driving our actions (thus anticipating Freud). But even he allowed that in aesthetic experience (above all, in music) and saintly renunciation we can occasionally rise above this view. He was the first major Western philosopher to be importantly influenced by Eastern thought, mainly Hinduism.

Tree- or Bush-Shaped Evolution?

"Evolution" is a word with multiple ambiguities. In its most general sense, it refers to any extended process with an identifiable end product: thus, we can talk of the evolution of the solar system, of the Constitution, and of the automobile. Chemists also talk of substances "evolving" (i.e., emitting) gases. There is often a suggestion that the process is *progressive*, in the sense that the latest product is supposed to be better than those that have gone before. But progress is not involved in the emission of gas, and even in political and technological change the latest model is not always an improvement on its predecessors (as you may have noticed).

Within Darwinian theorists an interesting distinction can be drawn between those who think the evolution of species is inherently *progressive* and those who deny this. The known series of life-forms on Earth seems to show some definite progress, for over geological time there has been a noticeable increase of the complexity of some animals, especially in brain size and power (though there are plenty of ancient primitive forms still around). And of course we humans tend to see ourselves as higher than all the rest!

In the Victorian era, the idea of progress had become part of the prevailing climate of thought, so popular philosophers like Herbert Spencer interpreted both biological evolution and human history as leading the whole world onward and upward. Darwin himself tended to go with this intellectual flow, writing at one point of Man being "the wonder and glory of the Universe"! The very word "evolution" tends to suggest progress, but in the *Origin* Darwin used the phrase "descent with modification," which does not carry the same connotation.

However, some Darwinians in the twentieth century have questioned whether the process of species change is necessarily progressive. Natural selection does not imply that the later forms are *better* as judged by some human criterion—only that they are *better adapted* to the prevailing set of environmental conditions. And a species does not have to be *ideally* adapted to its ecological niche, only well enough to survive and reproduce. Ecosystems can be finely balanced and upset by an apparently small change. Notoriously, a plant or animal introduced from another part of the world may flourish better than a related native species, and even drive the natives to extinction. If climactic conditions change suddenly, more complex or "higher " species may get wiped out. Apparently this happened to the dinosaurs, when a large asteroid hit the earth and the resulting ash and smoke obscured the sunlight. If we humans mess up the environment sufficiently, we might become extinct too.

The difference between progressive and nonprogressive understandings of evolution can be pictured by different shapes of the pathway of evolution that the two sides postulate. It has usually been presented as a *tall tree*, growing steadily upward, with many diverging branches, but some definitely higher than others, and a topmost twig on which sit—guess who?—human beings. Richard Dawkins and Edward O. Wilson are prominent evolutionists who think of evolution as progressive in that way. But Stephen Jay Gould has offered instead the picture of a *bush*, which tends to grow sideways and outward in all directions, according to opportunity, with no standard shape and no obvious topmost branch. On this view, there was no predetermined necessity about the evolution of mammals, apes, and humans with their impressive brains. If it had not been for that asteroid impact and other contingencies such as dramatic climate changes in the past, the dinosaurs or their reptilian descendants might still reign supreme.

Progress in Human History?

In Chapters 7 and 8 we saw how Kant, Hegel, and Marx developed philosophies of history. They each claimed to discern an overall pattern in human history and made their predictions and expressed their hopes on that basis. This historicizing mode of thought was something rather new in Western philosophy. It was partially anticipated by the eighteenth-century Italian philosopher Giambattista Vico, who, however, had a cyclical theory of history, unlike the linear, progressive understanding of the later Enlightenment philosophers.

Of course, the Judeo-Christian tradition had always offered an interpretation of history against the backdrop of God's creative and redemptive purposes. The Jews still define their very identity as a people in terms of events dating back some four millennia—namely, God's deliverance of the people of Israel from their captivity in Egypt and their entrance into the "promised land." Despite their many exiles and persecutions from the time of the prophets down to our own era, Jews have retained a messianic hope that God will eventually intervene in the world. Christianity claimed that in the person of Jesus, God has already entered uniquely into history with universal redemptive effect. And Christians have traditionally expected a "second coming" of Christ, at which the world will come to an end and everyone will be judged. Both religions have maintained a faith in God's "providence" (sorely tested by events), that all the events of history somehow work toward His divine purpose.

The belief in human progress that is so characteristic of the Enlightenment philosophies of Kant and Hegel, the revolutionary program of Marx, and of much humanist social and political thought ever since can be seen as a secular echo of the religious belief in providence. Hope is now more often put in human powers, human intelligence, technical ingenuity, education, political sophistication, or military prowess, rather than in divine providence. But it can well be said that if hope in God is fragile in the face of the manifest evils of the world, how much more fragile is hope in human powers?

There have been some times and places in which all seemed to be well, or if not quite *all* (it never is!), at least it seemed that things were generally moving in the right direction and that there were grounds to hope that most of humanity (or at least those "we" care about) would be happier in the future. The century of peace in Europe between 1815 and 1914 was one such time; indeed, it was the great high-water mark of belief in secular progress. The descent of the most highly developed nations into mutual slaughter in the First World War shook that belief, and arguably it has never fully recovered. Perhaps the first two decades after the Second World War allowed a briefer period of confidence in America, until the Vietnam War began to divide the nation.

I have no grand theory to offer in reply to the question: Will there be progress in human history? That some kinds of progress are possible is not in doubt. Of course, there can be scientific discoveries and technological innovations, maybe even new sources of energy. And there *could* be wiser political leadership than much of what we have had; there could develop cultures with higher levels of education, greater tolerance of harmless diversity, and (dare one say it?) deeper spiritual values. But this is only to say that the *potential* is there. Will it be realized?

A long view of human history does not support any very confident answer. The civilization of the ancient world was practically wiped out with the fall of the Roman Empire, and it took nearly a thousand years for Europe to emerge from the so-called Dark Ages. Many empires and cultures have come and gone elsewhere in the world, notably in India and China. Like the contingencies of climate and asteroids that have affected the evolution of species, there have been "close-run" events in human history, e.g., the battles of Hastings in 1066 and Waterloo in 1815, or the "hanging chads" and the vote of a single Supreme Court justice in the U.S. presidential election of 2000. If any of those contests had gone the other way, history might have been importantly different. And for the future, there are horrific possibilities of nuclear or biological war, or catastrophic climate change. But if we are skeptical about grand narratives of history, whether secular or religious, that does not prevent us from hoping for realizable improvements and working toward them.

THEORY OF HUMAN NATURE

Kant's distinction between different kinds of truth—a priori and a posteriori—allows us to find a place both for philosophical reflection on the concept of person and for empirical facts about human beings in physiology, psychology, anthropology, sociology, history, and biography. There are plenty of important facts about our bodies, about our mental capacities (e.g., for facial recognition and for interpreting other people's motives), and about our emotional dispositions (e.g., a tendency toward pair-bonding, and the need of infants and children for loving care from parents or others).

Philosophy of Mind—Rationality and Free Will

We can formulate a conceptual definition (influenced by Plato, Aristotle, and Kant) of the criteria for any creatures (on this earth or anywhere in the universe) to count as rational thinkers and agents. They must be capable of having reasons for their beliefs and their actions, and of giving their reasons in language. It would be too much to require that rational creatures *always* have good reasons for their beliefs and actions, since for much of the time we judge and act without thinking or explaining why. (Indeed, we sometimes find ourselves unable to give any plausible reason for what we have just said or done!) All that is required for this basic notion of rationality is that the subjects be able to formulate intelligible reasons for *some* of what they believe and do.

What is it about human beings that makes such rationality possible? Plato and Descartes believed that we have immaterial souls (or more precisely, that we essentially *are* immaterial souls), and many people have thought that our distinctively rational nature therefore lies beyond scientific investigation. This long-standing issue of dualism or materialism has to be faced. Do minds, consciousness, and rationality imply the existence of nonmaterial minds or souls, or are we made of matter alone? Are our mental states—sensations, emotions, dreams, imaginings, beliefs, and desires—merely a product of the goings-on in our brains that the neurophysiologists investigate?

There is, of course, no question of resolving this long-debated issue here. But I make bold to suggest that Aristotle and Spinoza have supplied us with the outlines of a promising approach. As we saw in Chapter 5,

Aristotle conceived of the rational, human mode of mental functioning as superimposed on the animal way of functioning, which is itself superimposed on the basic functions common to all living things, even plants. What then makes our linguistic and rational abilities possible? It is surely our brains, which are much more developed than those of other animals. Such powerful brains have surely evolved as an adaptation that enabled our apelike ancestors to survive and reproduce in complex, changing social environments.

The biblical talk of men and women as made "in the image of God" and as being given "dominion" over the rest of creation (Genesis 1:27–28) implies some vitally important difference between us and all other animals. But it remains to be elucidated what exactly that difference is. There is still a tendency for many theists to postulate some moment(s) in human evolution when some absolute change took place. For those who conceive of the soul as a separable substance, there is a difficulty in locating a metaphysical break—the coming into existence of a human soul—in the two empirical continua of the evolution of the human species and the development of the human embryo in the womb.

It is true that humans have many important properties that our apelike ancestors lacked, and similarly for the human adult compared to the embryo. But it does not follow that there must be some definite point in development where the new features first appear. There are plenty of concepts that we now apply (e.g., marriage, crime, war, scientist, novel, symphony), but for which we should not expect there to have been some exact point in history when they became applicable for the very first time. (Given the fact of evolution, there will have been no first elephant, either.) These questions involve vague borderlines, so they have no determinate answers. We cannot say precisely when concepts such as consciousness, free will, sin, classical music, democracy, or supermodel came into play in the gradual, often messy, development of human mentality and culture. But that does not prevent us from applying such concepts quite determinately in many cases now. A gradualist account of the genesis of a human capacity or practice is consistent with saying that what it has now become is different in kind from its predecessors.

Evolution may still seem to many people, not only theists, to pose a threat to our rationality, moral responsibility, and free will. The latter two concepts—which surely come as a package—seem to add something important to mere rationality, as explained earlier. It seems conceivable that future robots/machines/computers (whatever they may be called) might be equipped with abilities to use language to give reasons for what they say and do, without thereby endowing them with free will and responsibility. Nor need they have emotions or desires (except in the sense of whatever they have been programmed to try to do). Such artifacts might be rational in one sense of the word, but we would not count them as *persons*.

It is not obvious, however, that the perceived threat to the reality of persons from evolution is any greater than that already posed by materialist and determinist accounts of human nature in the seventeenth and eighteenth centuries, before Darwin. Perhaps evolution just makes the issues more vivid. To begin to see how the threat can be seen off without appeal to metaphysical dualism, an Aristotelian approach to personhood may help. If we identify the mind or soul with whatever the brain enables us to do (the "software" of the brain), we are still left with a duality of *aspects* (or properties or vocabularies)—as Spinoza realized. The mentalistic vocabulary figures essentially in the reasons we give for our actions, beliefs, desires, hopes, and fears. The physical descriptions of neuron firings, neurotransmitters, activation of brain regions, and so on figure in scientific explanations of other physically described events. These two levels of language are irreducible to each other, for there is no necessity that the same belief or desire, identified in terms of its content (i.e., *what* is believed or desired), is embodied in exactly the same physiological kind of brain state, in two individuals, or even in the same person at different times. (If there are extraterrestrial beings, they might have some of the same beliefs as us, at least about science and math, but the physics and chemistry of their brains might be very different.)

There is an irreducible duality of *kinds of explanation* involving either reasons or causes—as Kant struggled to express in his idiosyncratic vocabulary, and as emerged in our discussions of Sartre and Darwin. On one hand, we explain human actions and beliefs in terms of *reasons*, appealing to intelligible conceptual connections between premises and conclusions in theoretical or practical reasoning. The giving of agents' reasons for their actions also features in social science. On the other hand, in the physical sciences we explain events—including brain events—by citing their *causes*, appealing to universal (or probabilistic) laws of nature, plus particular preceding initial conditions.

There is a connection with the traditional concept of free will. Rationality may not be sufficient for free will, but it is certainly necessary for it; so if free will is possible, rationality must be possible. If we can get to understand how there is conceptual room for rationality in a physical world—how creatures whose brain functioning consists in electrical and chemical events can also be said, quite truly, to have reasons for their beliefs and actions—then there may be hope of understanding how there is room for free will in a world of determining (or probabilistic) causes.

Giving reasons for a proposition is trying to *justify* belief in it, and this is a conceptually different thing from giving putative causes for someone coming to believe that proposition. Rational justification offers reasons in favor of the proposition being true—and those reasons must be universal, in the sense that anyone who understands them should be capable of recognizing that they are indeed reasons for accepting that proposition. But a causal story tries to explain why a state of belief came into existence in a certain individual—and the relevant causal conditions may apply only to some kinds of people, or to people under social pressure, stress, advertising, or cultural conditioning. Causal explanation of someone's belief formation is equally possible whether one thinks the belief is true or false or unproven. But giving reasons for a belief is giving reasons for its truth.

Since everyone has beliefs, nobody—least of all the biological scientist, who wants to be intellectually responsible to the evidence—can opt out of giving reasons for their beliefs. The fact that our mental faculties are products of evolution is no threat to the rationality or indeed the truth of (many of) the beliefs that we arrive at by using those faculties. Our giving reasons for our beliefs (on any subject matter), and our holding those beliefs to be true, is not undermined by the fact that our mental capacities for forming any such beliefs have evolved from more primitive levels of mentality by a long process of natural selection.

Ethical Values and Evolution

Darwinian evolution may still seem to threaten a radical challenge to our values. If humans are descended from animals, then some may say that we are "nothing more than" apes and conclude that none of our values have any objective validity. Human life, like other life, may thus be seen as *merely* a struggle for survival and reproduction. Fear of this bleak conclusion, this apparent lack of meaning in human life, is surely part of what underlies the religious resistance to evolution. More precisely, it may be alleged that the only motives for all human behavior are individual survival and reproduction; anything else—such as the pursuit of ethical, political or religious, artistic, or sporting ideals—must come down to these motivations that we share with other animals.

But it is very unclear what that "coming down to" is supposed to be. It suggests a reductionist program, to try to show that any nonbiological reasons offered for human actions—e.g., in pursuit of artistic or scientific excellence, charitable giving, or religious renunciation—are not the "real" reasons, since they can be shown to be derivative from our biology. In a similar way, Freud claimed that all human striving is ultimately motivated by hunger and love (sexual desire, that is). But how can such claims be tested? Recent biologists have shown that what may appear to be "altruistic" behavior in ants is really governed by genetic relatedness. But there is, to date, no such genetic reduction of all human altruism, for we are (sometimes!) kind to people we are not related to.

Why should our *ethical* beliefs be undermined by evolutionary reflections, any more than any other beliefs? Why shouldn't we hold that we do have some objective values to guide our lives by—whether we express them in terms of Platonic harmony of soul, Aristotelian flourishing, Kantian respect for all persons, Marxist social justice, Judeo-Christian love of neighbor, Confucian benevolence, or Buddhist mindfulness? It is not obvious that the mere fact of human evolution implies that the human species lacks any goal external to its own biological nature. There may be *other* good reasons for doubting the objectivity of ethics, aesthetic judgments, or religious claims (especially the notorious absence of consensus on such matters)—but the mere fact of human evolution is not one of them.

Our reasons for action involve our beliefs and values, and are expressible in terms of our culturally developed concepts. Culture is at least as crucial to our contemporary human nature as evolution. It is superimposed on basic human biology, of course. That we have *some* innate tendencies is indisputable—for our sexual behavior is obviously rooted in our biology. But even that obvious example raises questions, for the forms sexuality takes have varied between societies, and in devotedly celibate individuals like monks and nuns, that its expression may be suppressed. We have some innate biological drives, certainly—but we seem to be unique in the extent to which human behavior depends on the culture we have been brought up in—and it also depends on individual choices. The possibility of reliable contraception, the option for women to give birth by cesarean section, and to feed their infants synthesized rather than breast milk show how modern life has, for better or for worse, given us ways to transcend our biology.

Rudimentary cultural differences have been discerned in some of the apes, but to nothing like the human extent. Although Skinner was wrong to treat human culture in terms of the mechanisms of operant conditioning that he studied in his experimental animals, he was right to recognize the enormous difference that the social environment makes to the development of every human individual. Freud made us realize just how crucial is the influence of parents and other caretakers on the growing infant. After that, peer groups and the wider society begin to take over education and socialization. In the high-tech capitalist economy that now dominates the world, much of the social influence is exerted through the power of money, advertising, and the media. And yet—we must insist—the individual has some degree of choice, and hence responsibility.

Some sorts of evolutionary explanation of the origin of human ethical beliefs and feelings may make us more aware of their social function and perhaps more skeptical of the unreflective deliverances of ethical "intuition," including our own. There is nothing new in *that* kind of thought; it has been put before us in Feuerbach's account of religion, Marx's theory of ideology, Nietzsche's genealogy of morals, Freud's account of the psychological development of moral feelings, and Durkheim's sociology of religion.

But no one can opt out of valuing some kinds of behavior and character dispositions as better than others. No scientific theory, even one as wide-ranging in its implications as the Darwinian theory of evolution, could carry the value implications and give the guidance for life that religions have traditionally offered. Future human societies might pursue pure knowledge and yet could vary widely in their values. Some might promote the dominance of a master race, or one powerful nation, or a fundamentalist religion, while others may value everyone as an end in themselves. That we need more than science as a source of values is surely a conceptual truth.

DIAGNOSIS

Any diagnosis of something wrong presupposes some standard of how things ought to be. Like Plato and Aristotle, Kant offered an objective yet nonreligious (or at least, not explicitly theological) basis for ethics, appealing both to pure reason and to empirical facts about human nature. The particular ethical systems of these three greatest philosophers differ, but this broad-brush description applies to all of them.

Kant is sometimes interpreted as proposing (implausibly) to derive morality from rationality alone, but I see him as appealing at root to a fundamental *moral* principle of respect for all rational beings (expressed in his principle of treating all persons "as ends in themselves"). In this, he was surely influenced by the Judeo-Christian ideal of love for one's neighbor as oneself, more than by Plato and Aristotle, who were less universal and more aristocratic in their bestowal of care or recognition of rights. The Confucian notion of benevolence and the Hindu and Buddhist ideal of detachment from ego or self would seem to point in the same direction of universal compassion. Marx's burning sense of injustice and exploitation was surely inspired by the Judeo-Christian ideal. And Sartre, in his "second ethics," also presupposed a universal conception of human potentiality and its ideal fulfillment in "a city of ends."

Kantian respect for all rational beings as ends in themselves implies recognition of the rights and needs of *all* human beings. Some may propose to restrict this to those who meet a certain standard of rationality and personhood, thus perhaps excluding fetuses, infants, the mentally handicapped, and the senile. But a broader, more humane, and surely safer interpretation is to accord rights to all humans in virtue of their human potential, even if this is impaired in particular cases. The rhetoric of human rights has expanded in recent years, but I suggest that the most appropriate talk of rights is in the negative cases: the rights *not* to be killed, injured, tortured, enslaved, imprisoned without trial, or exploited for someone else's benefit. In these cases, the corresponding negative obligations (on everyone) are generally acknowledged.

As we saw in Chapter 9, Sartre thought of human *needs* as objective values that "demand" to be fulfiled, if human beings are to flourish. Put in another way, given a basic value attached to human flourishing, and facts about what things human beings need to flourish, we attach a derived, but still objective, value to those things. The notion of need applies at several levels. There are things we need to maintain life and health: air, water, protein, vitamins, medicine. There are also psychological needs such as the need of children for loving care if they are to grow up feeling valued, and there are typical adult needs for friendship, for sexual fulfilment, and for children of one's own. Beyond the family, we may recognize needs for education and group membership, and needs to work or contribute in some way to society.

If we can agree on these human rights and needs (or most of them), a diagnosis immediately follows, given the facts about the world. All down history and into the present, human rights have all too often been denied and abused, and crying human needs remain unfulfiled. But *why* is this the case? Why is there so much human suffering in the world? The question is ancient and enormous—and it arises not just for believers in God, but for everyone.

One part of the answer is, of course, sheer accident. Earthquakes, volcanic eruptions, and asteroid impacts are beyond human control. Epidemics, famine, floods, drought, and climate change have usually been put in the same category, but we are now realizing that in many cases, the unintended side effects of human activity contribute to their causation. And there are smaller-scale accidents and illnesses that kill or disable individuals. So there is a category of events beyond human control that is traditionally called "Fate" (Confucius talked of "Destiny"). Theists may call them "the Will of God" (or at least, things that God allows, for He does not seem to act to prevent them), but that does not make them any easier to bear.

A large part of the rest of the answer is economic scarcity. The world, rich in resources though it is, does not provide enough for unlimited numbers of human beings to reproduce themselves, as Malthus saw. Of course, technological ingenuity often finds out ways to utilize more of the resources of nature, and thus makes economic and social advances possible, as Marx analyzed. But population growth and economic development generate new needs and desires, not all of which can be met at any one time. So there will always be some degree of scarcity, some competition for resources, and awkward questions of economic justice.

Another large part of the answer must be human culpability. If a human need is not met, it is not always the case that someone is to blame. But when a human right is abused, then someone is responsible—someone, some group or agency—has ordered or done the killing or torture, the enslavement or exploitation. And why? The answer will typically involve some advantage to themselves. There are a few sadistic individuals who take pleasure in causing pain, and there are plenty more who are prepared to do damage to others in the name of some "greater" cause, such as the Nation, the Party, or even the Church. But in most cases, people simply do what they see as best for themselves (and often that is simply to follow orders). We put other people's interests second, if we recognize them at all. Kant called this the "radical evil" in human nature.

We should not see this entirely in terms of individual culpability, because given our social nature and the immense influence of culture upon us, there is an important social dimension to sin, pride, and selfishness. It only needs some charismatic but perverted individual to gain influence and power, and many people will follow, motivated by some mixture of inspiration and perceived self-interest (consider Hitler, Stalin, and various cult leaders). Often there is *structural* injustice, enshrined in economic, social, or legal systems, the exploitation of one set of people by another, whether distinguished by class, race, ethnicity, or simple vulnerability, e.g., to sweatshop conditions of labor imposed by the market forces of global capitalism.

Those acculturated into a favorable position in such a system and its conceptions of superiority and inferiority, rights and lack of rights, may bear no direct responsibility for it. It may need a feat of imagination, or a stimulus from a different ethical or religious ideal, even to realize that something is morally wrong. But when some such realization "hits home" to people, they have some responsibility to do something about it, whatever little they can. I am thinking here not just of extreme cases from the past such as Nazi Germany, South Africa under apartheid, or our slave-owning ancestors, but of those who are presently involved in oppression, whether in the third world, in Palestine, in Chechnya, or elsewhere.

PRESCRIPTION

In the light of scarcity, individual selfishness, and social injustice, can we entertain any hope, as Kant and the Enlightenment did, for progress in the future? And what, if anything, can we do about it? More enormous and ancient questions, which arise both for religious believers and for humanists! I do not presume to have anything original to say about them; answers are likely to be quite ancient too.

As noted, some forms of scarcity may be alleviated by scientific discovery and technological ingenuity. If we can find an effective way of harnessing the radiation that continually pours down upon us from the sun, our problem of energy supply might be solved. But new affluence breeds new needs and desires. This is not just an economic truth, but a psychological one. For there seems to be an inherently competitive streak in human nature; we constantly compare ourselves with others and want to equal them or outdo them. There is a moral point here, for though our competitive tendencies may be acceptable and even laudable in sport and in scientific, scholarly, artistic, or professional achievement, they all too easily go "over the top" into ruthlessness, cheating, and greed. They may help drive social and cultural progress (as Kant suggested), but they stand in need of limitation by higher ideals of unselfishness and compassion.

What remedies are there for individual and social evil? The first step is surely to name the evils, to try to make everyone vividly aware of what is wrong, both in ourselves and in society. For human beings are adept at finding good names for the shabby things they do: there are almost infinite possibilities of self-justification, self-deception, Freudian repression, or Sartrian bad faith. There are similar devices at the social level, especially what Marx called "ideology," systems of belief that cover up or try to justify the underlying exploitation. Our first duty must be to look to "the beam in our own eye," as Jesus said. But institutional evils may deserve public, organized campaigns of dissent and resistance.

Besides naming and opposing evil, we can do something more positive by upholding standards of goodness, expressing our ideals of how human life ought to be. Of course "preaching" can be counterproductive. None of us can lay claim to unique or infallible insight, and our primary duty is to try to follow and embody the ideals ourselves: as the old saying has it, "Actions speak louder than words." But given our social nature and our individual fallibility, there is always need for some institutional, ongoing presentation of ideals, and some kind of spiritual practice to help people rise to them.

The Christian churches and the other religious traditions (including Confucianism, Hinduism, and Buddhism) have to some extent played this role, each in their own peculiar way, overlaid with various sacred traditions and metaphysical beliefs. Kant hoped that these differences would come to be seen as optional, and that a common set of moral duties and ideals would emerge as the essential ethical core of all religions. But it has to be admitted that in the two centuries since his time, there has been little sign of this happening (with the possible exception of the Unitarians and Quakers, who appeal to minority tastes). Religious traditions, in their supernatural and divisive forms, obviously retain a powerful hold over many human minds.

There is always need for education in the widest sense, including moral education, as Plato and Aristotle argued. This applies to young people especially, but we all remain capable of learning throughout life. None of us is omniscient or perfect, and each of us may need teaching or reminding at any time in our lives about what is true or good or beautiful. There are always spiritually enlightening resources available; we do not have to rely on our frail and fallible selves. There are immense riches (as well as a good deal of dross!) to be found in the sciences, the philosophies, and the arts. The religions offer various forms of spiritual practice, some of which are described as leading us out of this world; but most of them also claim to make us better persons in this world. There may be insoluble disagreements about metaphysics and theology, but perhaps we are more likely to agree about the test for being "a better person." Remember St. Paul's writing that "the harvest of the Spirit is love, joy, peace, patience, kindness, goodness, fidelity, gentleness, and self-control."

This book has concentrated on general theorizing and has hardly mentioned the arts. In closing, let me mention how literature, painting, theater and opera present us with imaginary, but in another sense very "real," cases of men and women in thought and feeling, action and song. In the greatest works of art, our understanding of human nature is extended and deepened, though often not in ways we can put into words. In contrast, many of the movies or soap operas that enjoy wide but passing popularity reinforce stereotypes rather than deepen our understanding. (Plato realized long ago just how influential the "media" of popular communication can be, for better or for worse.) The arts at their best can liberate our imaginations from the tyranny of the familiar, the parochial, and the contemporary.

Human nature is a topic that breaks down the boundaries between the sciences, the humanities, and the religions. Social and political problems in our own societies, and all around the world, cry out for better understanding of other human beings and cultures. Often the technical problems are soluble, but what seem insuperable are the political, social, and cultural problems. Some policy analysts seem to assume that nations or civilizations are going to remain enemies indefinitely, so they keep looking for new technologies and strategies of defense, rather than ways of reducing tensions, addressing injustices, and making conditions for lasting peace.

Even in peace and affluence, individual existential dilemmas, relationship problems, and family tensions remain. There is no contradiction between the hope for social progress and the need for each person to come to terms with his or her individual destiny. My concluding thought is that we need an awareness of the dark side of human nature as well as the possibilities of progress, and that our sense of light and darkness still needs to be informed and educated by the great philosophical and religious thought systems of the past that we have explored in this book.

FOR FURTHER READING

A reference book full of fascinating articles on a huge variety of topics is *The Oxford Companion to the Mind*, edited by Richard. L.Gregory (Oxford University Press, 1987). A comprehensive set of philosophical readings is *Philosophy of Mind: Classical and Contemporary Readings*, edited by David J. Chalmers (Oxford University Press, 2002).

There are many good modern introductions to the philosophy of mind: George Graham, *Philosophy of Mind*, 2nd ed. (Oxford: Blackwell, 1998); John Heil, *Philosophy of Mind* (London: Routledge, 1998); Samuel Guttenplan, *Mind's Landscape* (Oxford: Blackwell, 2000); Tim Crane, *The Mechanical Mind*, 2nd ed. (London: Routledge, 2003); and Margaret A. Boden, *The Creative Mind*, 2nd ed. (London: Routledge, 2003).

Iris Murdoch, *Metaphysics as a Guide to Morals* (London: Chatto & Windus, 1992), though long-winded and wandering, is full of fascinating, insights into the basis of ethics and religion, inspired especially by Plato and Kant.

Roger Scruton's *Intelligent Person's Guide to Philosophy* (London: Duckworth, 1996) is an unconventional introduction, fired by his conviction that "scientific truth has human illusion as its regular by-product, and that philosophy is our surest weapon in the attempt to rescue truth from this predicament"—a message that I hope this book has reinforced. See also Scruton's *Intelligent Person's Guide to Modern Culture* (London: Duckworth, 1998).

Mary E. Clark, retired from a Chair in Conflict Resolution, has written a wide-ranging interdisciplinary book, *In Search of Human Nature* (London: Routledge, 2002), in which she offers hope for the future, despite our manifold problems.

John Cottingham, *On the Meaning of Life* (London: Routledge, 2003), is a delightfully clear, concise, and balanced discussion that ends up recommending some form of nondoctrinal spiritual practice to develop our responses to objective truth, goodness and beauty, and our faith, hope, and love.

Index